PENGUIN CLASSICS

The Penguin Book of the Prose Poem

Jeremy Noel-Tod is a Senior Lecturer in the School of Literature, Drama and Creative Writing at the University of East Anglia. His literary criticism has been widely published and he has been the poetry critic for the *Sunday Times* since 2013. His books as an editor include the revised edition of the *Oxford Companion to Modern Poetry* (2013) and the *Complete Poems* of R. F. Langley (Carcanet, 2015).

T0053702

The Penguin Book of the Prose Poem

From Baudelaire to Anne Carson

Edited and introduced by JEREMY NOEL-TOD

PENGUIN BOOKS

PENGUIN BOOKS

UK | USA | Canada | Ireland | Australia
India | New Zealand | South Africa

Penguin Books is part of the Penguin Random House group of companies
whose addresses can be found at global.penguinrandomhouse.com

First published 2018
Paperback edition published 2019

008

Selection and editorial matter copyright © Jeremy Noel-Tod, 2018

The moral right of the editor has been asserted

Set in 11.13/13.96 pt Dante MT
Typeset by Jouve (UK), Milton Keynes
Printed and bound in Great Britain by Clays Ltd, Elcograf S.p.A.

A CIP catalogue record for this book is available from the British Library

ISBN: 978-0-141-98456-8

www.greenpenguin.co.uk

Penguin Random House is committed to a
sustainable future for our business, our readers
and our planet. This book is made from Forest
Stewardship Council® certified paper.

Contents

Contents

Contents

THE POSTMODERN PROSE POEM

Contents

Contents

Contents

Contents

Introduction: The Expansion of the Prose Poem

I

What is poetry and if you know what poetry is
what is prose – Gertrude Stein[1]

How do you define a prose poem? I have often been asked this question since I began to put together what follows: two hundred poems from around the world which have been chosen to represent the exciting, surprising, and memorable possibilities of a form that has sometimes been regarded with suspicion but is now suddenly everywhere. Collections of prose poems – such as Claudia Rankine's *Citizen* (2014) – win major prizes, and anyone who picks up a poetry magazine will almost certainly spot one. This book includes a range of names that might be expected to feature in any representative anthology of modern poetry in English: John Ashbery, W. H. Auden, Elizabeth Bishop, Rita Dove, T. S. Eliot, Allen Ginsberg, Seamus Heaney, Adrienne Rich. But it also celebrates neglected poets who have written with brilliance in a form habitually overlooked by anthologists. Together, they comprise an alternative history of modern poetry and an experimental tradition that is shaping its future.

How, then, to define the prose poem? After reading so many, I can only offer the simplest common denominator: a prose poem is a poem without line breaks. Beyond that, both its manner and its matter resist generalization. The prose poem has been called a 'genre with an oxymoron for name' (Michael Riffaterre), yet it may be doubted whether it is in fact a genre at all; another critic has positioned it on 'the boundaries of genre', between the many kinds of other writing it may mercurially resemble.[2] Surveying the 175 years of poetry represented here, what emerges for me is the prose poem's wayward relationship to its own form – and it is this, I believe, that makes it the defining poetic invention of modernity. In an age of mass literacy, our daily lives are enmeshed in networks of sentences and paragraphs as extensive as any urban grid. The prose poem drives the reading mind beyond the city limits.

Poets, of course, have long known that the border between verse and prose is porous. Is the prose soliloquy in which Hamlet exclaims 'What a piece of work is man . . .' really any less a piece of Shakespearean poetry than the blank verse of 'To be or not to be . . .'? Sir Philip Sidney informed Renaissance readers that although 'the inside and strength' of Plato's dialogues was philosophy, 'the skin, as it were, and beauty depended most of poetry'; in the Romantic era, Percy Bysshe Shelley contended that 'the distinction between poets and prose writers is a vulgar error'; and the French Symbolist poet Stéphane Mallarmé believed that 'there is no such thing as prose: there is the alphabet, and then there are verses'.[3] Put letters together to make words, that is, and you are already working with the basic units of poetic rhythm.

As the critic D. W. Harding noted in his study of rhythm in literature, 'all the prose we ever read is chopped up into lines; we rightly pay no attention to them'.[4] This is because page margins do not mark metre as line breaks do. Yet it is not uncommon for verse-like currents to eddy beneath the placid surface of a paragraph. 'Prose', wrote Samuel Johnson in his *Dictionary* of

1755, is 'language not restrained to harmonick sounds or set number of syllables, discourse not metrical'. But Johnson's own eloquence as an essayist, observed William Hazlitt – who thought it a fault – was often 'a species of rhyming in prose [in which] each sentence, revolving round its centre of gravity, is contained with itself like a couplet, and each paragraph forms itself into a stanza'.[5] There is one kind of prose poem that employs such cadences to raise its voice very close to verse, from Oscar Wilde's echoing of the parallelism of the King James Bible (sometimes known as 'thought-rhyme') in his homoerotic parables of desire 'The Disciple' (p. 380) and 'The Master' (p. 381) to Allen Ginsberg's companionable shadowing of Walt Whitman's long verse line in the paragraph-stanzas of 'A Supermarket in California' (p. 273). But our habitual expectation when we see a passage of prose is that it will explain, not sing. The information-giving sentence – logical, functional, linear – is the conveyor belt that carries the business of our lives. The rhythm of prose, believed the Russian literary theorist Viktor Shklovsky, contributes to the 'automatizing' of perception, which the images and rhythms of poetry work to disrupt – a theory that his friend the poet Velimir Khlebnikov illustrates in 'Menagerie' (p. 368), with its startling pen-portraits of the animals of Moscow zoo, often dashed off in a single sentence.[6] Poetry, we might say, bends the bars of the prose cage.

As Hermine Riffaterre has observed, the 'formal framework' of the individual prose poem is 'ad hoc', and often makes its home among other forms and genres.[7] These may be recognizably literary, such as the anecdote, the aphorism, the sketch, the dialogue, the essay, the fairy tale, the fragment, the joke, the myth, or the short story.[8] But prose poets are also attracted to the poetic possibilities of other kinds of writing, the official purpose of which is to record and inform: for instance, the cut-up journalism of Charles Madge's 'Bourgeois News' (p. 312); the graffitied game rules of Bernadette Mayer's 'Gay Full Story' ('Change one letter in each essential vivacity missing word to spell a times taking place defunct bird's name', p. 213); or the 'intense yet eccentric research in the rhetorical structure of English meteorological description' that Lisa Robertson undertook for her book *The Weather* (p. 104) – beginning with the famously incantatory rhythms of the BBC radio shipping forecast.[9] The prose of information, we begin to realize, comes in many forms, and all have the potential for poetry to be injected, like coloured ink, into their ostensibly transparent sentences.

With the exception, however, of the neatly 'trimmed' abattoir notice presented as a found poem by Laurie Duggan's 'Hearts' (p. 192), this anthology's definition of prose poetry does not extend to the wholesale reframing of prose as poetry by certain recent conceptual poets.[10] Instead, it attempts to map a tradition of lyric writing in prose form, which begins in the latter half of the nineteenth century with the French poet Charles Baudelaire and a posthumous volume known by two titles: *Le Spleen de Paris* or *Petits Poèmes en Prose* (1869). By the end of the century, Baudelaire's innovation had exerted a wide-reaching influence: on the prose reveries of later Symbolists such as Arthur Rimbaud and Mallarmé; on the *fin-de-siècle* decadence, across the English Channel, of Oscar Wilde and Ernest Dowson; on *Poems in Prose* (1883), the Russian novelist Ivan Turgenev's last book, written while living in Paris; and, in America, on Emma Lazarus's biblical evocations of the journeying of Jewish refugees, 'By the Waters of Babylon' (1887), which features the Baudelairean subtitle 'Little Poems in Prose' (p. 382). A generation later, the international literary revolution known as modernism saw prose and verse mingling in little magazines unconcerned with dividing their table of contents strictly into one or the other. In France, the dream-like strangeness of the Symbolists was redoubled under the influence of

Surrealism by young prose poets such as Pierre Reverdy ('Street Circus', p. 355) and Max Jacob ('Hell is Graduated', p. 337); in America, Gertrude Stein (*Tender Buttons*, p. 356) and William Carlos Williams (*Kora in Hell*, p. 339) made poetry from the same kind of stop-start paragraph employed to carry the stream-of-consciousness monologue in modernist fiction; and in China – which already had an ancient tradition of poetic rhyme-prose, known as *fu* – the term 'prose poem' (*sanwen shi*) was first used in 1918 by Liu Bannong, who translated poems by Turgenev. (A decade later, Lu Xun's great collection *Wild Grass* (pp. 332–5) evinced the continuing influence of Baudelaire.)[11]

At the same time, the question persisted as to whether prose poetry was a subject to be mentioned in polite society at all. Oscar Wilde had made the term notorious in 1895 when, in court, he described a letter he had written to his lover, Lord Alfred Douglas, as a 'prose sonnet' (an association that later prose poems, such as Dulce María Loynaz's 'Love Letter to King Tutankhamun' (p. 279), have continued). Its reputation was not improved a generation later, when, in 1915, Aleister Crowley, the so-called 'wickedest man in the world', published translations from *Paris Spleen* in *Vanity Fair* magazine. In the same year, one of the best-known prose poems in English, T. S. Eliot's 'Hysteria' (p. 345), made its first appearance in an anthology edited by Ezra Pound. But even Eliot had his doubts about the form as a critic, calling it 'an aberration which is only justified by absolute success'. Inside his personal copy of Stuart Merrill's *Pastels in Prose* (1890), a popular anthology of French prose poetry, he kept a clipping of a newspaper parody called 'The Latest Form of Literary Hysterics'. The title of his poem about a man made (hysterically) anxious by a laughing woman can, therefore, be read as an ironic comment on its own 'bad form' ('I decided that if the shaking of her breasts could be stopped, some of the fragments of the afternoon might be collected'). Later, Eliot privately dismissed 'Hysteria' as 'a kind of note for a poem, but not [. . .] a poem'.[12]

In casting doubt on the sanity of the prose poet, Eliot may have had in mind the infamous example of Gertrude Stein. Once much mocked for her emphatically repetitive, under-punctuated style, Stein now deserves to be recognized as the most original prose poet in the English language. With the vividly abstract domesticity of *Tender Buttons* (1914), she invented a verbal Cubism in which household objects and foodstuffs are evoked in enigmatically glancing ways ('a way of naming things that would . . . mean names without naming them'), just as the Cubist still-life broke up the solid contents of café tables into overlapping planes.[13] The aftershock of *Tender Buttons* was not widely felt until the second half of the twentieth century, when Stein's sideways manner can be heard everywhere in the experimental canon of American prose poetry, from the wry obliquity of John Ashbery – represented here by the poems 'For John Clare' (p. 244) and 'Homeless Heart' (p. 59) – to the kaleidoscopic autobiography of Lyn Hejinian's *My Life* (p. 186) and Clark Coolidge's erotically textual 'Letters', from *The Book of During* (p. 156). In such writing, Rosmarie Waldrop (p. 144) remarks, 'the cuts, discontinuities, ruptures, cracks, fissures, holes, hitches, snags, leaps, shifts of reference, and emptiness' that we associate with modernist free verse (such as Eliot's *The Waste Land*) occur, instead, '*inside* the sentence'.[14]

The freedom of the prose poem to follow the unmetrical pathways of thought can also take it in the opposite direction, towards a plainer style, imitative of speech. In this mode, the prose poem employs the formulas and rhythms of story-telling, with all their alluring familiarity and suspense. Among the handful of prose poems famous enough to be anthology pieces already are Joy Harjo's 'Deer Dancer' (p. 165), which draws on the Native American oral tradition to imagine a modern myth, and Carolyn Forché's 'The Colonel' (p. 207), which was written after travelling to El Salvador during the country's civil war. 'What you have heard is true', Forché begins, before recounting an almost unbelievably horrifying encounter with a military man in simple, declarative sentences that read like an eye-witness report. This is a poem, it seems, that has been written in defiance of the colonel who mocks: 'Something for your poetry, no?'

The story-telling prose poem also lends itself to the comic anecdote, and this has been its most popular manifestation in America and Britain since the 1960s, under the influence of up-the-garden-path absurdists such as Russel Edson (p. 228), James Tate (p. 211), and Maxine Chernoff (p. 212). Prose poems in this vein often feel like jokes that overshoot their punchlines into something more serious. When Peter Didsbury titles his downbeat monologue about a divorcé, a lodger and some stray dog hairs 'A Vernacular Tale' (p. 206), he is studiously avoiding its vernacular name: a shaggy dog story. To quote Cathy Wagner's 'Chicken' (p. 48) in full:

A poem goes to the other side. It's different there, but that's not why I wrote it. There's all there is, in the chicken joke. Where are you going with this.

Another kind of fabulism in which post-war poets have excelled is the mythology of an everyday object. Foreshadowed by the elemental meditations of Gabriela Mistral ('In Praise of Glass', p. 319), the prose object-poem is pioneered in French by Francis Ponge, with his first collection, *Le parti pris des choses* (1942) – a title recently translated by Joshua Corey and Jean-Luc Garneau as *Partisan of Things*. Ponge employs a seemingly clean, scientific prose to muse upon humdrum subjects (a door, a crate, rain) as if they were the most exquisitely fascinating phenomena, with secret lives of their own. The punchline of a Ponge poem, how-ever, is that words themselves are elusively alive. At the end of his hyperreal description of 'Rain' (p. 298), 'the brilliant appar-atus' of language evaporates into the simplest syllables: 'it has rained' ('il a plu'). Ponge's combination of simplicity and sophis-tication has made him the postmodern prose poet's postmodern prose poet, and the fine line he draws between mind and matter can be traced through many later poems here, including James Schuyler's 'Milk' (p. 246), Robert Bly's 'A Caterpillar' (p. 226), Shuntarō Tanikawa's 'Scissors' (p. 224), and Brian Catling's 'The Stumbling Block Its Index' (p. 168), which catalogues a shape-shifting sculpture that exists only in words ('**The Stumbling Block** is a graphite font').

The prose poem's tendency to dwell on image over narrative begins with the curious book that Baudelaire acknowledged as his model: Aloysius Bertrand's *Gaspard de la Nuit* (1842), a col-lection of historical vignettes offered to the reader as the vision of an old man who may be the Devil. Its first piece, 'Haarlem' (p. 408) – the last poem in the present anthology's reverse chronology – exemplifies the picturesque quality of Bertrand's work. Distilling scenes from seventeenth-century Flemish genre painting into sentences that suspend time by omitting a main verb, 'Haarlem' captures a little world in the amber of the ongoing moment ('And the drinkers smoking in some dark dive, and the inn-keeper's servant hanging up a dead pheasant in a tavern window'). The realism of Bertrand's prose derives from the novel, but its haunting amplification of image – its hanging-up of dead pheasants – leaves it in the realm of dream, a place the prose poem has repeatedly explored. In his first 'Manifesto of Surrealism' (1924), André Breton cited several prose poets among the movement's influences, including Baudelaire, Rimbaud, Mallarmé, Reverdy, and Saint-John Perse, as well as the wild prose nightmares of the Comte de Lautréamont's *Les*

Chants de Maldoror (1869). Breton sought to liberate the poetry of the unconscious mind by jotting down sentences while on the verge of sleep, a method he believed Rimbaud had also followed.[15] By the 1930s, the sleeping mind was speaking in prose poems written in many countries, from David Gascoyne in England to George Seferis in Greece, Anzai Fuye in Japan, and César Vallejo in Peru. In 1941, the Martiniquais poet Aimé Césaire praised the 'strange cities, extraordinary countrysides, twisted, crushed, dismembered worlds' of Rimbaud's *Illuminations* as 'the most authentic vision of the world'.[16] A century after the midnight visions of Aloysius Bertrand, the prose poem bore prophetic witness to the way that modern life itself had become violently surreal.

II

Prosaic France passed over to poetry. And everything changed.
– Aimé Césaire[17]

Versification varies from language to language and its subtleties are notoriously difficult to translate. One convention is simply to accept the loss of poetic form and render verse as prose – and one subgenre of the prose poem is to perform the translation of an absent original, as in Allen Upward's invented classical Chinese poems, 'Scented Leaves – from a Chinese Jar' (p. 367); Don Paterson's mock-scholarly recollection of a 'scrawny Orpheus' (p. 122); or Éric Suchère's exacting ekphrasis of comic book panels collaged from Hergé's Tintin adventure *The Shooting Star* (p. 40). The translation of prose into prose, however, does not so obviously require the sacrifice of formal effects, allowing the prose poem to move with relative ease between national traditions. This is its implicit role in Seamus

Heaney's 'Fiddleheads' (p. 89), a poem which offers itself to a friend from Japan as a 'basket' containing a delicacy common to both countries. As my selections have tried to show, prose poets themselves have significantly contributed to the translation of prose poems, and thereby helped to create an international tradition. Nor does it seem entirely coincidental that so many Nobel Laureates should figure in the history of a form that is uniquely cosmopolitan in its origins: Rabindranath Tagore, Gabriela Mistral, T. S. Eliot, Juan Ramón Jiménez, Saint-John Perse, Pablo Neruda, Eugenio Montale, Czesław Miłosz, Wole Soyinka, Octavio Paz, Wisława Szymborska, Tomas Tranströmer, and Heaney himself. As the American Frank O'Hara joked of one of his own poems in the 1950s: 'it is even in / prose, I am a real poet'.[18]

Without the visual architecture of verse, the prose poem is not immediately identifiable on the page. When read aloud, however, it is often characterized by the kind of echoic patterning that we associate with verse, arriving at its conclusion with a resonant neatness – what Amy Lowell, writing in defence of her own 'polyphonic prose', called the 'spherical effect' of poetic form.[19] One marker of form in the prose poem is the drawing of a verbal circle, as in Ernest Dowson's narcotically languid 'Absinthia Taetra' (p. 376), which repeats its first line as its last, or Barbara Guest's unsettling film-making fantasy 'The Cough', which calls back to its title with its last words (p. 115). Mark Strand's 'Chekhov' (p. 170) is an especially ingenious instance of the looped monologue, repeating the same six words at the end of its sentences according to a pattern borrowed from a 'fixed' form of verse, the sestina. The thematic emphasis on word choice introduced by such a conceit suggests Samuel Taylor Coleridge's distinction between the two modes: 'prose = words in their best order; poetry = the *best* words in the best order' (Gertrude Stein was getting at something similar when she said that 'poetry has to do with vocabulary just as prose does not').[20] Less traditional constraints that enforce a similar poetic economy include Christian Bök's *Eunoia* (p. 97), which is written in chapters that only allow themselves to use one of the English vowels ('Enfettered, these sentences repress speech'); Harryette Mullen's 'Denigration' (p. 99), in which every sentence turns on a word that might be cognate with the Latin for black (*'niger'*), itself only one letter away from the unspoken racial slur; and Peter Reading's *C* (p. 195), which begins with the speaker, having received a diagnosis of cancer, planning to write '100 100-word units. What do you expect me to do – break into bloody haiku?' (He then does this anyway: 'Verse is for healthy / arty-farties. The dying / and surgeons use prose.')

But if poetry is *not* synonymous with verse – as canonical anthologies such as *The Oxford Book of English Verse* assume – how do we define a poem at all? This question, at least, has been answered by many authorities. 'All good poetry', wrote William Wordsworth in the 'Preface' to *Lyrical Ballads* (1802), 'is the spontaneous overflow of powerful feelings.'[21] Verse serves as a mould to a moment of emotion, shaping it to a rhythmic pattern. Without line breaks, the prose poem is free – like this paragraph – to extend across and down the page as far as the printer's margins will allow. And it is in this freedom that we can locate the distinctive feeling to which the prose poem gives form: expansiveness. Unchecked by metre or rhyme, prose poetry flows by soft return from margin to margin, filling the empty field of the page, like the vision of Aloysius Bertrand's 'Mason' who, on his scaffolding above the cathedral roof, sees further into the surrounding landscape with every sentence, from 'gargoyles spewing water' to 'a village set afire by troops, flaming like a comet in the deep-blue sky' (p. 406). If the prose poem had a motto for itself as an ideal form, waiting to be realized, it might be from John Ashbery's 'For John Clare': 'There ought to be room for more things, for a spreading out, like' (p. 244).[22]

As Ashbery's artfully banal sentence suggests, prose is a mode of writing that allows the stylist plenty of slack. In the critical vocabulary of everyday English we use 'poetic' as a term of high praise, 'prosaic' to express disappointment with something unimaginative. Poetry is the beautiful ideal, prose the unlovely real: 'You campaign in poetry. You govern in prose', as the New York politician Mario Cuomo is reported to have said.[23] The challenge for the prose poet is to undo the distinction: to make the prosaic poetic, so that it expands a powerful feeling without dissipating its force. Agha Shahid Ali ('Return to Harmony 3' (p. 128)) saw this as a question of bringing the same 'energy' to prose as to strict forms such as the sestina and the sonnet, 'by making the sentence (and paragraph) rather than the line (and stanza) the be-all and end-all of my emotion. I had to teach myself to discard the line completely'.[24]

The prose poem's genius for expansiveness is not only due to its freedom from formal constraint, however. The linguist Roman Jakobson distinguished the 'poetic' and 'prosaic' uses of language as being dominated respectively by the figures of metaphor (which finds resemblance between things) and metonym (which assumes continuity between things).[25] Poets are famous, of course, for 'comparing stuff to other stuff', in the words of Hera Lindsay Bird (p. 9), and for Aristotle, to have mastered the imaginative use of metaphor (which in Greek means 'to carry over') was the mark of 'great natural ability' in poetry.[26] But the poet's talent for noticing resemblances is a matter of the ear as well as the eye: the verbal repetitions of versification – alliteration, metre, rhyme – depend on similarities of sound, which implicitly invite us to make connections between words. So verse itself can be considered part of poetry's tendency to stimulate the metaphorical movement of the mind. Prose, on the other hand, puts one thing after another in a logical chain, and this is why it tends to be dominated by metonym (which means 'change of name'). If, for example, I refer back at this point to 'Jakobson', I am using the surname as a metonym for 'Jakobson's theory of poetry and prose'. Metonymy is the preferred trope of the prose writer because it is unobtrusive and efficient, a shorthand that assumes the reader's understanding of an abbreviated meaning. And because metonymy leads the mind by meaning rather than metre, it subordinates the sound of words in order to streamline the flow of sense – thus making it the ideal figure of speech for news reports, legal documents, and realist novels.

Virginia Woolf, a novelist intensely concerned with the poetry of prose, saw its continuous nature as what kept it earth-bound: 'it rises slowly off the ground; it must be connected on this side and on that.'[27] The expansiveness of feeling that characterizes the prose poem is often created by a moment of metaphor giving it a sudden lift, like the flare of the burner in a hot-air balloon. This is what happens in the poem 'Pulmonary Tuberculosis' by Katherine Mansfield, a writer best known for her short stories, who in 1918 experimented with poems in free verse – that is, verse with no fixed rhythm or rhyme – but decided that the results read better when printed as a form of 'special prose':[28]

The man in the room next to mine has the same complaint as I. When I wake in the night I hear him turning. And then he coughs. And I cough. And after a silence I cough. And he coughs again. This goes on for a long time. Until I feel we are like two roosters calling to each other at false dawn. From far-away hidden farms.

In the first sentence, Mansfield sets the scene with a diary-like frankness. We are in the prosaic world of one thing next to another: 'the man in the room next to mine' serves as a metonym for the whole sanatorium of TB patients. The second sentence introduces the real-time narration of night waking, with four short sentences that imitate the lonely, arrhythmic volleying of coughs, which – like the most tedious prose – 'goes on for a long time'. The poetic only enters with the penultimate sentence, which employs metaphor to imagine a deeper affinity between the suffering human beings: they are transformed into 'roosters', fulfilling their animal instinct of crowing for sunrise. The final, verbless sentence expands the landscape from the roosters to the farms they metonymically imply, while at the same time deepening the metaphor as a fantasy of escape: to live on 'far-away hidden farms' would be the opposite of life in the sterile and crowded sanatorium.

Of course, powerful feelings of expansiveness are not in themselves exclusive to the prose poem. Wordsworth's sonnet 'Composed upon Westminster Bridge, September 3, 1802' evokes the whole of London in a single line of metonymic compression – 'Ships, towers, domes, theatres, and temples' – then rapturously expands this landscape with a metaphorical double exposure of city and countryside:

> Never did sun more beautifully steep
> In his first splendour, valley, rock, or hill;
> Ne'er saw I, never felt, a calm so deep!
> The river glideth at his own sweet will:
> Dear God! the very houses seem asleep;
> And all that mighty heart is lying still![29]

If Wordsworth had been moved to compose his sonnet in prose, the period covered by this anthology would itself have to expand by almost half a century. It's not an impossible alternative history: in the 'Preface' to *Lyrical Ballads*, published the same year, Wordsworth argued that there was no essential distinction between the language of poetry and the language of prose, and that the 'more philosophical distinction' would be between 'Poetry and Matter of Fact, or Science'.[30] The idea of the prose poem, and even the term itself, crops up in various places before Baudelaire, including as the subtitle of one of Edgar Allen Poe's last published works, *Eureka: A Prose Poem* (1848) – an extraordinary, unclassifiable essay, both mystical and scientific, in which Poe seems to anticipate modern cosmology with his vision of an expanding universe.

The form did not come to fruition as a lyric poem, however, until the 1850s, when Baudelaire began to write and publish, over the course of a decade, the fifty short prose texts that would be gathered in *Paris Spleen*. In the private letter to his publisher that serves as the book's preface, the poet asks:

> Which of us has not, in his ambitious days, dreamed of the miracle of a poetic prose, musical without rhythm and without rhyme, supple enough and choppy enough to fit the soul's lyrical movements, the jolts of consciousness?
>
> This obsessive ideal came to life above all by frequenting enormous cities, in the intersection of their countless relationships.[31]

Thus the prose poem, at the moment of its birth, is associated with two kinds of expansiveness, one private and one public, one old and one new: the 'lyrical impulses' of the sensitive soul, and the rapidly enlarging modern world, in whose cities that soul is jostled by thousands of others every day. When Wordsworth stood on Westminster Bridge, the population of

London was just over one million; by 1840, it had doubled. The same exponential growth happened in Paris over the same period, where it was made even more visible in the 1850s by Baron Haussmann's sweeping programme of urban reconstruction, which accelerated the public 'confluence' of Parisian life with a web of wide new boulevards that routed the busy lives of the affluent through the traditional neighbourhoods of the poor, to the disturbance of both: in the bright, wide-open spaces of Haussmann's Paris, in Marshall Berman's words, 'there is no way to look away'.[32]

The Baudelairean prose poem, and all its 'jolts of consciousness', is a record of this historical moment: a private journal made public, as it were, with all the violent ambivalence towards art and humanity that Parisian life provoked in the poet (see 'The Bad Glazier' (p. 400)). But even as lyric poetry, in Baudelaire's prose, expands to map the public spaces of this new world, it is at the same time retreating into 'the ebbs and flows of revery', and the private depths of feeling to be found there. In doing so, Baudelaire combined the historical word-painting he discovered in *Gaspard de la Nuit* with the influence of two contemporary writers of hallucinatory English prose, Edgar Allen Poe and Thomas de Quincey, both of whom he had translated into French. Like Bertrand in his gothic poems, such as 'The Madman' (p. 404), de Quincey and Poe are masters of what might be called visions of lucid darkness, a paradox upon which Baudelaire's 'Windows' meditates (p. 399):

He who looks in through an open window never sees so many things as he who looks at a shut window. There is nothing more profound, more mysterious, more fertile, more gloomy, or more dazzling, than a window lighted by a candle. What we can see in the sunlight is always less interesting than what goes on behind the panes of a window. In that dark or luminous hollow, life lives, life dreams, life suffers.

For Baudelaire, the shut window is a symbol of the 'dark or luminous' mystery of modern life itself, as relished by the flâneur of a metropolis such as Paris, who drifts among the nameless masses of the street seeking a gleam of insight.

Walter Benjamin characterized Baudelaire as a poet haunted by 'the phantom crowd of the words', and the restless cacophony of urban life returns again and again as the raw material of the prose poem, from the 'blurring of horses and motors' in Amy Lowell's 'Spring Day' (p. 346) to Cathy Park Hong's stories of a sleepless Chinese mega-city viewed from 'an apartment without its last wall' (p. 53), and Clifton Gachagua's urgent enquiry into the unspoken secrets of Nairobi ('In the old streets I besiege a man to translate the poems on the walls', p. 27).[33] In a crowded world, the prose poem clears an imagined space for mind-expanding revelations, whether 'a tiny incident [...] hidden like a rare jewel in the casket of Time', as in Rabindranath Tagore's 'A Day' (p. 338); a moment of ramifying horror, as in Ottó Orbán's 'Chile' (p. 223); or an overwhelming feeling of love, as in Lisa Jarnot's 'Ode' ('the rest of the balance continuing huge', p. 107).

'The prose poem', Rod Mengham has recently suggested, 'is modernity's response [...] to our fear of the receding horizon [...] it is the circle we draw around our interactions with the world.'[34] However much the apocalyptic landscape of a prose poem reveals, more remains out of sight. As the critic Nikki Santilli has written, prose poetry resonates with 'the absences that it accommodates'.[35] 'I alone know the plan of this savage sideshow', teases Rimbaud in the final, standalone sentence of 'Sideshow' (p. 388). Prose poems love to hint that they are themselves metaphorical unveilings of their own elusive nature: 'I am dapper and elegant; I move with great precision, cleverly managing all my smaller yellow claws. I believe in the oblique, the indirect approach', reflects Elizabeth Bishop's 'Strayed Crab' (p. 256), slyly punning on the prose poet's own means of sideways travel: the clause. As David Lehman observes in his anthology of *Great American Prose Poems* (2003), certain ideas inevitably recur whenever a critic attempts to pin down the paradoxical nature of the form: 'it will be noted approvingly,' for example, 'that the prose poem *blurs boundaries*'.[36] The prose poem, however, is the wittiest theorist of its own liminality, inviting us to see the ambivalence of identity as the way of the world: 'Me and Molly, that's M and M, melt in your mouth', writes Thylias Moss in her poem about physically inseparable teenage girls who eventually give birth to each other (p. 161); 'the material of her actual body is loosely knit as steam or a colored gas [. . .] and is very close to emotion', muses Mei-mei Berssenbrugge of one of her happily freeform 'Fairies' (p. 38); 'Reason is Spirit', claims Hegel, but according to Anne Carson this is not so much a statement of fact as a sentence in which two words 'tenderly mingle in speculation' (p. 5).

Baudelaire's belief that poetic prose might articulate the modern experience of 'the intersection' of different lives continues to inform its contemporary ambitions. One of the most original exponents of the prose poem currently at work in Britain, Vahni Capildeo (p. 7), has reflected on how her Trinidadian childhood experience of religious ritual informs her openness to the possibilities of mixed form. At Deepavali, the family garage and part of the house would be transformed into a ritual space, with lamps lit and Sanskrit chanted, leading to 'other mixings: of space, and of language':

I see no problem, I take delight, within the space of the page, in crossing from mundane to heightened, elaborated, even opaque

codes, registers, allusions. [. . .] To this experience I can trace
my instinctive revolt against such terms as 'line break', 'white
space' or 'margins of silence'. Without meaning to, I developed
a poetics of reverberation and minor noise.

This attitude and practice, Capildeo reflects, 'may indeed have
a politics, as well as a poetics, belonging to a modernity rooted
in ways of life still not considered safe, polite or relevant to
admit to the canon'.[37] As Marguerite S. Murphy puts it in her
study of the form from Wilde to Ashbery, the prose poem
embodies, among other paradoxes, a 'tradition of subversion'.[38]
Over time it has attained sufficient respectability to be studied,
prized, anthologized. But ever since Baudelaire's dream of a
form 'musical without rhythm or rhyme' rejected the strict
conventions of classical French verse, the prose poem's free-
dom to expand on any subject, and in any style, has attracted
poets wanting to challenge restrictions imposed upon them –
powerfully so, in the case of Wole Soyinka's 'Chimes of Silence'
(p. 233), which was mentally composed while he was a political
prisoner in solitary confinement.[39] If the prose poem's form is
ad hoc, then so is its politics. The spirit of lyrical dissent that
informs *Paris Spleen* returns, for example, in Fenton Johnson's
monologue 'Tired' (p. 342), which is spoken by an African-
American who is 'tired of building up somebody else's
civilisation'; in Kim Hyesoon's 'Seoul's Dinner' (p. 124), which
liberates the descriptive appetite of prose in defiance of the
decorum expected of the South Korean *yŏryu siin*, or female
poet ('I let the snow collect, then shove it into my mouth');[40]
and in Sean Bonney's 'Letter Against the Firmament' (p. 20), a
gnostic invective against the rhetoric of the British politician
Iain Duncan Smith ('that talking claw').

'If prose is a house, poetry is a man on fire running quite fast
through it' (Anne Carson).[41] Far from becoming a literary party

trick, the twenty-first-century prose poem seems full of energy to discover what emergencies it can cause next. Some contemporary poets continue to employ fragmentary prose as a prism through which to refract the 'crystalline jumble' of modernity (to use John Ashbery's exquisite phrase from the preface to his translation of Rimbaud's *Illuminations*).[42] Others, however, are drawn to prose for the poetry of plain statement; what Vivek Naryanan calls, in his 'Ode to Prose', 'the only heart we can trust if only because it beat so firmly'.[43] The precise, documentary prose of a poet such as Claudia Rankine, for example – whose most recent books, *Don't Let Me Be Lonely* (2004) and *Citizen* (2014), are both subtitled 'An American Lyric' – evinces an ambition to rewrite literary tradition that recalls the radical claim made two centuries ago by Wordsworth, when, in *Lyrical Ballads*, he presented 'incidents and situations drawn from common life' in 'language really used by men'.[44] This anthology aims to capture something of the same moment of change and renewal in contemporary writing, as the prose poem dissolves and reforms along the same horizon that enraptured Baudelaire's 'stranger' on the first page of his *Little Poems in Prose*: 'the clouds that pass ... over there ... the marvellous clouds!' (p. 397)

On the Selection and Organization

Brevity has been associated with the prose poem ever since Baudelaire modestly acknowledged his own inventions as 'petit'. In my selection, I have also tried to represent the prose poem in its lengthier manifestations as an extended sequence, but I have refrained from excerpting longer works that have not obviously been composed in readily separable units (such as the book-length 'lyric essay', which is increasingly being recognized as a contemporary form in its own right). I have also not tried to represent related traditions of mixed form, such as the haibun and the prosimetrum, which juxtapose prose and verse in order to make poetry from the tension between the two. My main rule of thumb has been only to include things that have already been published as poetry; to quote Michael Benedikt, editor of an earlier anthology of the form, these are poems 'self-consciously written in prose'.[45] This does, I realize, beg the question of definition, and raises the possible answer that – as Jorge Luis Borges suggested – poetry is in the eye of the reader ('a passage read as though addressed to the reason is prose; read as though addressed to the imagination, it might be poetry').[46] It is also, I realize, unsatisfactory from the point of view of literary history: what comprehensive critical account of the poetic resources of modern prose could leave out, for example, the work of Samuel Beckett, James Joyce, or Virginia Woolf? But that way an infinite anthology lies. The secret poetry of prose can be uncovered even in popular fiction, as Margaret Atwood's 'In Love with Raymond Chandler' (p. 154) demonstrates, wittily rewriting *noir* realism as erotic languor. The published-as-poetry principle has also kept me away, with regret, from the neighbouring fields of short and flash fiction, despite the evident family resemblances here. I have also on the whole chosen poems over poets, with only a few notable figures represented by more than one selection.

My reading has been concentrated on Anglophone poetry published in the United Kingdom and the United States, which has inevitably placed a limit on its internationalism. But one guiding principle was also to find prose poems in which it seemed as though something new was being presented to readers in different times and places, and I have tried, where translations were available – from Arabic, Bengali, Chinese, Czech, Danish,

Dutch, French, German, Greek, Hebrew, Hindi, Hungarian, Icelandic, Italian, Japanese, Korean, Polish, Russian, Spanish, Swedish – to give at least a glimpse of the global variety of prose poetry over the last century. Once these various histories began to flow together in one channel, there seemed to be little meaningful way to part them, which led me to adopt a simple tripartite division of chronology. Everything from Bertrand and Baudelaire to 1945 I have gathered under the heading 'modern', on the grounds that the prose poem originates and develops at the same time as many of the other founding inventions of modernity: the railway, photography, the daily news (a number of Baudelaire's prose poems first appeared as 'feuilletons', short literary items for newspaper readers). My next broad umbrella, 'postmodern', is a term which, like 'prose poetry', has been employed as often as it has been found unsatisfactorily capacious. For practical purposes, I have taken it to cover the second half of the twentieth century, a period when all the arts were in self-conscious conversation with the modernists who invented so many new forms of artistic expression between the 1910s and the 1930s. By cutting off the postmodern at 1999, I don't mean to imply that a new literary period neatly began at the start of the new century. But there was undoubtedly a surge of interest in the prose poem around this time, which can be partly attributed to the rise of the defining invention of our own era – the internet – as a forum for literary experiment and exchange, and the evolution of new daily forms of prose such as the email, the blog, and the tweet.

All poems have been presented in fully justified paragraphs divided by a single line break, with other distinctive aspects of formatting (such as the hanging indent) preserved where found in the original printing of the text. Where possible, I have used the first book publication for the dating of poems, and the chronology of the book has been ordered in reverse so as to foreground the importance of the present moment in the history of the form.

Notes

1. Gertrude Stein, 'Poetry and Grammar', in *Look at Me Now and Here I Am: Selected Works 1911–1945*, ed. by Patricia Meyerowitz (London: Peter Owen, 1967), pp. 123–45 (p. 123).

2. Michael Riffaterre, 'On the Prose Poem's Formal Features', in *The Prose Poem in France: Theory and Practice*, ed. by Mary Ann Caws and Hermine Riffaterre (New York: Columbia University Press), pp. 117–32 (p. 117); Michel Delville, *The American Prose Poem: Poetic Form and the Boundaries of Genre* (Gainesville: University Press of Florida, 1998).

3. Sir Philip Sidney, 'The Defence of Poesy', in *Sidney's 'Defence of Poesy' and Selected Renaissance Literary Criticism*, ed. by Gavin Alexander (London: Penguin, 2004), pp. 3–54 (p. 5); Percy Bysshe Shelley, 'A Defence of Poetry', in *The Major Works*, ed. by Zachary Leader and Michael O'Neill (Oxford: Oxford University Press, 2003), pp. 674–701 (p. 679); Stéphane Mallarmé, 'The Evolution of Literature', in *Selected Prose Poems, Essays and Letters*, ed. by Bradford Cook (Baltimore: The Johns Hopkins Press, 1956), pp. 18–24 (p. 19).

4. D. W. Harding, *Words into Rhythm: English Speech Rhythm in Verse and Prose* (Cambridge: Cambridge University Press, 1976), p. 71.

5. William Hazlitt, 'On the Periodical Essayists', in *Lectures on the English Comic Writers* (London: Taylor and Hessey, 1819), pp. 195–201 (p. 200).

6. Viktor Shklovsky, 'Art as Technique' (1917), in *Russian Formalist Criticism: Four Essays* (Lincoln: University of Nebraska Press, 1965), ed. by Lee T. Lemon and Marion J. Reis, pp. 3–24.

7. Hermine Riffaterre, 'Reading Constants: The Practice of the Prose Poem', in *The Prose Poem in France*, pp. 98–115 (p. 115).

8. For a recent anthology which locates the prose poem among a number of these other forms, see *Short: An International Anthology of Five Centuries of Short-Short Stories, Prose Poems, Brief Essays, and Other Short Prose Forms*, ed. Alan Ziegler (New York: Persea Books, 2014).

9. Lisa Robertson, *The Weather* (London: Reality Street Editions, 2001), p. 80.

10. For example, Vanessa Place's *Tragodía 1: Statement of Facts* (2010), which is made up of redacted documents from her work as a criminal defence attorney specializing in sex offences.

11. See Nick Admussen, 'Trading Metaphors: Chinese Prose Poetry and the Reperiodization of the Twentieth Century', *Modern Chinese Literature and Culture*, 22.2 (2010), 88–129.

12. See *The Poems of T. S. Eliot*, ed. by Christopher Ricks and Jim McCue (London: Faber, 2015), pp. 444–6.

13. Stein, 'Poetry and Grammar', p. 139.

14. Rosmarie Waldrop, 'Why Do I Write Prose Poems/When My True Love is Verse' (2005), reprinted in *Atlantic Drift: An Anthology of Poetry and Poetics*, ed. by James Byrne and Robert Sheppard (Todmorden: Arc/Edge Hill University Press), pp. 315–18 (p. 316).

15. André Breton, 'Manifesto of Surrealism' (1924), trans. by R. Seaver and H. R. Lane, reprinted with corrections in *Modernism: An Anthology*, ed. by Lawrence Rainey (Oxford: Blackwell, 2005), pp. 718–41 (p. 726).

16. Aimé Césaire, 'Poetry and Knowledge', trans. by Jon Cook, in *Poetry in Theory: An Anthology 1900–2000*, ed. by Jon Cook (Oxford: Blackwell, 2004), pp. 276–87 (p. 285).

17. Ibid., p. 278.

18. Frank O'Hara, 'Why I am Not a Painter', in *Selected Poems*, ed. by Donald Allen (Manchester: Carcanet, 1991), p. 112.

19. Amy Lowell, *Can Grande's Castle* (New York: Macmillan, 1918), p. xv.

20. Samuel Taylor Coleridge, *Table Talk* (London: John Murray, 1835), I, p. 84; Stein, p. 136.

21. William Wordsworth, *The Major Works*, ed. by Stephen Gill (Oxford: Oxford University Press, 2000), p. 598.

22. In *Other Traditions* (Cambridge, Mass.: Harvard University Press, 2000), Ashbery notes that his poem was inspired by Clare's prose fragment musing on the neglected subject of 'House or Window Flies' (pp. 18–19).

23. *The New Republic*, 8 April 1985, p. 18.

24. Quoted in *The Best American Poetry 1997*, ed. by James Tate and David Lehman (New York: Scribner, 1997), p. 200.

25. Roman Jakobson, 'Two Aspects of Language and Two Types of Aphasic Disturbances', in *Selected Writings* (The Hague: Mouton), II (1956), pp. 239–59.

26. Aristotle, *Poetics*, in *Classical Literary Criticism*, trans. by Penelope Murray and T. S. Dorsch (London: Penguin, 2000), p. 88.

27. Virginia Woolf, 'Impassioned Prose', in *Collected Essays* (London: The Hogarth Press), I (1966), pp. 165–72 (p. 168).

28. See Keiko Mizuta, 'Katherine Mansfield and the Prose Poem', *The Review of English Studies*, 39.153 (1988), 75–83.

29. Wordsworth, p. 285.

30. Ibid., pp. 601–2.

31. Charles Baudelaire, 'Preface to *La Presse*, 1862', in *The Parisian Prowler*, 2nd edn, trans. by Edward K. Kaplan (Athens: The University of Georgia, 1997), pp. 129–30 (p. 129).

32. Marshall Berman, *All That is Solid Melts into Air: The Experience of Modernity* (London: Verso, 2010), p. 153.

33. Walter Benjamin, 'On Some Motifs in Baudelaire', in *Illuminations*, trans. by Harry Zorn (London: Jonathan Cape, 1970), pp. 152–90 (p. 162).

34. Rod Mengham, 'A Genealogy of the Prose Poem', *Countertext* 3.2 (2017), 176–86 (p. 186).

35. Nikki Santilli, *Such Rare Citings: The Prose Poem in English Literature* (London: Associated University Presses, 2002), p. 22.

36. David Lehman, 'Introduction', in *Great American Prose Poems* (New York: Scribner, 2006), pp. 11–26 (p. 13).

37. Vahni Capildeo, 'Letter Not from Trinidad', *PN Review* 221 (January–February 2015), 6.

38. Marguerite S. Murphy, *A Tradition of Subversion: The Prose Poem in English from Wilde to Ashbery* (Amherst: University of Massachusetts Press, 1992).

39. Wole Soyinka, *A Shuttle from the Crypt* (London: Rex Collings / Eyre, Methuen, 1972), p. vii.

40. See Ruth Williams, 'Kim Hyesoon: The Female Grotesque', *Guernica*, 1 January 2012, online.

41. Kate Kellaway, 'Anne Carson: "I do not believe in therapy" ' [interview], *The Observer*, 30 October 2016, online.

42. Arthur Rimbaud, *Illuminations*, trans. by John Ashbery (Manchester: Carcanet, 2011), p. 14.

43. Vivek Naryanan, *Universal Beach* (Mumbai: Harbour Line, 2006), p. 65.

44. Wordsworth, pp. 596–7.

45. Michael Benedikt, ed., *The Prose Poem: An International Anthology* (New York: Dell, 1976), p. 47.

46. Jorge Luis Borges, *Selected Poems 1923–1967* (London: Allen Lane, 1972), trans. by Norman Thomas di Giovanni, p. xv.

The Prose Poem Now

The End of Days

after Anselm Kiefer & for Elena Lydia Scipioni

A snake with honey-coloured eyes survived and told what had happened:

In our burning fields, Yesterday drew me with the spittle of its mouth on a charred wall, like a blackboard in front of frightened pupils. Thus you saw in me the image of my father, throwing my last pennies into the fountain of death, then sewing the buttons of his oil-green coat in the furrows of mud where you had planted seeds, arranged in the form of words, and they grew and blossomed when light rained down, warm as remorse, and again blood was made to flow on the palms of the earth. Canes grew high as poplars and we broke them to roof our refuge, and we jumped over our vein-streams to swim in our first sky. We fertilised our language with our debris. Mountains had become ripe heads for the fists of the sky and the slopes cheeks we ran down like melted ice, and at every point where the disappeared had fallen an unattainable flower sprang up, or a burning matchstick flickered before a school-boy could close his mouth over it to put out the flame – as he hurries to do his homework on forgetting fear.

We will remember for a long time how we were before this harvest. Each of us will visit his own grave, carrying a whip on

3

his shoulder, or behind his back a sickle or a knife. Time was a game. We bade farewell to our beds that had been smashed by our dreams. Gamblers offered us a moon that crumbled to dust at the touch of our fingers. Rats offered us their eyes as stars. Hunger blazed its suns behind our foreheads. Books we hadn't read flittered down and landed on our ulcers. Great silences seeped through our bandages. No one uttered a word. The dots and signs with which we ended our lines leapt towards the words scattered about them, and all meanings changed.

Golan Haji (2017), translated from the Arabic
by the author and Stephen Watts

Merry Christmas from Hegel

It was the year my brother died, I lived up north and had few friends or they all went away. Christmas Day I was sitting in my armchair, reading something about Hegel. You will forgive me if you are someone who knows a lot of Hegel or understands it, I do not and will paraphrase badly, but I understood him to be saying he was fed up with popular criticism of his terrible prose and claiming that conventional grammar, with its clumsy dichotomy of subject and verb, was in conflict with what he called 'speculation'. Speculation being the proper business of philosophy. Speculation being the effort to grasp reality in its interactive entirety. The function of a sentence like 'Reason is Spirit' was not to assert a fact (he said) but to lay Reason side by side with Spirit and allow their meanings to tenderly mingle in speculation. I was overjoyed by this notion of a philosophic space where words drift in gentle mutual redefinition of one another but, at the same time, wretchedly lonely with all my family dead and here it was Christmas Day, so I put on big boots and coat and went out to do some snow standing. Not since childhood! I had forgot how astounding it is. I went to the middle of a woods. Fir trees, the teachers of this, all around. Minus twenty degrees in the wind but inside the trees is no wind. The world subtracts itself in layers. Outer sounds like traffic and shoveling vanish. Inner sounds become audible, cracks, sighs, caresses, twigs, birdbreath, toenails of squirrel.

5

The fir trees move hugely. The white is perfectly curved, stunned with itself. Puffs of ice fog and some gold things float up. Shadows rake their motionlessness across the snow with a vibration of other shadows moving crosswise on them, shadow on shadow, in precise velocities. It is very cold, then that, too, begins to subtract itself, the body chills on its surface but the core is hot and it is possible to disconnect the surface, withdraw to the core, where a ravishing peace flows in, so ravishing I am unembarrassed to use the word *ravishing*, and it is not a peace of separation from the senses but the washing-through peace of looking, listening, feeling, at the very core of snow, at the very core of the care of snow. It has nothing to do with Hegel and he would not admire the clumsily conventional sentences in which I have tried to tell about it but I suspect, if I hadn't been trying on the mood of Hegel's particular grammatical indignation that Christmas Day, I would never have gone out to stand in the snow, or stayed to speculate with it, or had the patience to sit down and make a record of speculation for myself as if it were a worthy way to spend an afternoon, a plausible way to change the icy horror of holiday into a sort of homecoming. Merry Christmas from Hegel.

Anne Carson (2016)

Going Nowhere, Getting Somewhere

How was it that till questioned, till displaced in the attempt to answer, I had scarcely thought of myself as having a country, or indeed as having left a country? The answer lies peripherally in looming, in hinterland; primarily in the tongueless, palpitating interiority. Trinidad was. Trinidad is. In the same way, some confident speakers do not think of themselves as having an accent. They will say so: 'I don't have an accent! You have an accent!' In those accentless voices compass points spin, ochre and ultramarine flagella fling themselves identifiably towards this that or the other region. It is a motile version of that luxury, solidity, non-reflectivity that is the assumption of *patria*. So different is the expat from the refugee, who has her country on her back, or the migrant, who has countries at his back.

What would I have called home, before I began creating home? Before I had to learn to ravel up longitude, latitude, population, oil rigs, mobile phone masts, prayer flags, legality of fireworks, likely use of firearms, density and disappearance of forests, scarlet ibis, other stripes of scarlet, into a by-listeners-unvisited, communicable, substantial image of 'Trinidad'?

Language is my home. It is alive other than in speech. It is beyond a thing to be carried with me. It is ineluctable, variegated and muscular. A flicker and drag emanates from the idea

7

of it. Language seems capable of girding the oceanic earth, like the world-serpent of Norse legend. It is as if language places a shaping pressure upon our territories of habitation and voyage; thrashing, independent, threatening to rive our known world apart.

Yet thought is not bounded by language. At least, my experience of thinking does not appear so bound.

One day I lost the words *wall* and *floor*. There seemed no reason to conceive of a division. The skirting-board suddenly reduced itself to a nervous gentrification, a cover-up of some kind; nothing especially marked. The room was an inward-focused container. 'Wall', 'floor', even 'ceiling', 'doorway', 'shutters' started to flow smoothly, like a red ribbed tank top over a heaving ribcage. Room grew into quarter. Room became segment. Line yearned till it popped into curve. The imperfections of what had been built or installed: the ragged windowframe or peeling tile: had no power to reclaim human attention to 'floor' or 'wall' as such. Objects were tethered like astronauts and a timid fringe of disarrayed atmosphere was the immediate past that human activity kept restyling into present. The interiority of the room was in continuous flow. *Wall, floor* became usable words again in a sort of silence.

I had the sense to shut up about the languageless perception. Procedure for living.

Language is my home, I say; not one particular language.

Vahni Capildeo (2016)

Children are the Orgasm of the World

This morning on the bus there was a woman carrying a bag with inspirational sayings and positive affirmations which I was reading because I'm a fan of inspirational sayings and positive affirmations. I also like clothing that gives you advice. What's better than the glittered baseball cap of a stranger telling you what to strive for? It's like living in a world of therapists. The inspirational bag of the woman on the bus said a number of things like 'live in the moment' and 'remember to breathe' but it also said 'children are the orgasm of the world'. Are children the orgasm of the world like orgasms are the orgasms of sex? Are children the orgasm of anything? Children are the orgasm of the world like hovercraft are the orgasm of the future or silence is the orgasm of the telephone, or shit is the orgasm of the lasagne. You could even say sheep are the orgasm of lonely pastures, which are the orgasm of modern farming practices which are the orgasm of the industrial revolution. And then I thought why not? I like comparing things to other things too. Like sometimes when we're having sex and you look like a helicopter in a low-budget movie, disappearing behind a cloud to explode. Or an athlete winning a prestigious sporting tournament at the exact moment he realises his wife has been cheating on him. For the most part, orgasms are the orgasms of the world. Like slam-dunking a glass basketball. Or executing a perfect dive into a swimming pool full of oh my god. Or travelling into the past to forgive yourself and creating a time paradox so complex it forces all of human history to reboot, stranding you naked on some rocky outcrop, looking up at the sunset from a world so new looking up hasn't even been invented yet.

Hera Lindsay Bird (2016)

Antico Adagio

Bring down the lights. Bring out the stars. Let the record sing; the vibraphone; the violin; the gong. We call this charm a festooned gazebo in twilight. We call night and her creatures to the summer screen; every beat a wheel every wheel aglow. The soft tight musical light a freshet. And happy who can hear the wood, the ferns bobbing, the stars splashing down. I wanted this glad tight happy light inside the gloaming. I wanted glow. The piping anthem of a voyage listing in lamplight, oboe light; hear it and fly. Hear it fly like friendship like modernism beginning like a steamer pulling out to sea in an old reel dreaming. Married to a song; to a pebble of song.

Peter Gizzi (2016)

Knife

It has a broad axe shape, but is sliver-thin. Even at the blunt end, the ochre-coloured flint, smoothed and polished, is a slim-line product. It looks like a small spatula, and would be something of a puzzle to archaeology, but speculation is point-less, rendered futile at a touch. The obliging object tells the hand exactly where it wants to go.

As soon as I picked it up, the long haft made itself at home, slung between first finger and thumb on the elastic webbing of skin. The first fingerpad went straight to the back of the blade. After three thousand years of dumb neglect, the instrument was attuned, responsive, prompt to its ancient cue.

The leading edge is minutely pecked. Broken small craters, overlapping scoops, were quickly opened up in the glassy stone by the same degree of force aimed repeatedly, dozens of times, at the same hard margin of a few fingers' breadth.

The life-knowledge of the flint-knapper dwells in the sparing of exertion at the very point of landing a blow. The effects of this knowledge, the depth and shape of indentations in the stone, are accordingly generic if not uniform. An even more precise and unthinking calculation is needed for end-on strokes that split the individual flint.

At some point the maker, under the spell of making, no longer sees the use to which the blade is put, seeing instead the bloom of a new shape begin to emerge from the flint's uncertain depths. Sometimes this shape is only poorly divined, or glimpsed and avoided; sometimes it is nursed into life, by craftsmen who watch for the ideal form of knife-being, especially if this is a votive blade, intended for ritual deposit. Best of all is when the artist, setting his sights on perfect function, sees it rise above the horizon at the same point as beauty of form.

This tool for cutting was neither deposited nor lost. I think it was left beneath the roots of a broad oak with a clutter of flints, worked but unfinished, until the maker should return, and return soon. There it lay until the sea covered all the oaks whose stumps are now below the tides at Holme-next-the-Sea.

Lying there through storms that uncovered the massive inverted bole of roots at the centre of Seahenge, close by, it found another hand to belabour, to switch on, to gear up, when just enough sand had been swished aside for its pale surface to draw the eye.

It may never have been used, but was made for a hand that used others like it, and it would always transmit the same feeling for action, the same possible uses for butchery: severing, slicing, scraping. It was the lever between inner and outer worlds, it showed that the airs and waters, rocks and earth, moving and combining and resisting one another, obeying the spirits that ruled them, had their equivalent workings, their times of calm and upheaval, under the skin; in the wallowing lungs, the weeping flesh, the flowing heart, and in all the symmetries of bones and muscles, the asymmetries of lower organs, the random belt of the guts. It brought the cross-sections of life within grasp. Behind it, the physician's trial and error, the surgeon's initiative; the whole breathing, faltering body of science.

Rod Mengham (2015)

A Woman Shopping

I will soon write a long, sad book called *A Woman Shopping*. It will be a book about what we are required to do and also a book about what we are hated for doing. It will be a book about envy and a book about barely visible things. This book would be a book also about the history of literature and literature's uses against women, also against literature and for it, also against shopping and for it. The flâneur is a poet is an agent free of purses, but a woman is not a woman without a strap over her shoulder or a clutch in her hand.

The back matter of the book will only say this: *If a woman has no purse, we will imagine one for her.*

These would be the chapters:

On a woman shopping
On men shopping, with and without women
On children with women as they shop
On the barely moving lips of the calculating and poor
On attempting to open doors for the elderly and in the process of this, touching their arms
On the acquiring of arms in action movies
On Daniel Defoe
On the time I saw a homeless man murdered for shoplifting

On whether it is better to want nothing or steal everything
On how many of my hours are gone now because I have had
to shop
On how I wish I could shop for hours instead

There would be more; lavish descriptions of lavish descriptions of the perverse or decadently feminized marketplace, some long sentences concerning the shipping and distribution of alterity, an entire chapter about *Tender Buttons* in which each sentence is only a question. And from where did that mutton, that roast beef, that carafe come?

But who would publish this book and who, also, would shop for it? And how could it be literature if it is not coyly against literature, but sincerely against it, as it is also against ourselves?

Anne Boyer (2015)

Notes Towards a Race Riot Scene

In April 1979, I was ten years old.

This is a short talk about vectors. It's about Brueghel's Icarus. It's about a girl walking home from school at the exact moment her neighbour laces up his Doc Martens, tight. It's about a partial and irrelevant nudity. It's about the novel as a form that processes the part of a scene that doesn't function as an image, but as the depleted, yet still livid mixture of materials that a race riot is made from. Think of the sky. Think of the clear April day with its cardigans and late afternoon rain shower. Think of the indigo sky lowering over London like a lid. Think of Blair Peach, the anti-racism campaigner and recent emigrant from New Zealand, who will die before this day is out.

Think about a cyborg to get to the immigrant.

Think of a colony. Think of the red and white daikon radishes in a tilted box on the pavement outside Dokal and Sons, on the corner of Uxbridge Road and Lansbury Drive. Think of the road, which here we call asphalt: there, it is bitty. It is a dark silver with milky oil seams. A patch up job, *Labour* still in power, but not for long. It's 1979, St. George's Day, and the Far Right has decided to have its annual meeting in a council-run meeting hall in Southall, Middlesex, a London suburb in which it would be rare – nauseating – to see a white face.

To see anyone, actually. Everyone's indoors. Everyone can tell what's coming. It's not a riot, at this point, but a simple protest in an outlying area of London, an immigrant suburb: a *banlieue*. Everyone knows to board the glass up, draw the curtains and lie down. Lie down between the hand-sewn quilts shipped from India in a crate then covered in an outer cotton case stitched to the padding with a fine pink thread. The quilts smell of an antiseptic powder, an anti-fungal, Mars. We lie down beneath the blankets in front of the fire. It's 1979, so there's a small gas fire and a waist-high fridge, where we keep our milk and our bread and our cheese, right there, in the living room. It's 1979, and so I live in Hayes, though in two months, we'll put our house on the market and move.

Move away. As would you.

Bhanu Kapil (2015)

'There were barnacles . . .'

Once there were . . . – Cormac McCarthy

There were barnacles that marked the edges of oceans. Late scramblers on the rocks could feel their calcic ridges stoving sharply underfoot. The wet rocks glittered beneath and in the wind they smelled of verdigris. The barnacles fused in intricate settlements. For their whole lives they cleaved, and in turn the fragile rock cleaved to them. Volcanoes and thimbles and strange constellations. Together they mapped distant cities and willed the sea to overtake them. And when the russet tide came they opened themselves like unfamiliar lovers. The whole thing some actinic principle: a forest grew up in a second, to grace a world where the sun was a watery lamp. Where none had been before, white mouths frilled softly in the current and squat armour issued forth the unlikeliest of cilia: transparent, lightly haired, cherishing each updraft as, feathered, they moved with it. They only existed for that half-sunk terrain. And as they briefly lived, those tender quills wrote of their mystery.

Sarah Howe (2015)

from *Letter Against the Firmament*

I know. I'd been hoping to spare you any further musings I might have had on the nature of Iain Duncan Smith, that talking claw. But perhaps we're at a point now where we need to define him, to recite and describe, occupy his constellations. Because to recite the stations of the being of Iain Duncan Smith, as if they were a string of joy-beads, and they are, would be to recite the history of the law, if we take that law to be something as simple as a mouth is, and each noise, each syllable that emits from that mouth is only ever and never more than the sound of animals eating each other, a gap in the senses where the invisible universe goes to die, and we become like ghosts or insomniacs stumbling through the city, we become the music of Iain Duncan Smith, his origin in the chaos of animals and plants, of rocks and metals and the countless earths, where over and again he breaks children's teeth with gravelstones, covers them with ashes. Because to classify those stations, the cancer-ladder of the dreams of Iain Duncan Smith might, at a push, be to consume him, and to define those stations, those marks on the hide of Iain Duncan Smith, might be to trap him, to press granite to the roof of his mouth, the stations of the law. And at this point, obviously, I really wish I could think of something to say that was hopeful, that was useful, that was not simply a net of rats blocking the force of the sun, till it crawls on its fists and knees, screaming like a motherfucker, sarcastic and wrathful, boiling the mountains as if they were scars, laughing, laughing like a crucifixion, modular and bleached. Bleached with the guts of Iain Duncan Smith, of each of the modest number of words he actually understands, such as grovel and stingray and throat, chlamydia, wart. And those five words are the entirety of the senses of Iain Duncan Smith, the gates to his city, his recitation of the germs of the law, a clock that never strikes and never stops, where we are not counted, wiped from the knots of statistics, comparable to fine gold, receptacles of song, shrieking gulls. It's all I can bear to listen to, that shrieking. It blocks out the stars, the malevolent alphabet he's been proposing.

Sean Bonney (2015)

from *Citizen: An American Lyric*

When you are alone and too tired even to turn on any of your devices, you let yourself linger in a past stacked among pillows. Usually you are nestled under blankets and the house is empty. Sometimes the moon is missing and beyond the windows the low, gray ceiling seems approachable. Its dark light dims in degrees depending on the density of clouds and you fall back into that which gets reconstructed as metaphor.

The route is often associative. You smell good. You are twelve attending Sts. Philip and James School on White Plains Road and the girl sitting in the seat behind asks you to lean to the right during exams so she can copy what you have written. Sister Evelyn is in the habit of taping the 100s and the failing grades to the coat closet doors. The girl is Catholic with waist-length brown hair. You can't remember her name: Mary? Catherine?

You never really speak except for the time she makes her request and later when she tells you you smell good and have features more like a white person. You assume she thinks she is thanking you for letting her cheat and feels better cheating from an almost white person.

Sister Evelyn never figures out your arrangement perhaps because you never turn around to copy Mary Catherine's answers. Sister Evelyn must think these two girls think a lot alike or she cares less about cheating and more about humiliation or she never actually saw you sitting there.

*

The new therapist specializes in trauma counseling. You have only ever spoken on the phone. Her house has a side gate that leads to a back entrance she uses for patients. You walk down a path bordered on both sides with deer grass and rosemary to the gate, which turns out to be locked.

At the front door the bell is a small round disc that you press firmly. When the door finally opens, the woman standing there yells, at the top of her lungs, Get away from my house. What are you doing in my yard?

It's as if a wounded Doberman pinscher or a German shepherd has gained the power of speech. And though you back up a few steps, you manage to tell her you have an appointment. You have an appointment? she spits back. Then she pauses. Everything pauses. Oh, she says, followed by, oh, yes, that's right. I am sorry.

I am so sorry, so, so sorry.

*

A friend writes of the numbing effects of humming and it returns you to your own sigh. It's no longer audible. You've grown into it. Some call it aging – an internalized liquid smoke blurring ordinary ache.

Just this morning another, What did he say?

Come on, get back in the car. Your partner wants to face off with a mouth and who knows what handheld objects the other vehicle carries.

Trayvon Martin's name sounds from the car radio a dozen times each half hour. You pull your love back into the seat because though no one seems to be chasing you, the justice system has other plans.

Yes, and this is how you are a citizen: Come on. Let it go. Move on.

Despite the air-conditioning you pull the button back and the window slides down into its door-sleeve. A breeze touches your cheek. As something should.

Claudia Rankine (2014)

My Funeral

Remove any remaining teeth which still have amalgam fillings, and dispose of them in a hazardous waste facility. Cast a rectangular coffin in inch-thick magnesium, 6 feet by 3 feet by 2 feet, total surface area approx. 19,700 square inches, the equivalent of 409 A5 pages. Use letter punches to stamp the inner and outer surfaces of the coffin with the text of this book, and of the *Poésies* of Stéphane Mallarmé. Pour a layer of white granulated sugar into the coffin, to a depth of half the difference between the interior height of the coffin and the thickness of my corpse. Lay my corpse on its back, fully dressed, on the sugar. Place an Elrathia kingii trilobite, free of all matrix, over each of my eyes; an enrolled Phacops rana trilobite in my navel, under my shirt; and the large, testicles-shaped fragment of mediaeval masonry you will find among my personal effects, over my genital area, with the balls pointing down. Put the polished section of Madagascan ammonite I always carry with me into my left-hand trouser pocket. Lay two small canisters of oxygen, and two small canisters of propane gas, beside my corpse, one of each on either side. Fill up the remaining volume of the coffin with powdered ammonium nitrate fertilizer, and figure out how to hermetically seal a magnesium coffin. Lay the coffin on a pyre of sustainable Scottish oak wood, built wherever seems most appropriate and constructive to you at the time. Invite everyone. Light the pyre. Run away. Don't actually do this.

Peter Manson (2014)

Flower, Quartet, Mask

To dignify a room needs no more than unusual attention to the usual. The corner of a glass table with the CD case lying on it, the orchid above still flowering after six months. It's as though a challenge has been issued to time itself. The bronze face of a girl in sleep or ecstasy makes no comment upon the competing efforts of these things to behave as if they could control time. The orchid's petals, like pink propellers frozen in a downwards plunge, a suspended cataclysm, have dared to endure; the music, whose case it is, has moved away on its own, as if to expend itself. One is still, one enlarged. Yet only one is growing unpredictably; the other knows its direction and directions. Does it matter? Both are doomed. Each outwits regulation for the time it takes, and for what time takes from it. The laser will eventually have nothing left spinning to decode, and the stalk will cease to transmit the life that qualifies stillness in the veined blush of the flower. Only the bronze face is content to be measured by time. Her eyes are narrowed, and her slight smile suspends all clocks. Sharing this for the moment that I drain my glass, I reflect that the page is no partisan. Everything has some claim upon it equally. They were all set upon their courses, and must see them through. The page woos them, but they make no response other than to be themselves. Eventually the page apologises, and is silent.

John Fuller (2014)

Reclaiming a Beloved City

I approach Nairobi, thrown into the mass of old avenues. I have
a map of the old town and what the streets used to be called,
government road and the little place where Lord Delamere
liked to be the asshole, all regards to the dead.

And in the eyes of people are azaleas blooming and popping
like bubblegum carried up to perch in the branches of a blue
I&M tree, there where the transmission has been telling us
consumption begins and ends when our bodies decide. We are
lapping against each other, our bodies not touching, our inten-
tions quite clear, our beds unmade.

A naiad, completely given up to sighs and biting its fingernails,
winks at me. I am the inconsolable. She gives me back a second
of my celebratory youth.

I am not approached by beggars although to feel at home my
eyes beg for some reprieve from the eyes of another traveler
who has misplaced his airplane in the middle of the street
where it is okay to hold the arms of a stranger until you have
crossed the road.

In the old streets I besiege a man to translate the poems on the walls, on the bodies of women, on the lumps that are hanging from their men. Gross desire is a river tapestry with water like ribbons – he tells me.

Clifton Gachagua (2014)

Imagined Sons 9: Greek Salad

For a week I travel on business, and on the fourth afternoon, I go to a restaurant to have yet another meal alone. I order a Greek salad and read a Dickens novel to escape my loneliness.

When the salad arrives, I barely look. How will Jenny Wren respond to news of her drunken father's death? I push the fork into the lettuce, and it yields slowly to the tines. The balance of balsamic vinegar and olive oil, with the sweetness of the red lettuce, is perfect, and I pause, relishing the flavour.

I hear the smallest of shrieks. I think I must have anticipated Jenny, that I must have been that engrossed, when I hear it again. I put my book down so its open pages press the plastic tablecloth and keep my place, and my fork dives again, spearing a cube of feta.

'Stop! Stop!' The sound rises from the salad.

'Who – what are you?' I whisper. '*Where* are you?'

A black olive wiggles atop a romaine leaf, as though to wave. 'I am your son, brutally transformed!'

I glance around the restaurant and see the other diners, all in groups, engaged in conversation. 'When I last saw you, you were an infant. How did you get into this state?' I say with some sharpness.

I think I see him cringe. Meekly, he says, 'I fell in love with the virgin mistress of the god's own olive grove. When I made love to her, I was turned into an olive tree!'

'When you made love to her?'

The softest of whispers: '*They* say, when I raped her.'

'So you are a tree as well as this olive?' I ask, trying to move my mouth as little as possible as I see the waiter coming from the kitchen. 'So she tends to you, there in the grove?'

'She only knows I disappeared,' the olive whines. 'She tends to me, yes, but without thought, without love. It is a fate worse than –'

'Delicious,' I say to the waiter, swallowing the small olive whole. 'Just delicious.'

Carrie Etter (2014)

Place Name

Flog Man, for them days when man could get nine-and-thirty
just cause he hold his head so high that Missus call him
uppity. Nigger man admit he sometimes feel the curl of
whips, their stinging S's – tips soaked in horse piss – more
than he feel sun on his skin. Flogging was so common it was
odd that they call this place Flog Man, why not rename the
whole damn country Flog Island? But it had one beating so
brutal, no one could cork their ears from it; both black and
white man fail in the long practice of deafness; years pass;
like salve but they was still hearing it, the cow whip flicking
up flecks of skin, and this Mandingo man who they did think
was too big, too proud to ever let eye water grace him eye
was bawling out a bruck-spirit sound even larger than the
barrel of him chest. Blood did sprinkle the ground like
anointing and now people walk by and cringe as memory
curl like S and lash them owna skin.

Kei Miller (2014)

Rape Joke

The rape joke is that you were nineteen years old.

The rape joke is that he was your boyfriend.

The rape joke it wore a goatee. A goatee.

Imagine the rape joke looking in the mirror, perfectly reflecting back itself, and grooming itself to look more like a rape joke. 'Ahhhh,' it thinks. 'Yes. *A goatee.*'

No offense.

The rape joke is that he was seven years older. The rape joke is that you had known him for years, since you were too young to be interesting to him. You liked that use of the word *interesting*, as if you were a piece of knowledge that someone could be desperate to acquire, to assimilate, and to spit back out in different form through his goateed mouth.

Then suddenly you were older, but not very old at all.

The rape joke is that you had been drinking wine coolers. Wine coolers! Who drinks wine coolers? People who get raped, according to the rape joke.

The rape joke is he was a bouncer, and kept people out for a living.

Not you!

The rape joke is that he carried a knife, and would show it to you, and would turn it over and over in his hands as if it were a book.

He wasn't threatening you, you understood. He just really liked his knife.

The rape joke is he once almost murdered a dude by throwing him through a plate-glass window. The next day he told you and he was trembling, which you took as evidence of his sensitivity.

How can a piece of knowledge be stupid? But of course you were so stupid.

The rape joke is that sometimes he would tell you you were going on a date and then take you over to his best friend Pee-wee's house and make you watch wrestling while they all got high.

The rape joke is that his best friend was named Peewee.

OK, the rape joke is that he worshiped The Rock.

Like the dude was completely in love with The Rock. He thought it was so great what he could do with his eyebrow.

The rape joke is he called wrestling 'a soap opera for men.' Men love drama too, he assured you.

The rape joke is that his bookshelf was just a row of paperbacks about serial killers. You mistook this for an interest in history, and laboring under this misapprehension you once gave him a copy of Günter Grass's *My Century*, which he never even tried to read.

It gets funnier.

The rape joke is that he kept a diary. I wonder if he wrote about the rape in it.

The rape joke is that you read it once, and he talked about another girl. He called her Miss Geography, and said 'he didn't have those urges when he looked at her anymore,' not since he met you. Close call, Miss Geography!

The rape joke is that he was your father's high school student – your father taught World Religion. You helped him clean out his classroom at the end of the year, and he let you take home the most beat-up textbooks.

The rape joke is that he knew you when you were twelve years old. He once helped your family move two states over, and you drove from Cincinnati to St. Louis with him, all by yourselves, and he was kind to you, and you talked the whole way. He had chaw in his mouth the entire time, and you told him he was disgusting and he laughed, and spat the juice through his goatee into a Mountain Dew bottle.

The rape joke is that *come on*, you should have seen it coming. This rape joke is practically writing itself.

The rape joke is that you were facedown. The rape joke is you were wearing a pretty green necklace that your sister had made for you. Later you cut that necklace up. The mattress felt a specific way, and your mouth felt a specific way open against it, as if you were speaking, but you know you were not. As if your mouth were open ten years into the future, reciting a poem called Rape Joke.

The rape joke is that time is different, becomes more horrible and more habitable, and accommodates your need to go deeper into it.

Just like the body, which more than a concrete form is a capacity.

You know the body of time is *elastic*, can take almost anything you give it, and heals quickly.

The rape joke is that of course there was blood, which in human beings is so close to the surface.

The rape joke is you went home like nothing happened, and laughed about it the next day and the day after that, and when you told people you laughed, and that was the rape joke.

It was a year before you told your parents, because he was like a son to them. The rape joke is that when you told your father, he made the sign of the cross over you and said, 'I absolve you of your sins, in the name of the Father, and of the Son, and of the Holy Spirit,' which even in its total wrongheadedness, was so completely sweet.

The rape joke is that you were crazy for the next five years, and had to move cities, and had to move states, and whole days went down into the sinkhole of thinking about why it happened. Like you went to look at your backyard and suddenly it wasn't there, and you were looking down into the center of the earth, which played the same red event perpetually.

The rape joke is that after a while you weren't crazy anymore, but close call, Miss Geography.

The rape joke is that for the next five years all you did was write, and never about yourself, about anything else, about apples on the tree, about islands, dead poets and the worms that aerated them, and there was no warm body in what you wrote, it was elsewhere.

The rape joke is that this is finally artless. The rape joke is that you do not write artlessly.

The rape joke is if you write a poem called Rape Joke, you're asking for it to become the only thing people remember about you.

The rape joke is that you asked why he did it. The rape joke is he said he didn't know, like what else would a rape joke say? The rape joke said YOU were the one who was drunk, and the rape joke said you remembered it wrong, which made you laugh out loud for one long split-open second. The wine coolers weren't Bartles & Jaymes, but it would be funnier for the rape joke if they were. It was some pussy flavor, like Passionate Mango or Destroyed Strawberry, which you drank down without question and trustingly in the heart of Cincinnati, Ohio.

Can rape jokes be funny at all, is the question.

Can any part of the rape joke be funny. The part where it ends – haha, just kidding! Though you did dream of killing the rape joke for years, spilling all of its blood out, and telling it that way.

The rape joke cries out for the right to be told.

The rape joke is that this is just how it happened.

The rape joke is that the next day he gave you *Pet Sounds*. No really. *Pet Sounds*. He said he was sorry and then he gave you *Pet Sounds*. Come on, that's a little bit funny.

Admit it.

Patricia Lockwood (2014)

from *Fairies*

2

Fairies begin their day by coming together a moment and sharing joy.

They love the feeling, which dew on the leaves draws from grass, lilacs and the response of meadow and flowers to the dawn.

Diminutive green sylphs now run in the grass, whose growth seems intimately associated with theirs, a single line of · concentration.

They talk to themselves, constantly repeating, with an intensity causing their etheric doubles, grass, to vibrate as they pass, vivifying growth.

To rabbits and young children they're visible, but I see points of light, tiny clouds of color and gleams of movement.

The lawn is covered with these flashes.

In low alyssums along a border, one exquisite, tiny being plays around stems, passing in and out of each bud.

She's happy and feels much affection for the plants, which she regards as her own body.

The material of her actual body is loosely knit as steam or a colored gas, bright apple-green or yellow, and is very close to emotion.

Tenderness for plants shows as rose; sympathy for their growth and adaptability as flashes of emerald.

When she feels joy, her body responds all-over with a desire to be somewhere or do something for plants.

Hers is not a world of surfaces – skin, husks, bark with definite edges and identities.

Trees appear as columns of light melting into surroundings where form is discerned, but is glowing, transparent, mingling like breath.

She tends to a plant by maintaining fusion between the plant's form and life-vitality contained within.

She works as part of nature's massed intelligence to express the involution of awareness or consciousness into a form.

And she includes vitality, because one element of form is action.

Sprouting, branching, leafing, blossoming, crumbling to humus are all form to a fairy.

Mei-mei Berssenbrugge (2013)

from *Mystérieuse*

24

Observatory dome, vertical and horizontal curves, mobile staircase leading to a large telescope, wheels, cranks, large gyration systems, eyepieces, lens, and in front, table and chair: two figures seated at the table, scholars leaning over their calculations in puzzlement, drops of sweat splash, the figure comes towards them – concentration.

Simple background, table and chair: the figure approaches one of the scholar figures who indicates silence, drops of sweat splash – imperative gesture.

Simple background, table and chairs: whilst one of the scholar figures sits and calculates, symbols all around, drops of sweat splash, the other scholar justifies or tries to explain – invitation to go and look.

Mobile staircase leading to a large telescope: the figure climbs up – impending explanation.

Simple background, telescope, lens: the figure looks in and cries out in terror, drops of sweat splash – horror.

Simple background: two concentric circles in which the silhouette of a hairy spider shines out among the stars – an unlikely vision.

Simple background, chair: the figure comes back all excited by what he has seen, drops of sweat splash, addresses the scholar figure sitting at the table: falling on deaf ears.

Simple background, chair: the figure, all excited, tries to explain what he has just seen to the scholar figure sitting at the table, drops of sweat splash: falling on deaf ears.

Simple background, chair: the figure, all excited, explains what he has just seen to the scholar figure sitting at the table who understands none of it, drops of sweat splash – lack of understanding.

Simple background: the figure, all excited, explains what he has just seen to the scholar figure who gets up, drops of sweat splash – lack of understanding.

Simple background: the figure invites the scholar figure who gets up to go have a look, follows him to go see, drops of sweat splash – verification.

Simple background, telescope, lens: the scholar figure looks in, drops of sweat splash, agrees and comments to the other standing by his side – barely surprised.

Simple background, telescope, lens: the scholar figure looks in and describes precisely what he is seeing, drops of sweat splash – truly scientific.

Simple background, telescope, lens: the scholar figure looks in, drops of sweat splash, while the other thinks, formulates a hypothesis – a guess.

Éric Suchère (2013), translated from the French
by Sandra Doller

Some Fears

Fear of breezes; fear of quarrels at night-time; fear of wreckage; fear of one's reflection in spoons; fear of children's footprints; fear of the theory behind architecture; fear of boldness; fear of catching anxiousness from dogs; fear of ragged-right margins; fear of exposure after pruning back ivy; fear of bridges; fear of pure mathematics; fear of cats expressing devotion; fear of proximity to self-belief; fear of damp tree trunks; fear of unfamiliar elbows (all elbows being unfamiliar, even one's own); fear of colour leaking from vegetables; fear of the mechanics of love affairs; fear of slipping; fear of ill-conceived typography; fear of non-specific impact leading to the vertical ejection of the spine from the body; fear of leaf mulch; fear of the timbre of poetry recitals; fear of balcony furniture; fear of colour leaking from the heart; fear of internal avalanche; fear of the notion of a key engaging with the inside of a lock; fear of psychoanalytical interpretations; fear of dregs; fear of book titles; fear of particular hues of sky glimpsed from aeroplane windows; fear of text stamped into metal; fear of promises; fear of alienation brought on by hospitality; fear of unexplained light; fear of comprehensive write-off; fear of fear; fear of help. Fear of asking for, receiving, refusing, giving, or being denied help.

Emily Berry (2013)

from *Odes to TL61P*

5: I.i

I stupidly broke the catch. I slammed the door shut and the catch encased in the door is now broken. The catch inside the rim is fine, and if I lodge a spoon in there it continues to function, but obviously then the door isn't closed. I am having a nightmare finding a replacement door. I have managed to take the door off. But I can't seem to get the door apart to remove the catch itself. A liquid sieve was slicked on mock extinct. The grating is a waste grown empty, ground up in the missing cogs; the ultimate multifacets grow facetiously immortal. For who knows well it isn't; she wants more than that, and so should you; please as if gradually read all the notes on your coding notice; it's good to know the worst, it's good to know that it's only that; Perturbation theory leads to an expression for the desired solution in terms of a formal power series in some small parameter that quantifies the deviation from the exactly solvable problem. Love can be trusted not to fade, as also faded out to trust; devour the wind that just washes over you, its meaning is its filling; your reflection in glass blown into the shape of your face to accommodate its progressive jutting; cracks appear in your shambolic argumentative scream learnt fresh from first orgasming, a rondo to oblivion *d'exécution transcendante*; excess levity leads to an unblessed strain injury for the dozen or so

marketing executives secretly pretending to get good enough
at free improvisation; they're out back; whatever the fuck that
thought is, *get it back*; commissioning variations on your
theme – the screen blinks, Yemen for cubist; get it back; mor-
tality is scrambled to the précis of our meaning, to make life
comprehensively succinct; the immutable is better than the
mutable, the inviolable is better than the violable, and the
incorruptible is better than the corruptible: look at teeth, or
Africa. Or Wales. Look at yourself. You don't need to be Dante.

I go on to the mound. It is snowing a bit. The fence at the cor-
ner is obscurely associated with being loved and doing the
creosoting for a meagre sum which I think is a lot but is also a
way of rounding into the street with your feeling of disappoint-
ment. Twigs scratch and knock on it, later redone in local
colour. People are dragging back the sled. On the top the snow
is packed onto the muddy grass oddly hard by all their feet.
That is the efficiency of feet. People go down the mound. In the
summer when the snow was gone under the mud I went there
with David and ended up agreeing to be the one who was
fucked so long as I did not have to be the one who would fuck
back, and put myself on my hands and knees with my pants
down, in front of him, facing away; I felt myself become a hole,
I now think I emerged as a hole for him; I now emerge as a hole
for you. We didn't get to do it, our mothers came looking for us
and stopped it even before fear did, but I suspected even then
that he was frightened or just indifferently disgusted, since
otherwise surely he would have done it to me quicker, since I
think so; I mean that him fucking me would have come first,
but not me fucking him, or our mothers; we should have made
our mothers come too late; I heard that he told people about it
and I was angry because I was ashamed at having again capit-
ulated to secrecy; secrecy was my enemy, like God engrossed in

someone else; in the caravan in his garden I tried pressing him to agree to one last fuck without touching with his father figure who was a man I now give a cartoon nose, white skin, a beard, and idly establish was 40. I'm colouring in his hair, it's brown. It wasn't love, but it hurt and left me complex; I am a real hole for you, not a barely noticeable flimsy crack; David had a stupid way of laughing and a fucking ugly blush. Hasten defections. I swapped stickers with him, and went on to exchange my motorbike for Christian's tank, an agreement which my father unhappily replied was a sort of extortion from infancy, but which made me sexually delight in having given away more than I had got back, for the delight was secret; I made my sister wear the fantasy lieutenant's shirt with the felt tip arrows pinned to the collar. To propitiate invasion. Nylon for Insignia. I lay under a cushion and asked her to jump on my head. She did. I like Roxette, *Elite* and cocoa butter on carrots.

Keston Sutherland (2013)

The Mysterious Arrival of an Unusual Letter

It had been a long day at work and a long ride back to the small apartment where I lived. When I got there I flicked on the light and saw on the table an envelope with my name on it. Where was the clock? Where was the calendar? The handwriting was my father's, but he had been dead for forty years. As one might, I began to think that maybe, just maybe, he was alive, living a secret life somewhere nearby. How else to explain the envelope? To steady myself, I sat down, opened it, and pulled out the letter. 'Dear Son,' was the way it began. 'Dear Son' and then nothing.

Mark Strand (2012)

Chicken

A poem goes to the other side. It's different there, but that's not why I wrote it. There's all there is, in the chicken joke. Where are you going with this.

Cathy Wagner (2012)

Birthweights

for Freya Potts, born 22 Jan 09

When the baby arrives we announce the birthweight. To make it real. You were driving at midnight, woke us to tete-a-tete the network with Fuckin' hell: all perfect, not a freckle. So welcome Freya, at eight pounds ten.

Birth is the only operation that runs itself, medical science just helps it along. The op involves removing live flesh from flesh, undertaken not to simplify but make life more complicated. Or *various*. We take it out and watch it mould us.

One father looked back: the first time was like a bloodbath. But the last was like a bar of soap.

So welcome Freya without freckles. Is it Freya with Phoebe's face? Or the face of Potts? Or Freya with her own face, an afterthought of resemblances? All the birthweight declare is: I am here. I thought: could genetics make for babies announcing their own names in the minutes after they're born? Then the wait for the phonecall.

Past midnight, we wake. The baby's here: all perfect, not a freckle.

She says her name is Freya.

Chris McCabe (2012)

Other Things

To plant a garden is to believe in tomorrow.
– Amana Colony, Iowa

To buy a potted plant is to admit both faithlessness and need. To water the plant, perhaps daily, perhaps once in a while when you remember and the leaves start to droop, is as close to love as it gets.

Other things mean other things.

To light a lamp is to hide darkness in the same closet as sleep, along with silence, desire, and yesterday's obsessions. To read a book is to marry two solitudes, the way a conversation erases and erects, words prepare for wordlessness, a cloud for its own absence, and snow undresses for spring.

The bedroom is where you left it, although the creases and humps on the sheets no longer share your outline and world-view. In that way, they are like the children you never had time for.

A cooking pot asks the difficult questions: what will burn and for how long and to what end.

TV comes from the devil who comes from god who comes and goes as he pleases. To hide the remote control in someone's house is clearly a sin, but to take the wrong umbrella home is merely human.

The phone is too white to be taunting you. The door you shut stays shut. The night is cause enough for tomorrow, whatever you believe.

Remember, the car keys will be there after the dance. Walls hold peace as much as distance. A kettle is not reason enough for tears.

The correct answer to a mirror is always, yes.

Alvin Pang (2012)

from *Adventures in Shangdu*

Of Lucky Highrise Apartment 88

The contractors were in a hurry to catch up with the rest of the world so they rushed off before they finished building Highrise 88. So here is my apartment without its last wall, gaping out to a panoramic view of Shangdu's river. Across the river, all the white-tiled factories hum anxiously. This hum of 2,000 factories can inspire or drive you mad. Yesterday, a drunk man and a suicide used 88's unencumbered views to fall to their deaths and now there are ads for new roommates. I am one of the few women who live alone in this building. My last roommate married as quickly as she moved in with me. I see her in the neighborhood, pregnant and gloating, with men who fetch her footstools.

Of the Millennial Promenade Along the River

Vendors line along the promenade to serve passersby – they sell pinwheels, pancakes, and roast meats of all kinds, even sticks of prickly little sea horses. One female vendor keeps peeled apples under her armpit until they are saturated with her scent and then she sells them so customers can luxuriate in both the scent of fruit and her ripeness. Along the promenade, the rabble is enraptured by the new tower across the river but the vendors grumble of slow business. Officials installed cameras behind the vendor's umbrella fringes to catch conspirators. Today, there is no drama so the vendors gossip.

It is true that the fried prawn vendor tilted his surveillance camera so it caught nothing but the sun. Officials executed him after they watched the useless footage of a sun bobbing up and down for 100 days. Why did he do such a stupid thing? He was a saboteur! said one. We should all destroy the cameras. Everyone knows about them and it takes away business! Said a third, It was for personal reasons. He was stupid in love and his lover walked out on him for – and the vendors stopped short for the cameras were recording.

Cathy Park Hong (2012)

Cry Break

The day the news rolled in that half of the world's population had perished via an anticipated but still shocking chemical explosion, even the Country Music Station recanted on its promise: 'All Country All The Time.' Death on a large scale always takes precedence and allows one to act swiftly and without guilt. I kissed my brother-in-law at my mother-in-law's funeral, the ill-fitted plank of his torso hewn to my grief, so that afterward it was easier to be around the happy stuff everyone seemed to remember. It was all very confusing, as the radio put it, 'complete mayhem.' I thought about going to the school early to pick up my daughter, but decided against it – all those children parroting sorrow, what did they know? Sure, a few of them had been slapped, spit upon, held down and raked over – some had been told the truth: YOU WON'T GO FAR, YOU WON'T GO ANYWHERE AT ALL. I love my daughter, the pale gloaming of her hair a minor song of my continuance. Unlike the Country Music Station, the day the news rolled in that half of the world's population had perished, I did my chores as usual, putting the dirty clothes into the washer and removing the clean ones from the dryer as if the world could be soothed by the delicate cycle and the loving heat of my steady machine. It was as though I knew I was not going anywhere until an anticipated but still shocking chemical explosion allowed me to perish from my daughter, my swift, guiltless death an event that would bring context to her sorrow and allow her to remember, unbidden, the happy stuff, which I'm sure happened daily, like writing your name in the fog on the shower door, for example. I thought of the way the singers that particular station favored created a chest-pulse, commonly known as the cry-break in Country Music, and how I had, while doing the laundry or tending that which required my tenderness, until that moment, been really listening for it.

Paige Ackerson-Kiely (2012)

Short Prayer to Sound

Sound has the particular quality of being visible. It is the greater god. Vision, in evening's fog, shows a man on the cycle with his newspaper bags, the threaded breeze of his hair, the holes of his eyes; yet, though riveting, vision knows nothing of his pain.

Sound does, for sound *is* pain, curled and garbled by the ganglia, stunned and suppressed, dim thundering from some secret window. Never regular, though it may sometimes seem so. Never present, though it may seem. Rivet of moment to moment. A sack on the face with holes to see.

Imprecise, as a world seen through cloth, ease of the friend that follows. Agony internal to the shape. The tinier holes through which a quality refines. A private lack, a riveting in some riveting act.

What does sound carry? It will not tell. It refuses to be known. So close to us, clinging, it will not tell. He wants to gather memories in its sack, as if memories in the brain's shifting imagos had actually the tangible quality of being gatherable. Alas, sound is forgetting. It has already been forgotten. It is the hole into which all knowhow disappears. A hole we can only call: *the future*.

Yet, like peas in a pod, like arguments in the agora, it follows tracks.

Vivek Narayanan (2012)

Homeless Heart

When I think of finishing the work, when I think of the finished work, a great sadness overtakes me, a sadness paradoxically like joy. The circumstances of doing put away, the being of it takes possession, like a tenant in a rented house. Where are you now, homeless heart? Caught in a hinge, or secreted behind drywall, like your nameless predecessors now that they have been given names? Best not to dwell on our situation, but to dwell in it is deeply refreshing. Like a sideboard covered with decanters and fruit. As a box kite is to a kite. The inside of stumbling. The way to breath. The caricature on the blackboard.

John Ashbery (2012)

Black Sunlight

From amid a grove of poplars it appears – and perhaps this testifies to how uninspiring the late morning walk had been – a little aspen tree, shimmering in the heat. It was not so long before this that he had set out, with his boxes and pencils, eager to do some drawing. The sun had been scalding, but despite the heat transfixing him, gouging his forehead, the dusty cart road had been easy underfoot, fringed by oaks and box scrubs. It wasn't long before he had come to a turn in the path and saw the tree: black, sickly, ancestral. By presenting itself in this way, close to the cattle wandering deep in the fields, straining to stand upright amid tightly spaced trees where shafts of light fell in a dense bluegreen, it was as if it were performing a courtesy for those passing through. And further; that it should form a stand in such a hot parched landscape suggested to him the most hopeful of signs – a circle of connection, a return. He decided to sit down and draw it. Beside him he placed a jug of water and a basket of strawberries. He felt content. Thoughts of restlessness abated; his mind grew rooted and still. It was as though something inside him were slowly uncoiling, wanting to burst forth into an act of pure attention. He felt himself recede into the present – as if hit by a sudden cold wave. As he begins to draw the tree seemed to arrange itself into an image of the eternity he craved rather than the brute emptiness he feared. But close up he saw something that clutches at his heart: something like a shadow, or a delayed pain, a gaze overflowing from the tree. He didn't know what to do with that ardour overflowing from a tree. Or that gaze. Think instead of a mind trembling under its own weight, trying to glimpse its own undoing; then subtract the feeling of something formless surging on the forested floor; waiting to flow back to the source. Or you could imagine that the tree itself, trying to resist the forces that shaped it, had burrowed back into this black earth. As though it had given up on its treeness — tired at last of its offices, unwilling to be woven from the earth. As though it had misread its own nature, refusing the illusion of its own form. He had engineered the encounter. He had wanted to see the tree free from artifice, whatever that may be. But it did not. It wanted nothing. Nothing at all. Better stop here. Better to simply stand, serving your purpose, waiting for the world to appear elsewhere.

D. S. Marriott (2011)

Nightmare Pink

It's raining. Here. There. Where you're singing. Raining very hard. I'm sitting in the house in a deep swivel chair. It's night-time. I spin the chair around and listen to the rain. You're singing. The rain is loud enough to hear. I listen. To the rain. Another person arrives. With a pink lampshade. Brand new. He switches off the light, unscrews the bulb, takes off the black shade, puts on the pink one, then switches the light back on. We sit bathed in pink light and talk about shades. Lamp-shades. I open the balcony doors. You're singing. But the rain is louder. It comes into the house. Hits the lampshades. Knocks over the lights. Collides with reality. The cherry trees in the neighbor's garden haven't had fruit for years. Four men enter carrying sticks. They enter the neighbor's garden along with the rain. They've come to discipline the trees and chop them down if they don't blossom. I watch the men hit the trees. I watch the rain hit the men.

Elena Penga (2011), translated from the Greek
by Karen van Dyck

Conversations About Home
(at the Deportation Centre)

Well, I think home spat me out, the blackouts and curfews like tongue against loose tooth. God, do you know how difficult it is, to talk about the day your own city dragged you by the hair, past the old prison, past the school gates, past the burning torsos erected on poles like flags? When I meet others like me I recognise the longing, the missing, the memory of ash on their faces. No one leaves home unless home is the mouth of a shark. I've been carrying the old anthem in my mouth for so long that there's no space for another song, another tongue or another language. I know a shame that shrouds, totally engulfs. *Allah Ceebta*, I tore up and ate my own passport in an airport hotel. I'm bloated with language I can't afford to forget.

*

They ask me *how did you get here?* Can't you see it on my body? The desert red with immigrant bodies shot in the face for trying to enter, the Gulf of Aden bloated with immigrant bodies. I wouldn't put my children on the boat unless I thought the sea was safer than land. I hope the journey meant more than miles because all of my children are in the water. I want to make love but my hair smells of war and running and running. Look at all these borders, foaming at the mouth with brown bodies broken and desperate. I'm the colour of hot sun on my face, my mother's remains were never buried. I spent days and nights in the stomach of the truck, I did not come out the same. Sometimes it feels like someone else is wearing my body.

*

I know a few things to be true. I do not know where I am going, where I have come from is disappearing, I am unwelcome and my beauty is not beauty here. My body is burning with the shame of not belonging, my body is longing. I am the sin of memory and the absence of memory. I watch the news and my mouth becomes a sink full of blood. The lines, the forms, the people at the desks, the calling cards, the immigration officers, the looks on the street, the cold settling deep into my bones, the English classes at night, the distance I am from home. But Alhamdulilah all of this is better than the scent of a woman completely on fire, or a truckload of men who look like my father, pulling out my teeth and nails, or fourteen men between my legs, or a gun, or a promise, or a lie, or his name, or his manhood in my mouth.

*

I hear them say, *go home*, I hear them say, *fucking immigrants, fucking refugees*. Are they really this arrogant? Do they not know that stability is like a lover with a sweet mouth upon your body one second and the next you are a tremor lying on the floor covered in rubble and old currency waiting for its return. All I can say is, I was once like you, the apathy, the pity, the ungrateful placement and now my home is the mouth of a shark, now my home is the barrel of a gun. I'll see you on the other side.

Warsan Shire (2011)

O Elegant Giant

And Jehovah. And Alzheimer. And a diamond of extraordinary size on the hand of a starving child. The quiet mob in a vacant lot. My father asleep in a chair in a warm corridor. While his boat, the Unsinkable, sits at the bottom of the ocean. While his boat, the Unsinkable, waits marooned on the shore. While his boat, the Unsinkable, sails on, and sails on.

Laura Kasischke (2011)

Via Negativa

My mother was not Christ, but she was spat at. My father was not Christ, but he didn't always know this. The two of them met in a garden, but they were not Adam and Eve. And when my mother became pregnant, this was considered a miracle, and when pregnant again, this was nothing short of Blake's sunflower vision. But we are none of these things. When my mother had an epileptic attack, she looked like a monster. Of course, she was not possessed, but as children we didn't always know this. What she was, was spat at. Someone we didn't know, who was more needle than skin, more threadbare than whole, turned his mouth to her as she fitted on the pavement; emptied his tongue, and told her to get up. Beside her, flowers shook their heads behind a newly built wall. She'd made the bricks bleed on her way down, and narrowly missed the plaque that named them the city's best roses.

Jane Monson (2010)

The Experience

I hadn't meant to go grave robbing with Richard Dawkins but he can be very persuasive. 'Do you believe in God?' he asked. 'I don't know,' I said. He said, 'Right, so get in the car.' We cruised around the cemetery with the headlights off. 'Here we go,' he said, pointing to a plot edged with clean, almost luminous white stone. I said, 'Doesn't it look sort of . . .' 'Sort of what?' 'Sort of fresh?' I said. 'Pass me the shovel,' he said. Then he threw a square of canvas over the headstone, saying, 'Don't read it. It makes it personal.' He did all the digging, holding the torch in his mouth as he chopped and sliced at the dirt around his feet. 'What the hell are you doing?' he shouted from somewhere down in the soil. 'Eating a sandwich,' I said. 'Bacon and avocado. Want one?' 'For Christ sake, Terry, this is a serious business, not the bloody church picnic,' he said, as a shower of dirt came arcing over his shoulder.

After about half an hour of toil I heard the sound of metal on wood. 'Bingo,' he said. Then a moment or two later, 'Oh, you're not going to like this, Terry.' 'What?' I said, peering over the edge. Richard Dawkins's eyes were about level with my toes. 'It's quite small,' he said. He uncovered the outline of the coffin lid with his boot. It was barely more than a yard long and a couple of feet wide. I felt the bacon and avocado disagreeing with one another. 'Do you believe in God?' he said. I shrugged

67

my shoulders. 'Pass me the jemmy,' he said. The lid splintered around the nail heads; beneath the varnish the coffin was nothing but clean chipboard. The day I found little Harry in the bath, one eye was closed and the other definitely wasn't. Flying fish can't really fly. With both feet on the crowbar Richard Dawkins bounced up and down until the coffin popped open. But lying still and snug in the blue satin of the upholstered interior was a goose. A Canada Goose, I think, the ones with the white chinstrap, though it was hard to be certain because its throat had been cut and its rubber-looking feet were tied together with gardening twine. Richard Dawkins leaned back against the wall of the grave and shook his head. With a philosophical note in my voice I said, 'What did you come here for, Richard Dawkins?' He said, 'Watches, jewellery, cash. A christening cup, maybe. What about you?' 'I thought it might give me something to write about,' I replied. 'Well, Samuel Taylor Coleridge, we've got a murdered goose in a child's coffin in the middle of the night, and mud on our boots. How would you finish this one?' he said. I looked around, trying to think of a way out of this big ugly mess. Then I said, 'I've got it. What if we see the vicar over there, under the yew tree, looking at us? He stares at us and we stare back, but after a while we realise it isn't the vicar at all. It's a fox. You know, with the white bib of fur around its neck, which we thought was a collar. A silent man-size fox in a dark frockcoat and long black gloves, standing up on his hind legs, watching.'

Simon Armitage (2010)

Folkways

My grandmother called me into the yard. She'd wrapped sacred seals around her head and was standing under the guava tree staring at the sky. Half the canvas had bled black tar with scattered beads of yellow, green and purple globularity. A hideous wound. Well, death groove my brush broom.

At alternate breaths I remembered the small supermarket where I packed brown paper bags. An old woman with bandaged glasses bought two pounds of birdseed, a soprano saxophone and two tins of fried chicken ice cream. Well, death groove my brush broom and I began to paint: Harmolodic portraits in oxides and oils.

Afraid to climb down now between Bermudez biscuit factory and the old rail line is a gutter. A deep stream of silt to hop over. And under: a bulbous snake. The old man was waiting on the other side with a strap soaked in cat piss an pepper and a bible in the other hand. Perched on a lime tree branch like a parrot; he'd done four weddings that day, all down backroads of the mythic.

Anthony Joseph (2009)

from *Virtual Airport*

1

And the moment it takes to blink your eyes and stare, and feel as if you recognise the place you are in, is just long enough for the air to cool off again or the lights to dim, and for the entire feeling of familiarity to drift away to nothing.

The public address plays a mumbling kind of music. The corridor becomes less crowded. A group of girls goes by.

The colour of the light is like new aluminium. A sugary orange-smell carries into the air.

2

The cups of weak coffee and the nylon-colour lighting, the noisy rows we go through and the drifting, hollow music.

4

There is a kind of completeness to these families camping out around the restaurant, altogether different from the completeness

there is in the colour of the sun, and how it swims over the
floor, shifting beyond the shadows of the stools and the chairs.

6

There is a sad kind of surprise in the way the steel-colour light
takes up the space between the cafeteria and the corridor, giving
an even emphasis to the low metal banisters, the pigeon-colour
flooring, the wall lamps, the mirroring, the open double doors.

The space itself has the feel of something imagined or some-
thing not quite recognised, like getting to your destination and
feeling you are still in the place you departed from. Or like
returning home and finding no house there, no street, no pave-
ment lined with hedges, your town not even mentioned on the
regional travel map.

9

The light is like something only dimly understood.

The light is like greaseproof paper.

II

The chairs are the colour of blue chocolate-papers. The depar-
tures board is unreadable. The ceilings are low.

The light is like a kind of lengthy explanation – the light is like
two thoughts occurring at once.

13

The fluorescent yellow lighting in the upper-storey corridors is not absolutely like anything you remember.

14

That feeling of sourness you get in the gut, stepping onto a descending escalator, is not unrelated to that trembling sensation – that other feeling you sometimes get – of actually being two places at once.

This is probably something it is better not to talk about.

17

The first thing is how much the light from the chandelier brings to mind a pan of bubbling caramel chocolate, and the other's the way the angles of the fluorescent ceiling-tubes are like something from the diagram page of an organic chemistry textbook.

18

Sometimes the light is a soft vanilla-colour; sometimes it is a colour like the yellow of an egg.

21

Waiting out the morning in the roped-off restaurant area, the feeling of looseness and unreality that keeps on bringing us back to ourselves is not unrelated to the certainty we feel as we sit and watch the planes pulling off into the distance, that if we fix our eyes on the names painted along the bodies of the aircraft then we will continue to be able to read those words, never losing focus as the planes become speckles in the vivid deep blue of the sky.

This is nothing much more than a trick to do with distance, like the way our childhoods fasten themselves in the memory always just so far off, so they never seem any more distant or any less real, though further and further away from us they grow.

Warmth comes like a murmur, and the minutes go round. The sunlight at the windows is like honey and butter.

24

The middle-morning sunlight, becoming bluish against the windows, creates simple shadows on the sand-colour flooring.

We sit at a table and speak in low voices, and ask for coffee and new ashtrays and paper serviettes.

Matthew Welton (2009)

Photographs, Undeveloped

Somewhere a tourist book was warning the reader that this capital was grey. I depicted it. I saw a grey childhood. Swinging the Soviet Horizont in one hand wandering amongst art nouveau houses shooting around down town. Under arches of courtyards black and white: those films I have never developed. What I mean is I have never taken them to the shop. I did not need to. What I mean is I did not need to see them at all.

My mother in that other era used to sit on the roof drawing the passing sky on her own. Her hair was thin, uncut, colourless. She needed to climb up the ladder to get up there to the loft and from there to the top onto the tiles. Later she used colours. But in that era those colours became neutral on the paper; I don't mean decolorized. That era was neither toneless nor grey. It was a thick white glass. Through that glass was my mother observing those clouds, I think.

Much later, in another millennium, I saw those galleries on a poster. The grey capital's apartments on sale. But it was in a different country. What I mean is that it happened in another century. What happened in another century in another country? I think it is 'it' I talk of that occurred then between the black and the white. If anything this capital is in-between.

It is painted naught, or it was. Light yellow, in January, when you look out of the train pulled by the rails, no, not too fast.

Why were we both disloyal? What I mean is why do we not live in the place, no matter where, that we actually live in? We meet here three times a year waiting for each other behind bins lining the dark at night. It is cold. A January. A January just before Christmas is what I mean. It is such a Christmas is what I mean. Those bins happen at each corner. One after another you hide from me and ask me to do the same for you. There is no plan in the future and so you leave the country on Christmas day.

Take the train to the border. What I mean is that border drawn between two pine-trees. They are pines of the same woods, of the same pine. In-between; take a walk in *tomb-land* where veterans of the Alps, of the same land of the same woods, still assemble from time to time. The bones used to be scattered. Sporadically. I see. Now . . . martially renovated stones . . . I fit my soles in your traces on a path of our sledge you used to pull in the snow. Forgive me if I don't spend any more time with you here. What I mean is don't I spend more time with you spending time with ghosts?

Don't blame the signs of the galleries in St Paul's. What I mean is there are no circular walls that could bring those voices back. We left them there in that discoloured era. Or is it that they only whisper in that white coloured glass? Leave the domes' troubles to the domes. And the trams' to bridges that can hold them no longer. I think domes should not talk at all and should not fool their visitors who pilgrimage from far-off lands, from black and white capitals. From white glass coloured capitals. From grey capitals.

Ágnes Lehóczky (2008)

from *Folklore*

20

All week they screw in the yellow bulbs red ones. Round in their hands. All the morning & talks. Saw them driving geese, the chicken men. Down from market. Greys and then orange beaks. The sound of their feathers. The heat inbetween. Holds a goose egg still warm. Electricity all over the May Fair. The lights on the cobbles.

You walks & breathe sugar in. Stares into the metal. They revolve & your teeth ache. Yellow lights make you sick. Footsteps on the uneven street. Wood and its stuccoed walls. Perspiration running down. The boys they all. Come down the street towards the wall of death all for fights &.

All I have is a hand. Coin passing from.

The big wheel arcs over and over the house & chained library &. Comes for you round & behind then the city. The little lights narrow. The wrought iron steel, below. Above them then. Castor & Pollux. The noise of the pump organ goes. Over the fields & houses & out. Rows then cells settle then darkness oaks and the black bluff of Hay. Black behind black then. Farewell to all stars.

Tongue in my tongue. It comes up on the wheel. Hanging out of our fingers. The cherry paint flakes. Ringing round. The drawn daggers hit cards. All from here. 3 through the heart's mark. Steer into each other's legs & the waltzer & on off & on. The darts diamonds hearts. The wall of death steals. Our breaths. One more time.

Hit a fox on the road. Halfway home. The lights go up dancing and after.

Inside the darkness, colour.

Tim Atkins (2008)

Edith

She was late home, she had gone out in an invitation blouse, a
post-work spritzer, & this whole creamy twin-set she liked. She
was advertising a hot political look. She was an idiot, she was
Freud, she was a sex fiend. She was, in truth, nothing more than
a discontinued type-cast made of polyester. She was responsible
for all of January's inverted oppression. I was in thrall. She came
at me with this smooth, military [slash] corporate 'cop-a-feel'
attitude & I let her, quaking in my rebel boots. She cast a dark
shadow over this love story that was going to practically write
itself – this girl Tracey I was after – she was – never mind. She
sugared up every young protégé, then left them on the seedy
corner she found them. Plus, she had made Ginny all sore, sort
of inside her heart, that's what Lisa had told me. I thought how
can she get away with this shit, with all this blabber in town?
But I fell for it hard, ignored all the salt-lick metaphors. So we
went back to hers, pulped all these ideologies, these texts, & I
sculpted her body with them, around this mesh we got from the
borderland fence. We ate hard-boiled eggs in the morning,
talked about categories, drew up lists of everyone we knew.
She did my makeup and hair to look like hers, gave me these
little ballet pumps & threw my boots out the window. She was
magic, & waited 3 weeks to drop me, the best 3 weeks of my life.

Sophie Robinson (2008)

The Wren

for V.

This will be your last life here. I see a dropsy helicopter, chor-
ing along. A heron like a sickle reaps an Iron-Age sun. I see a
Caravan. You've been travelling on your own but – Dear God –
like falling face down into warm mud, this is love – the sudden,
muddy sun.

You have the Polytunnel. Something about you will need pro-
tecting. A bust creel's a debt. You have a debt . . . doesn't
everyone? Money is a pile of anything. Cabbages mean money
as manure does. Cool leaves creak between your palms in the
evening. It's enough. Pull one.

I see the Wren. Behind and before, above and below you. That's
luck. And under the sun, the Dark-Haired Hammerer. In the
gleaming grass, the ducks will gleam like curling stones. You'll
get off scot-free, trusting everyone.

You will love the land. You will love the land like a bairn. The
Hammerer. The Wren. The dropsy helicopter choring along.
The heron like a sickle reaps an Iron-Age sun.

Jen Hadfield (2008)

from *Bird bird*

Troglodytes troglodytes (wren)

Must work without the wren their shiny coats there their fat small hands. They once were kind. Once they all faced the same way and sang. Once. Doubtful bird you have seen. The word that the wren said: 'shoes!' A wren doesn't cost any money. There! There! Dipping in northern europe. The story of its longer wings from england. Must buy ham. This will not be liked much either. Under the tractor I shoved it in her hard but each take was spoiled by the king wren. Tit parties in winter, small loose parties erupting westwards sometimes high up. Golden england. Down and down newington butts caught moths with the smaller birds, again wren-like. Wren as host, magpie as host, above whose clashing hands, business-like, now a wren costs a few pence.

Apus apus (swift)

Easily told around the houses and they went this way looking like quick and brown, the same as before only going. Going to a roding valley there to feel for the wrong bee. A fish carried forward in the hand, to soothe. There in time to motley. The head to lead to the circle. They fell down rhyming, lightly come, like a man at things in a wood. A poetry ring recent and wet. The point is outside and in, though scarcely so. Like scarcely weeping, or scarcely so. From town to form, from place to position. Or grazing on each other they work the suburb to a thin.

Coccothraustes coccothraustes (hawfinch)

That tapping. It's the rain or the rainiest day that nobody looked at the hawfinch and it's like a dixons in the springtime. It's massive its head in a conifer belt. We have streets and we have a dixons. We have streams and houses and fields on the borders of woods and we have like a dixons. That's where your iPod is. Like there was this shy gardener found with sixty iPods. Much more like that because he so rarely mixed with them. I mean the finches. Got to get to take them from the city for the white phase that they utter in. I mean again the finches. It's so dark it passes. The lores as they slide over each other. That's where your mouth is. Finches and iPods interchangeably. And that tapping. It's so thin it must be a display.

Jeff Hilson (2008)

The Hornsman

I was asleep, I remember that, when I first heard the sound of the horn. A thin, far-away simple horn-call – it gently woke me, and remained with me, awake. I stumbled across the room, thinking of strange alarm clocks, unusual mobile phone tones . . .

But this was a quite unusual tone – a two-note motif with a repeating rhythm, rather like 'aha! . . . aha! aha!' There was something classic in it, not the tinny precision of pre-recorded electronic farce, but a richer reality, friendly, urgent, as of a miniature cascade of harmonics, faithful but very, very remote – in a neighbouring valley or a distant cell?

There was only my one room. I shook myself alert, and fixed my eyes on the model watchman chess figure above the dud fire. He was only a copy of course, of some hand-worked Anglo-Norse original, perhaps three inches high, standing in fixed resin form, blank eyes pointed toward me. Yet, I thought, the sound had come . . . inside the room certainly . . . from this direction?

I looked more closely, as though daring him to repeat his call to life. From the top of a round turret, the body of the watchman was in place, a veteran soldier on an easy but important duty.

He had a fine moustache, flowing down into a beard; it was a cold dawn, maybe, where he lived, for he had a top tunic and also a cloak with its hood folded down behind; and a helmet, as if danger might be at hand, should be expected, as I was expecting it.

The instrument was little more than a wide curve, an animal horn inverted, and the tip cleared away to admit rasping breath. The tip was in his mouth. He blew.

Suddenly I saw.

I dashed across the room, opened the drawer, clawed out the Christmas bauble, and launched it mercilessly out through the top window I kept open this night and every night. In just that flash of time before the rams began to batter in the front door and vizored police, no inch of human left about them, grabbed their way in and flattened me to the floor.

Bill Griffiths (2008)

from *The Idylls*

I

One day the men were repairing the fence by the stream in the Bawn. Moss drove in the stakes with the sledge, while my father followed with Dan-Jo unwinding the barbed wire and stapling it loosely to the timber. Then the strands were pulled taut by the three men and made secure.

'We haven't seen or heard a soul all day,' my father remarked. 'Not even a tramp or the youngsters from school.'

'Everyone goes round by the road nowadays,' said Dan-Jo.

'And there's no work in the fields any more. No beet to thin. No sheep to count. No hay to turn and cock and wind.'

'Once you'd have seen twenty men and women in a field at harvest time.'

'Do you remember the pony races, Moss?'

'I do. The water jump was there by the alders and then the last jump was into Dillon's Field. The finishing post was by where the pylon is today.'

'The field black with people.'

'You'd see folk in the fields,' my father continued, 'whatever job you were at. Sometimes you'd meet a total stranger and they'd stop to talk.'

'I drove a pick-up through Manitoba,' Jo said, 'and neither man nor animal did I see for three days.'

'In the forestry,' Moss said, 'you'd be on your own a lot of the time. Though you'd hear an axe or a saw from the next section and you'd be glad of that.'

Maurice Riordan (2007)

Blue Dog

The blue dog is made of plastic. It is no more than two inches high. The blue dog is a pug and sits on its haunches. It is what she has been looking for all her life. 'You remember being a child, don't you?' she asks me. This is what I remember about being a child: Rows of horror films by the counter in the video store.

'No blue dogs,' I say.

'But I am in love with the blue dog,' she says. 'Don't you remember taking joy in the smallest things?'

'I have learned to group those things together,' I say, 'and take joy in none of them.'

'This is why we have wine connoisseurs and restaurant critics,' she continues, 'film makers and English teachers. This is why we have bird-watchers and moth-catchers, professional sports players and magazine journalists. When people say: *Everyone is searching for something*, they are talking about the blue dog and all that it could once evoke.'

The little blue dog sits proudly in the middle of the table. I consider snatching it – and throwing it in a river, or melting it.

Perhaps it is the way I am glaring at the blue dog – or perhaps, as I suspect, it is that she is so highly strung she can practically read my thoughts.

'If you ever take the blue dog away from me,' she says, 'I will cry. I won't want to live anymore.'

'You think I'm a monster, don't you?' I say, addressing the question to the blue dog.

Luke Kennard (2007)

If

If you open your mouth, ache. If you don't open your mouth, swelter. If you open your mouth but hold your breath, ether. If you look for colour, coral and tea leaves. If you follow the moon, wet and concrete. If you cling to the earth, pistol and candy apple. If you give up your garden, maze and globe, hydrangeas and moonvines. If you lose your shoes, pumice and strain. If you have no money, tin, linen and clang. If you lie down with dogs, pale and tender. If you watch television, carrot and yanking. If you embrace nothing, lustre and tar. If you know sorrow, whistle and salt. If you lie down with birds, currents and vertigo. If you can, software and lingerie. If you should, totem, forelock, tibia and stamen. If you are blonde, topple, flax, moraine. If you love flowers, do not fold. If you follow the sun, straw and oval. If you hide, velvet and myrrh. If you are a redhead, pepper and artichoke. If you eat only limes, Knossos and paddle. If you sing, ozone, crackle and stir. If you are wanting, scathed and shrouded. If you open your eyes, salt lick and clover. If you lie down with cats, ankle and dock. If you follow your heart, sledgehammer. If you embrace all, oarlock and tidal. If you look for light, spleen, splint. If you follow the earth, spade and compass. If you lie down with fish, ice cube and convection. If you know anger, detonate and flex. If you give up walls, columbine and feather. If you are still here, present and peel, dandelion and lemon hound.

Sina Queyras (2006)

Fiddleheads

Fiddlehead ferns are a delicacy where? Japan? Estonia? Ireland long ago?

I say Japan because when I think of those delicious things I think of my friend Toraiwa, and the surprise I felt when he asked me about the erotic. He said it belonged in poetry and he wanted more of it.

So here they are, Toraiwa, frilled, infolded, tenderized, in a little steaming basket, just for you.

Seamus Heaney (2006)

Captain of the Lighthouse

The late hour trickles to morning. The cattle low profusely by the anthill where brother and I climb and call Land's End. We are watchmen overlooking a sea of hazel-acacia-green, over torrents of dust whipping about in whirlwinds and dirt tracks that reach us as firths.

We man our lighthouse – cattle as ships. We throw stones as warning lights whenever they come too close to our jagged shore. The anthill, the orris-earth lighthouse, from where we hurl stones like light in every direction.

Tafara stands on its summit speaking in *sea-talk*, Aye-aye me lad – a ship's a-coming! And hurls a rock at the dumb cow sailing in. Her beefy hulk stupidly jolts and turns. Aye, Captain, another ship saved! I cry and furl my fingers into an air-long telescope – searching for more vessels in the day-night.

Now they low on the anthill, stranded in the dark. Their sonorous cries haunt through the night. Aye, methinks, me miss my brother, Captain of the lighthouse, set sail from land's end into the deepest seventh sea.

Togara Muzanenhamo (2006)

from *Angle of Yaw*

THE FIRST GAMING SYSTEM was the domesticated flame. Contemporary video games allow you to select the angle from which you view the action, inspiring a rash of high school massacres. Newer games, with their use of small strokes to simulate reflected light, are all but unintelligible to older players. We have abstracted airplanes from our simulators in the hope of manipulating flight as such. Game cheats, special codes that make your character invincible or rich, alter weather conditions or allow you to bypass a narrative stage, stand in relation to video games as prayer to reality. Children, if pushed, will attempt to inflict game cheats on the phenomenal world. Enter up, down, up, down, left, right, left, right, a, b, a, to tear open the sky. Left, left, b, b, to keep warm.

Ben Lerner (2006)

The Phases of the Moon in London

She and I were talking about the weather, the rusty key that opens conversations here in London. Mrs Morrison, our old neighbour, is the last English woman on our street, where the English have dropped off one by one once the population balance tipped toward the Asian immigrants. She said, 'the London sky was not like this in the past, but must have resembled your sky in India.'

I said, 'I am from Jordan', but she did not stop at my correction, which she may not have seen as a correction in the first place. In that English manner whose emotional resonances are hard to read, she continued that they too used to see the stars and detect the phases of the moon.

I was not convinced, but I played on in this game of English politeness. I said, 'What caused the stars and moon to disappear and the sky to turn into a blotted sheet even on these nights clear as a rooster's eye?'

'I don't know,' she said. 'Maybe the change in the weather, or our insatiable consumption of electricity, this excessive urbanization. We light the earth and the sky disappears. You're probably better off in India.'

'In Jordan,' I said.

Again, she did not pause at my correction. She smiled and directed her small shopping trolley toward her house, announcing the end of a conversation that politeness had imposed on two neighbours who otherwise try all they can to avoid each other when they meet at the door.

I wanted to tell her that the skies of eastern cities, bent under military rule and corruption, are also blotted out, and that the stars that freckled our childhood with comets have also disappeared, but I feared to lose the only gift for which she envied me.

Amjad Nasser (2004), translated from the Arabic
by Khaled Mattawa

Corruption

I am about to recite a psalm that I know. Before I begin, my
expectation extends over the entire psalm. Once I have begun,
the words I have said remove themselves from expectation &
are now held in memory while those yet to be said remain
waiting in expectation. The present is a word for only those
words which I am now saying. As I speak, the present moves
across the length of the psalm, which I mark for you with my
finger in the psalm book. The psalm is written in India ink, the
oldest ink known to mankind. Every ink is made up of a color
& a vehicle. With India ink, the color is carbon & the vehicle,
water. Life on our planet is also composed of carbon & water.
In the history of ink, which is rapidly coming to an end, the
ancient world turns from the use of India ink to adopt sepia.
Sepia is made from the octopus, the squid & the cuttlefish. One
curious property of the cuttlefish is that, once dead, its body
begins to glow. This mild phosphorescence reaches its greatest
intensity a few days after death, then ebbs away as the body
decays. You can read by this light.

Srikanth Reddy (2004)

from *echolocation*

The sky is fitted linen, stretched over sealine without a crease, pegged to the spikes and jags of mountains, kingsize, navy, preparing to be sunshot. Sooner than lovers can hide, no sooner than the taste of stars striking your lips, one by one stunned and falling to light.

It's all been said and yet, need, blowing between our lips, streams inside a tree. We flowed out of time and back so soon eating eggs our own. Through each other we pass like water.

At the sun to see how it never changes, at the moon to see how it does, algae slipping beneath our feet, roots travelling and dewdrops dying in visible speed. There is no such thing as a circular river.

Unlike bread, the body becomes softer with age. We tag our children with our names, store the plaits of our daughters, stash berries under rocks and look for them later.

Held in the fangs of a wristwatch, a well-worn path of a nail in our veins, heart-hammered time trail.

No matter who two are kissing, eternity arrives, jelly bean eyes black crystal balls. The longer we look, the more we recognize and anything we could say is too obvious. The songs we like are the songs we know, and every song on the radio is about us.

Mani Rao (2003)

from *Chapter E*

for René Crevel

Enfettered, these sentences repress free speech. The text deletes selected letters. We see the revered exegete reject metred verse: the sestet, the tercet – even *les scènes élevées en grec*. He rebels. He sets new precedents. He lets cleverness exceed decent levels. He eschews the esteemed genres, the expected themes – even *les belles lettres en vers*. He prefers the perverse French esthetes: Verne, Péret, Genet, Perec – hence, he pens fervent screeds, then enters the street, where he sells these letterpress newsletters, three cents per sheet. He engenders perfect newness wherever we need fresh terms.

Relentless, the rebel peddles these theses, even when vexed peers deem the new precepts 'mere dreck'. The plebes resent newer verse; nevertheless, the rebel perseveres, never deterred, never dejected, heedless, even when hecklers heckle the vehement speeches. We feel perplexed whenever we see these excerpted sentences. We sneer when we detect the clever scheme – the emergent repetend: the letter E. We jeer; we jest. We express resentment. We detest these depthless pretenses – these present-tense verbs, expressed pell-mell. We prefer genteel speech, where sense redeems senselessness.

Christian Bök (2002)

Denigration

Did we surprise our teachers who had niggling doubts about the picayune brains of small black children who reminded them of clean pickaninnies on a box of laundry soap? How muddy is the Mississippi compared to the third-longest river of the darkest continent? In the land of the Ibo, the Hausa, and the Yoruba, what is the price per barrel of nigrescence? Though slaves, who were wealth, survived on niggardly provisions, should inheritors of wealth fault the poor enigma for lacking a dictionary? Does the mayor demand a recount of every bullet or does city hall simply neglect the black alderman's district? If I disagree with your beliefs, do you chalk it up to my negligible powers of discrimination, supposing I'm just trifling and not worth considering? Does my niggling concern with trivial matters negate my ability to negotiate in good faith? Though Maroons, who were unruly Africans, not loose horses or lazy sailors, were called renegades in Spanish, will I turn any blacker if I renege on this deal?

Harryette Mullen (2002)

A Hardworking Peasant from the Idyllic Countryside

I was illiterate until yesterday. All these squiggly lines – tattooed on every available surface, all around me, all my life – suddenly started to make sense yesterday. Until yesterday I did not know that the invectives and commands constantly swarming around me were actually made of words. I thought they were mosquitoes, or dust, or flecks of paint, each one leaving a prickling sensation on my thin, almost transparent skin. Yesterday someone said something in my vicinity and I finally decided to write it down, a phonetic transcription, to the best of my abilities: FUAK YOW MOFTHEARFUAKIER.

I wrote that down with a blue pen on a yellow piece of paper. I finally wrote, I thought, now I'm a writer. If I had merely transcribed the above as a blue thought onto my yellow memory, I would still be seen as a hardworking peasant from the idyllic countryside.

Linh Dinh (2001)

Ted's Head

So there's this episode of Mary Tyler Moore where Ted's trying to get a raise & after finagling and shenaniganizing he puts one over on Lou & gets his contract changed to non-exclusive so's he can do commercials which is not cool w/ Lou & the gang because Ted's just a brainless gimp & it hurts the image of the news to have the anchorman selling tomato slicers & dogfood so Lou gets despondent because the contract can't be rescinded but then he gets mad & calls Ted into his office & says, you know his voice, 'You're going to stop doing commercials, Ted' & Ted says 'why would I do that Lou?' & Lou says 'Because if you don't I'll punch your face out' & Ted says 'I'll have you arrested' & Lou says 'It'll be too late, your face will be broken, you're not gonna get too many commercials with a broken face now are you Ted?' & Ted buckles under to force & everybody's happy, except Ted but he's so dumb nobody cares & everybody loves it that Lou's not despondent anymore he's back to his brustling chubby loud loveable whiskey-drinking football-loving ways. Now imagine if Ted were Lou, if Ted were the boss. You know how incredibly fucking brainless Ted is, but let's imagine he understands & is willing to use force. That's the situation we're now in as Americans.

Rod Smith (2001)

Hosea: A Commentary

Reaping a whirlwind, I remarked, pointing to the words on the sandwich board that was leaning against his chair as he sipped his cappuccino: a bit steep for a spot of adultery between consenting adults? He said he didn't think it was meant literally, it was more a figure of speech, and I warmed to him at once – not at all the uptight evangelical type I'd expected, the sort with metal fatigue who could crack open at any moment and spill their payload across the hinterland of a major industrial city. So the palaces devoured by fire, the slaying of the fruit of the womb, the infants dashed in pieces . . . ? He said he couldn't be one hundred per cent sure – he was only doing this job while Hosea was away on vacation, he had a place at college to read immunology in September – but basically, at the root of it all, the issue was pollution. We let the word rest between us for a while, it had the right anthropological ring, until we noticed a man walking past in sandals, muttering to himself through his long grey beard. I could feel my boy becoming a bit edgy – that was Isaiah himself, and the prophets were supposed to stick to their own streets, there was a gentleman's agreement. Luckily a hairdresser's over the road was still open, a few late customers were sitting on leather sofas reading up the tips on foreplay in glossy magazines. We each took one of Isaiah's arms and hustled him in for a haircut. He offered only token resistance, I think secretly he was quite happy.

Charles Boyle (2001)

The Skull Ring

I am very excited about the skull ring. I didn't know anyone would think I wanted a silver skull ring. Now, when I am rude to those who oppose me, I can just look down at the skull ring. It has ruby chips in the eyes! Ruby chips like the nasty flame in my own eyes when I am insulted or reviled. No one will dare oppose me now in my hometown. For a very long time I have avoided rings because none of them seemed right for me. A skull ring is actually a good complement to my diabolical will. Thank you very much for the skull ring.

Chelsey Minnis (2001)

from *The Weather*

Monday

First all belief is paradise. So pliable a medium. A time not very long. A transparency caused. A conveyance of rupture. A subtle transport. Scant and rare. Deep in the opulent morning, blissful regions, hard and slender. Scarce and scant. Quotidian and temperate. Begin afresh in the realms of the atmosphere, that encompasses the solid earth, the terraqueous globe that soars and sings, elevated and flimsy. Bright and hot. Flesh and hue. Our skies are inventions, durations, discoveries, quotas, forgeries, fine and grand. Fine and grand. Fresh and bright. Heavenly and bright. The day pours out space, a light red roominess, bright and fresh. Bright and oft. Bright and fresh. Sparkling and wet. Clamour and tint. We range the spacious fields, a battle-ment trick and fast. Bright and silver. Ribbons and failings. To and fro. Fine and grand. The sky is complicated and flawed and we're up there in it, floating near the apricot frill, the bias swoop, near the sullen bloated part that dissolves to silver the next instant bronze but nothing that meaningful, a breach of greeny-blue, a syllable, we're all across the swathe of fleece laid out, the fraying rope, the copper beech behind the aluminum catalpa that has saved the entire spring for this flight, the tops of these a part of the sky, the light wind flipping up the white undersides of leaves, heaven afresh, the brushed part behind, the tumbling. So to the heavenly rustling. Just stiff with ambition we range the spacious trees in earnest desire sure and dear. Brisk and west. Streaky and massed. Changing and appearing. First and last. This was made from Europe, formed from Europe, rant and roar. Fine and grand. Fresh and bright. Crested and turbid. Silver and bright. This was spoken as it came to us, to celebrate and tint, distinct and designed. Sure and dear. Fully designed. Dear afresh. So free to the showing. What we praise we believe, we fully believe. Very fine. Belief thin and pure and clear to the title. Very beautiful. Belief lovely and elegant and fair for the footing. Very brisk. Belief lively and quick and strong by the bursting. Very bright. Belief clear and witty and famous in impulse. Very stormy. Belief violent and open and raging from privation. Very fine. Belief intransigent after pursuit. Very hot. Belief lustful and eager and curious before beauty. Very bright. Belief intending afresh. So calmly and clearly. Just stiff with leaf sure and dear and appearing and last. With lust clear and scarce and appearing and last and afresh.

Lisa Robertson (2001)

Ode

For let me consider him who pretends to be the pizza delivery man and is instead the perfect part of day, for the fact he is a medium, for the eight to twelve inches of snow he tends to be, for he who covers the waterfront, for he that was handmade in a tiny village in japan, for that he is more than just an envelope or inside-out balloon, for that he can always find the scotch tape, for that he resembles a river in mid-December muddied over, for that he has seen the taxi cabs on fire in the rain, for that he is like the heat beneath the desk lamp, for that he is not a tiny teal iguana, for that it is he who waits for me inside cafes, for that he has hands and legs, for that he exceeds the vegetable, for that he is the rest of the balance continuing huge.

Lisa Jarnot (2001)

from *Letters to Wendy's*

September 2, 1996

I love the cleanliness of a Wendy's. Such a clean is not in any sense a banishing of genitalia; it is the creation of a quiet bright mind-space that allows for the deliciousness of genitalia to become obvious. I look out over the colorful clean tables and the pretty food posters and *I like people* again; each has a dick and balls, or a cunt and titties, which, clean, are simply enjoyable.

September 5, 1996

Naturally I think about smashing the skulls and rib-cages of the other customers. They stand in line so smug – like they were safe, *outside* the desires of or for an other. It's as if, for them, there is no *other*'s desire – as if desire was one thing, and was *ours*. Restraining myself is not *dishonest*. It's a way of maintaining a keen sense of the unforeseeable injuries which shall reunite us.

September 21, 1996

If I had to say what Wendy really was – if she had to be one thing instead of a field of various energies – I think I'd have to say that she was a penis. Something about her face and the shape of her hair, the muffled red coherence of head and torso, and perhaps too her lack of arms and legs. A penis is founded in just such a lack of limbs; it's really amazing when it arrives anywhere.

February 8, 1997

Wendy, will you not even poke me? Not even a slow poke? I wonder why you treat me so. Am I a wooden board? Am I to be thought of as a simple wooden board? Come on, just give me a slow poke. I'm not a wooden board, honey. Come on, just poke me like you used to. Just a slow poke. Look into my eyes – are these the eyes of a wooden board?

June 3, 1997

I took my Frosty into the bathroom and sat it on the floor. I pulled my pants down, got down on all fours, and buried the tip of my cock in the cold brown swirl. Then I forced my cock and balls all the way into the cup, Frosty spilling on to the floor. Then I thought sexy thoughts. My erection slowly forced more Frosty on to the floor. This is the real test of a drink's thickness.

June 28, 1997

My previous statements were made in haste. I was hungry and confused, and I longed for purpose. I wanted to seem like I was in the process of focusing in on something important. I wanted to feel purpose rising like an ancient city from the excavator's pick and shovel. I wanted this so much that I rushed – I swung my pick wildly, and I brought a great delicate city to the dust it had always verged on.

Joe Wenderoth (2000)

The Most Sensual Room

One wall of the bathroom of Jay's apartment has a cat's foot-prints. Absence is something like that. To leave evidence. I see it. By rolling the world back. The way the cat ran up the wall and escaped out of the window. The wind that came in just as the cat left knocked down everything it touched by reversing time, from the small past in which the cat had disappeared, toward the present. The wind, having substantially disturbed the proper position of a light letter on the desk, has now passed by. And it is no longer here. Jay and I are contained in the room. And yet, the room feels vacant, somehow. Am I here? Clearly exist here? I am passing through it. I will become absent.

From the open window I hear the sounds of the neighbour's house. Why aren't you finishing your homework? The noise of plates. Would you come here and help me a bit? The noise of plates. What did you do with that? The noise of a washing machine. The soft ringing of a telephone. Hello, hello? Hello, hello? The beep signalling that the washing machine finished its work. We don't know the faces of our neighbours. Nonetheless, they come in. Like a flood. Our neighbours' daily routines, into this vacant room.

Jay and I turn on music. A brief conversation. Sexual inter-course. Laughter. The sound of slapping flesh. Two people cursing each other. These noises, too, slowly go out. Toward our neighbour's house. Unobtrusively, directly. We languidly blend with one another, with voices alone. On the ground separating us ivy leaves overgrow.

The Sunday morning when I leave Jay's room. There is Jay's room where I no longer am. I don't leave a single footprint, but my invisible fingerprints are imprinted everywhere. Nights, I think of the room. I peer out of the window. I see the absences of myself and the cat. Jay is a man who is part of that room. His long body tightly coiled into hardness, he, the penis of the room, is quietly asleep. I stretch my hand and touch the room. The wall is soft. I push the room harder, and the room goes out of the room. The room that contains nothing, except Jay, at first with some bounce, like a soap bubble, goes out of the hard room, slowly.

Masayo Koike (2000), translated from the Japanese
by Hiroaki Sato

The Postmodern Prose Poem

The Cough

He felt an uncomfortable sensation in his throat. Perhaps his throat was struggling with words. Seated in the car next to this Japanese film director, Wilhelm began to cough. He feared the conflict going on in his throat might not stop. It might continue and interrupt their conversation in the long drive from the Japanese airport. He threw his body against the seat in an attempt to shake off his embarrassment.

'Allergy,' said Nagao with confidence, 'Allergy to our film.' On Nagao's unwrinkled skin were little ribbons of smile.

At the intersection of the road in Nagasaki where in Japanese films a short dark woman usually squats, Wilhelm pointed out a break between two buildings where light crept through like an oyster. He said he would like to use that oyster light. '*Cliche*,' said Nagao.

(Observing Nagao in his dark blue denims, he wondered if their film should be called *Dark Blue Denim*.) He wished the noise an oyster makes could get into the film. Nagao shook his head. 'Better noise the eye when it blinks. *"Pachi Pachi"* in Japanese.'

Wilhelm suggested the sound of creaking wood for the scene of the two people lost in the garden.

'*Pachi Pachi* better,' Nagao said. 'More subtle.'

The action was too slow and Wilhelm wanted a more violent crescendo. When the body fell down the cellar stairs, perhaps another body could fall on top of it?

'Could be liquid soap on stair,' said Nagao.

In the middle of a film, Wilhelm always had the feeling he was being chased. He complained that when he directed those shots up in the sky with two planes flying parallel to each other, he was also in a sky chase. 'Flower petals putting on the wings of a plane,' suggested Nagao.

Perhaps he might return to his home for awhile and the scenarist could work with Nagao. She could put her own story into the script, how she got hired, etc. Was there something going on between her and Nagao.

He thought of home as a possible sequence and *Home* started to roll with its camera views. *Home* needed editing, especially the scene with his analyst when they discussed his cough that now seemed like another room in the movie.

Nagao believed the film was too slow. It was old-fashioned to explain why gangsters upset the fish cart.

Wilhelm disagreed and told him the fish cart was like a scene by the painter, Utamoro, a capsule of real life. He suggested a new title, *Dreams of Real Life*.

'No,' said Nagao, both eyes blinking, *The Cough* is better.

Barbara Guest (1999)

Cinema-Going

One afternoon in a cinema in the East Neuk when I was about nine years old. The film was *Captains Courageous* with Spencer Tracy and Freddie Bartholomew, the child star. A story of the famous schooners out of Gloucester, Massachusetts, to fish the Grand Banks for cod. Astonishingly, the film projector, concealed in its flimsy little wooden cabin, was powered by the engine of an inshore fishing boat. It *put-putted* all through the 'picture' (as we called a film in those days): *put-put* in the grey fog of the banks, and *put-put* in the half-darkness of the summer afternoon stalls.

Ian Hamilton Finlay (1998)

from *Joan of Arc*

– Here's Joan drawing herself up forever tall against the sky with a stake at her back.

– Each vertebra presses against the trunk as if to enter it.

– The wind does not ruffle her dress, because of the ropes.

Of the kind of tree that shores her (oak? beech? alder? willow?), we know nothing, because it burned with her.

– Her final expression, hard to read on a face in flames: either dolorous, or joyous, or dolorous and joyous.

Can we see blood running down the burning body?

– A contemporary questions whether someone could pleasure and suffer at the same time, whether puissance and sufferance alternate, one rising as the other recedes.

The crowd forms a cresting sea before her. She can clearly see a little towhead.

In the center of the confusion, she is both calm and deaf (no cry filters through those wide open mouths).

– A course patiently pursued – from Domrémy to Auxerre, Gien to Bourges, Sens to Paris, Reims to Soissons, Arras to Rouen – starts its final progress, from feet to ankles, knees to soft thighs, nipple to neck's nape, vibrant chin to trembling nostrils (then from her mouth soars the dove).

– Lunula or patella, nothing's discreet anymore, this is a young (vain?) and compact body burning up, joyous blaze, mystic barbecue.

– Her spasmodic breathing is stopped by the coughing.
– And her eyes turn in their orbits.

Nathalie Quintane (1998), translated from the French
by Sylvain Gallais and Cynthia Hogue

Neglected Knives

The knives in the kitchens of single women who order a lot of takeaway sorely need whetting. The knives in the knife block are of no use to the bread crust or the proud tomatoes or the patient onion of the woman who unwittingly brings unprepared food into the kitchen of a woman who stops cooking when her lovers disappear.

Their impossible knives, completely impossible knives, neglected and dusty, in burdensome kitchens that only get plugged in if he who can return the proteins back into the abdomen of the kitchen's owner is nearby.

Still, the gardens display their finest. The lemons on the trees await hands that will squeeze them over the old asparagus. And the redcurrants spread over everything like inebriated lanterns, though that reminds me mostly of the kisses we didn't repeat.

And still it is also magnificent to slice vegetables into the stomach of one's love with a sharp knife slice and slice vegetables and again vegetables with a sharp knife into the stomach of one's love slice and slice the vegetables down with a sharp knife. Into the stomach of one's love.

Lovely unloved women, you who open the door to young delivery boys bearing lukewarm, fertile, plastic tubs of food, some in uniform, some in their own clothes but all with the waking young eyes that touch anything in their path, whet the knives in your kitchens, whet them.

Kristín Ómarsdóttir (1998), translated from the Icelandic
by Vala Thorodds

Little Corona

i.m. Radka Toneff

C: . . . true, but there is, however, often a real event which triggers what Jabès called our endocrine fantasies. For example, there was boy in our village, Goran . . . I don't recall his last name, but his family were from way up on the Ukraine border . . . who played peckhorn or euphonium with the local marching band, and had the most extraordinary skill: he was able to get a tune out of almost anything, and could make a whistle from piece of macaroni, a zither from a cigarette-packet . . . Once, I remember, he had us all spellbound as he blew the guts from a goose-egg and then fashioned a kind of primitive ocarina, and on this absurdly delicate instrument blew a strange little off-key melody, almost more breath than note . . . I hear it clearly in the lochrian mode of so many of the folk-songs of the region, but this is too convenient to be more than a trick of memory . . . Then this scrawny Orpheus, as soon as he knew we were all drawn into his magic, crushed it in his hand, as if out of pure scorn for us; this trick would always draw an involuntary groan from his audience, and the first time I witnessed it I burst into tears . . . the sudden, immaculate, irrevocable disappearance of both the singer and the song seemed such a terrifying thing . . . I can still see his terrible grin . . .

from *Armonie Pierduta şi Regăsita: Emil Cioran*, reprinted in *The Aquarian*, no. 12/13, trans. Tess DiMilo

Don Paterson (1997)

Seoul's Dinner

Flowers enter. The flowers with puckered lips. The flowers
that fill the back of a truck suck on the wall of the tunnel. The
tunnel reddens momentarily. She plucks off the new leaves and
shoves them into her mouth. Angelica shoots drop from angel-
ica trees and fall into the dish of seasoned soy sauce. A truckload
of angelica enters. Angelica shoots turn the mouth of Seoul
green. Flatfish enter. A thousand flatfish packed in ice enter,
swooning. A truckload of the East Sea enters. Pigs enter. The
pigs oink and suck on Seoul's lips. She dips the meat from the
pig's neck in pickled shrimp and eats. Her squirming throat is
omnivorous. Mudfish pour in like a muddy stream. The Tae-
baek range is shredded and enters, squirming. The fields of the
higher ranges of Mount Sŏrak enter, salted. Radishes revealing
only the top half of their white bottoms are neatly stacked onto
a truck. Trucks with their lights on enter. They line up and
enter in between the teeth. When the trucks leave the tunnel,
Seoul's blue stomach acid embraces them. Some of the trucks
with big eyes try to make their way through the sea of acid, but
the darkness inside Seoul's intestine is dense. Greens in sacks
enter. Thousands of chickens with reddened crowns follow
thousands of eggs just laid today and enter. Bulls as big as ele-
phants their eyes fiercely opened enter. Bulls charge the path
inside the body of someone who lives in Seoul. Tonight she
drinks too much soju. The tunnel where the liquor is poured is

long and dark. White milk that could overflow Lake Soyang pours out of the tunnel into the night's intestine. The plains of Honam enter. But in the opposite lane, trucks loaded with waste water purifiers have lined up in single file. Having left the party, I begin to vomit as soon as I step outside. Seoul eats and shits through the same door. My body curls up like a worm. It seems that every few days a big hand descends from the sky to roll out cloud-like toilet paper and wipe the opening of Seoul, which is simultaneously a mouth and an anus. Tonight, fat flakes fall as the last truck leaves the tunnel. I let the snow collect, then shove it into my mouth.

Kim Hyesoon (1997), translated from the Korean
by Don Mee Choi

Christopher Robin

*In April of 1996 the international press carried the news of
the death, at age 75, of Christopher Robin Milne, eternalized
in a book by his father A.A. Milne,* Winnie-the-Pooh,
as Christopher Robin.

I must think suddenly of matters too difficult for a bear of little
brain. I have never asked myself what lies beyond the place
where we live, I and Rabbit, Piglet and Eeyore, with our friend
Christopher Robin. That is, we continued to live here, and
nothing changed, and I just ate my little something. Only Chris-
topher Robin left for a moment.

Owl says that immediately beyond our garden Time begins,
and that it is an awfully deep well. If you fall in it, you go down
and down, very quickly, and no one knows what happens to
you next. I was a bit worried about Christopher Robin falling
in, but he came back and then I asked him about the well. 'Old
bear,' he answered. 'I was in it and I was falling and I was chang-
ing as I fell. My legs became long, I was a big person, I wore
trousers down to the ground, I had a grey beard, then I grew
old, hunched, and I walked with a cane, and then I died. It was

probably just a dream, it was quite unreal. The only real thing was you, old bear, and our shared fun. Now I won't go anywhere, even if I'm called for an afternoon snack.'

Czesław Miłosz (1997), translated from the Polish
by the author and Robert Hass

Return to Harmony 3

Two summers? Epochs, then, of ice.

But the air is the same muslin, beaten by the sky on Nanga Parbat, then pressed on the rocks of the nearer peaks.

I run down the ramp.

On the tarmac, I eavesdrop on Operation Tiger: Troops will burn down the garden and let the haven remain.

This is home – the haven a cage surrounded by ash – the fate of Paradise.

Through streets strewn with broken bricks and interrupted by paramilitaries, Irfan drives me straight to the Harmonies ('3' for my father – the youngest brother!), three houses built in a pastoral, that walled acreage of Harmonies where no one but my mother was poor.

A bunker has put the house under a spell. Shadowed eyes watch me open the gate, like a trespasser.

Has the gardener fled?

The Annexe of the Harmonies is locked – my grandmother's cottage – where her sons offered themselves to her as bouquets of mirrors. There was nothing else to reflect.

Under the windows the roses have choked in their beds. Was the gardener killed?

And the postman?

In the drawer of the cedar stand peeling in the verandah, a pile of damp letters – one to my father to attend a meeting the previous autumn, another an invitation to a wedding.

My first key opens the door. I break into quiet. The lights work.

The Koran still protects the house, lying strangely wrapped in a *jamawar* shawl where my mother had left it on the walnut table by the fireplace. Above, *If God is with you, Victory is near!* – the framed calligraphy ruthless behind cobwebs.

I pick up the dead phone, its number exiled from its instrument, a refugee among forlorn numbers in some angry office on Exchange Road.

But the receiver has caught a transmission: Rafi's song from a film about war: *Slowly, I so slowly, kept on walking, / and then was severed forever from her.* THIS IS ALL INDIA RADIO, AMRITSAR. I hang up.

Upstairs, the window too is a mirror; if I jump through it I will fall into my arms.

The mountains return my stare, untouched by blood.

On my shelf, by Ritsos and Rilke and Cavafy and Lorca and Iqbal and Amichai and Paz, my parents are beautiful in their wedding brocades, so startlingly young!

And there in black and white my mother, eighteen years old, a year before she came a bride to these Harmonies, so unforgivenly poor and so unforgivingly beautiful that the house begins to shake in my arms, and when the unarmed world is still again, with pity, it is the house that is holding me in its arms and the cry coming faded from its empty rooms is my cry.

Agha Shahid Ali (1997)

Thought (1)

You walk through the room and point out things. 'Table, bowl, chair, photograph, scissors.'

Then you watch how rain drips down the windowpane. You try to remember the drops. 'Now, now, now', you say, but the drops fall too quickly; their now is over as soon as you pronounce it.

The drops are people, you think. When they are at the top they are young; at the bottom they are old. You look at the drops just above the window sill. Poor drops. Do they realise that they will die?

You watch how the rain falls on the street. With each drop a little sailboat of water splatters upward. A great many sailboats that exist for no longer than a second. They think they are on their way, you think. Suddenly they exist and believe that they had always been there, and then it is over, then they think nothing anymore.

You look at the boats and think: I think 'I'! My I thinks with this head!

You think: I am this head!

Esther Jansma (1997), translated from the Dutch
by Scott Rollins

The Poet

I made myself into a poet because it was the first thing I really loved. It was an act of will. I realize that now. I was always afraid of asking for things from the devil. I would probably get them. Then I stumbled onto this idea about the purity of the heart. This is a way I could get what I want. To desire one thing, that's the idea. I knew I could do that. And I already knew what I wanted. To keep doing what I was doing, but to know that it was true. It was right for me to keep doing that, to want nothing else but that. I felt free at last. My life had become a dream. My dream. My life was the cloth of that. Days spent sharing an egg with a cat were good days. With my little red floor & white walls. & millions of men in my bed. It meant nothing. I liked alcohol. What poet didn't. I woke up in the dreaming poem of the day & made myself a hot black cup of coffee. I would begin. Soon I would want something. A cigarette. That was good. The place I bought them was far enough, a walk, good for my body, something blue for my hand. Who did I think the poet was. A talking dog. Who felt her lips with her fingertips & wrote that down. You see the page for me has terrific dimension. I can go into the white & I do. The lines are designs for something real, how much space around the slender bars I bend and shape in the name of my world. A comma is a little fish, a dash sort of a raft. When we say capitals we mean apples. German words about the same size as God. When you want to refer to that. Its comedy. Sometimes the poem wants to come home. It has a firm back, its left hand margin, sometimes it feels just fine about that. The page is the sky. My typewriter, classic, a wispy one had no spine & so my poems floated like clouds, globs of sunlessness & I marked the world free. Sensationally flat poems I know each line went from there to there was ironic as print felt that way soothed by the cruelty of wasps and was crisper than them, just a season of flat poems. Lonely the loss of rock 'n roll. It was receding. My poems were flat. A woman made me ache, I was love on the page not yet I had always felt like a brick shit house. I was the poem. The incident in the afternoon the folded sheet, I was the mouth the sounds emitted from I was the pipes of god, me this structure in eternity. Enter it. The oldest dream I remember an important one was about a train in the night going to Germany & I must get on & save myself. Once in a while I say be full, and it is, be slow, oh tear holes in me as the day dies. I have truly become my poems, but do note the sculpture of others, their obliviousness, like architects leaving crumbs. It is not lost my century, thanks to us. We are the liars & thieves, we are the women we are the women I am full of holes because you are. I am the only saintly man in town. Don't be afraid to be feminine. A girl on a rowboat, full of holes. She saw words shooting through.

Eileen Myles (1995)

Prose Poem

The morning coffee. I'm not sure why I drink it. Maybe it's the ritual of the cup, the spoon, the hot water, the milk, and the little heap of brown grit, the way they come together to form a nail I can hang the day on. It's something to do between being asleep and being awake. Surely there's something better to do, though, than to drink a cup of instant coffee. Such as meditate? About what? About having a cup of coffee. A cup of coffee whose first drink is too hot and whose last drink is too cool, but whose many in-between drinks are, like Baby Bear's porridge, just right. Papa Bear looks disgruntled. He removes his spectacles and swivels his eyes onto the cup that sits before Baby Bear, and then, after a discreet cough, reaches over and picks it up. Baby Bear doesn't understand this disruption of the morning routine. Papa Bear brings the cup close to his face and peers at it intently. The cup shatters in his paw, explodes actually, sending fragments and brown liquid all over the room. In a way it's good that Mama Bear isn't there. Better that she rest in her grave beyond the garden, unaware of what has happened to the world.

Ron Padgett (1995)

from *Kuchh Vakya*

The Well

Mother's money lies hidden under a sheet of paper in a green box.

Father stands before a dark almirah.

Late at night, my brother gazes into the deep well. He searches for the glass he can never find near the earthen pot.

Father is delighted to see the red tomatoes in the field. The gardener drags himself after him. In a corner of the field, the gardener's wife lulls her child to sleep sitting on the black soil.

Walking in her sleep, mother finds her way to the well. They fail to recognize each other.

Grandmother mumbles: 'On dark nights ghosts fill water at the well.'

'I can never find the glass,' my brother screams, parched with thirst. Petrified, mother does not move.

The harsingar tree in the courtyard covers father's dead body with white flowers.

Sari

Father is sitting at a long dining table eating a *roti* with a knife and fork. Fascinated, I sit beside him watching his strange performance.

Mother sits in an empty room as finely spun shadows drown her. Father's death slowly spreads over her *sari*.

Grandfather's lonely hands grope over a wall for the hook on which he can hang his cap.

Grandmother mumbles quietly, 'Is the old man asleep again?'

When I insist, Mother changes her white *sari*.

Where the road takes a sharp turn, Father walks towards the sky.

Udayan Vajpeyi (1995), translated from the Hindi
by Alok Bhalla

The Ice House

Every Sunday afternoon we used to go on our Sunday afternoon run. There were two routes. Route one: from Darfield via Goldthorpe to Hickleton with its churchyard with the skulls in the gate, turn left at Hickleton crossroads for a Danny's ice cream, then past Bilham Sand quarry to Hooton Pagnell, described by Arthur Mee in his *Counties of England* as a Jewel in a sea of coal, then past the mysterious church in the middle of a field at Frickley and back home. Route two: through Darfield to Millhouses, turn left at Holly House, the old pit owner's house where the beekeeper lived, through Middlecliffe, once called Plevna, and Great Houghton, past Houghton Woods to a Danny's ice cream at Brierley crossroads. A childhood of Sundays dominated by mysterious buildings and Danny's Ice Cream. And my dad would always say the same things as we drove along. Past a house at the edge of Great Houghton he'd point and say 'We now pass the famous house of Dick Turpin, famous for his horse Black Beauty. And now we approach the ducky pond, famous for the ducks.'

And for all those years of Sundays as we sat at Brierley crossroads eating ice cream, I never knew this place was here: the ice house, deep in the woods that the man at Burntwood Hall created for his pleasure. A treasure under the ground, melting away.

Ian McMillan (1994)

How Everything Has Turned Around

We are relieved at last to have left the shadowlands. You will remember he sat at the table looking straight at me with tears in his eyes. He was tame and composed, he was faithful. Nothing he could do when having to love seemed like too much of an effort, like playing sport, like getting fit. Perhaps that endurance, the pining away, the sexless resignation, became old and tedious. Now everything has turned, is all lit up, the afternoon sun covers the walls with shimmering shadows. The difference is dazzling, worth bright gouache paintings and on these different days he can throw rice for the doves. Now he can carry you out of your fainting, pick up the lipsticks dropped from low windows, search with great care for dry parts of the tissue, switch on car radios and hope for Bach preludes. How everything has turned around as we never know things will things do.

Pam Brown (1994)

Hammer and Nail

'Would you like to see where our little girl is buried?' my friend asks as we walk between stucco shrines and wreaths of brilliant flowers. Even a plane's propeller is attached to a pilot's grave as if the whole thing might spin off into the wind. One man's relatives built a castle over his remains, with turrets and towers, to match the castle he built for his body in life. If you stand at a certain angle you can see both castles at once, the bigger one he lived in off on the horizon. An archway says in Spanish, 'Life is an illusion. Death is the reality. Respect the dead whom you are visiting now.' We hike down the hill toward the acres of 'free graves'. Here people can claim any space they want without paying, but also risk having someone buried on top of them. In the fields beyond the cemetery, women walk slowly with buckets slung over their shoulders on poles. Black cows graze on knee-high grass. The crossbar from the marker to my friend's child's grave has come loose and lies off to one side. My friend kneels, pressing the simple blue crossbar back into the upright piece, wishing for a hammer and nail. The cross has delicate scalloped edges and says nothing. No words, no dates. It reminds me of the simplicity of folded hands, though I know there were years of despair. My friend says, 'Sometimes I am still very sad. But I no longer ask, "What if . . . ?" It was the tiniest casket you ever saw.' On the small plots in either direction, families have stuck tall pine branches into dirt. The needles droop, completely dried by now, but they must have looked lovely as miniature forests for the first few days.

Naomi Shihab Nye (1994)

In the Off-Season

The sea has frozen to a stop. Ice stretches to the horizon. Little humps of sand, of water mixed with sand so thoroughly that granules of this new matter have the texture of firn, stick out smartly where the surf used to pound the shore, and beyond that a great frozen slab opens out like a cold hand, lined with the details of waves, crests, white horses of snow: a fleeting image of air in a furtive coupling of wind and spray, an alphabet of meanings receding to the horizon, repeated to infinity, an infinity of vibrations and still-born interferences. I think of a deserted Venice. I move without a shadow and enter the deep, lost in the sound of ice scrunching under my feet. But if I stop there will be a withering silence wrapped in the whisper of melting snow, of crumbling crests and friezes more delicate than soot. Here and there are cracks, as flashy as lightning, the contours of ice-floes, the blueprints of disintegration. And I imagine that I could mistake it all for one huge jigsaw puzzle, sit down and wait till water washes away the pattern, the frozen craziness of it, until I sink, slowly, to the bottom.

From up there, you won't hear me. Perhaps heaven is like this. So white, you can't look at it, so silent, you can't hear a word. I lie down on the snow and try to feel, running my fingers over the fragile summits, frozen geysers, gelid eruptions, icy foliage. The sky is reflected in this . . . mirror, so completely that when I lie on my back the clouds seem to pass through me like sand in an hourglass and – stiffening, coagulating into ribbons of snow – they unfurl in long lines of print which in a moment will be quickened by a touch of sunshine. A few more turns of the body and the sea is like the roof of a white cave, beneath which I hang like a bat, with the sky underneath like a sea.

And at night – I stay for the night – that crash and creak of ice, grinding and rumbling as it plays with the cables of ships, in a violent effort – to keep things moving? On the moon's behalf? Or some other satellite's? To mould these snowy crests into a smile? A stealthy smile when no-one is looking? And when no-one looks I spot a whirlpool and a welter of the waves, a blizzard of shapes: shadowy headless forms, of serpents coiled into rings, of the frenzied dance of the Maenads, and Athenian magistrates.

Andrzej Sosnowski (1994), translated from the Polish
by Rod Mengham

from *Lawn of Excluded Middle*

1

When I say I believe that women have a soul and that its substance contains two carbon rings the picture in the foreground makes it difficult to find its appearance back where the corridors get lost in ritual sacrifice and hidden bleeding. But the four points of the compass are equal on the lawn of the excluded middle where full maturity of meaning takes time the way you eat a fish, morsel by morsel, off the bone. Something that can be held in the mouth, deeply, like darkness by someone blind or the empty space I place at the center of each poem to allow penetration.

2

I'm looking out the window at other windows. Though the pane masquerades as transparent I know it is impenetrable just as too great a show of frankness gives you a mere paper draft on revelations. As if words were passports, or arrows that point to the application we might make of them without considering the difference of biography and life. Still, depth of field allows the mind to drift beyond its negative pole to sun catching on a maple leaf already red in August, already thinner, more translucent, preparing to strip off all that separates it from its smooth skeleton. Beautiful, flamboyant phrase that trails off without predicate, intending disappearance by approaching it, a toss in the air.

3

I put a ruler in my handbag, having heard men talk about their sex. Now we have correct measurements and a stickiness between collar and neck. It is one thing to insert yourself into a mirror, but quite another to get your image out again and have your errors pass for objectivity. Vitreous. As in humor. A change in perspective is caused by the ciliary muscle, but need not be conciliatory. Still, the eye is a camera, room for everything that is to enter, like the cylinder called the satisfaction of hollow space. Only language grows such grass-green grass.

4

Even if a woman sits at a loom, it does not mean she must weave a cosmogony or clothes to cover the emptiness underneath. It might just be a piece of cloth which, like any center of attention, absorbs the available light the way a waterfall can form a curtain of solid noise through which only time can pass. She has been taught to imagine other things, but does not explain, disdaining defense while her consciousness streams down the rapids. The light converges on what might be the hollow of desire or the incomplete self, or just lint in her pocket. Her hour will also come with the breaking of water.

5

Because I refuse to accept the opposition of night and day I must pit other, subtler periodicities against the emptiness of being an adult. Their traces inside my body attempt precariously, like any sign, to produce understanding, but though nothing may come of that, the grass is growing. Can words play my parts and also find their own way to the house next door as rays converge and solve their differences? Or do notes follow because drawn to a conclusion? If we don't signal our love, reason will eat our heart out before it can admit its form of mere intention, and we won't know what has departed.

6

All roads lead, but how does a sentence do it? Nothing seems hidden, but it goes by so fast when I should like to see it laid open to view whether the engine resembles combustion so that form becomes its own explanation. We've been taught to apply solar principles, but must find on our own where to look for Rome the way words rally to the blanks between them and thus augment the volume of their resonance.

Rosmarie Waldrop (1993)

The Word-Gulag

They've opened a new gulag. The word-gulag.

I go there every week, and take a shopping bag filled with fresh fruit, a bar of soap and a few tins of condensed milk. I call out a prisoner's name at random, then wait in the visitors' room with the gesturing crowd. One by one, the words file out of a little door and stand in front of us on the other side of the wire. Pale. Trembling. Haggard. Shattered.

'Speak!' the guard barks while he patrols the corridor that divides us, clanging his keys against the grille.

No one responds. The words can't reply because their jaws are visibly broken. Nor can the visitors because, as they've just suddenly realised – they really should have wised up to this earlier – the gulag has robbed them of all their best words.

'Visiting time is over,' the guard shouts, drawing a curtain we hadn't noticed before.

Some barely audible words burst out, but nobody could tell which side of the grille they were coming from. They were probably words of goodbye.

Abdellatif Laâbi (1993), translated from the Arabic
by André Naffis-Sahely

Dustie-Fute

When I opened my window and reached for the yoghurt cooling on the outside ledge, it had gone. All that remained was a single Scottish word bewildered by the Paris winter frost and the lights of its riverbank motorways. What can *dustie-fute* have to say to a night like this? How can it dangle its hyphen down into the rue Geoffrey L'Asnier where Danton stayed on the eve of revolution? How can it tame this strangeness for me or change me into the cupolas and flagstones I so desire yet still notice every time I walk among them? Does the 'auld alliance' of words and things stand a chance among the traffics and pimps in the Publicis Saint-Germain? For it's not as if *dustie-fute* were my familiar. I could easily confuse *dustie-fute* with *elfmill* which is the sound made by a worm in the timber of a house, supposed by the vulgar to be preternatural. These words are as foreign as the city they have parachuted into, dead words slipping on the sill of a living metropolis. They are extremes that touch like dangerous wires and the only hope for them, for us, is the space they inhabit, a room Cioran speaks of, veering between dilettantism and dynamite. Old Scots word, big French city and in between abysmal me: ane merchand or creamer, quha hes no certain dwelling place, quhair the dust may be dicht fra hes feete or schone. Dustie-fute, a stranger, equivalent to *fairand-man*, at a loss in the empty soul of his ancestors' beautiful language and in the soulless city of his compeers living the 21st century now and scoffing at his medieval wares. Yet here, precisely here, is their rendez-vous and triumphantly, stuffed down his sock, an oblique sense, the dustie-fute of 'revelry', the acrobat, the juggler who accompanies the toe-belled jongleur with his merchant's comic fairground face. He reaches deep into his base Latinity, into his *pede-pulverosi* and French descendants pull out their own *pieds poudreux*. Dustie-fute remembers previous lives amid the plate glass of Les Halles. They magnify his motley, his mid-oranges, his hawker lyrics and for a second Beaubourg words graze Scottish glass then glance apart. In this revelry differences copulate, become more visible and bearable and, stranger than the words or city I inhabit, I reach for my yoghurt and find it there.

David Kinloch (1992)

dropped on the ground • the small coin

People were gathered on the square watching a man make popcorn. At that time I was about three or four years old. The crowd was large and it was dusk. I slyly wound my way among the heels and dirty leather shoes of the adults. I was wearing split-pants, my round chubby bottom must have stuck outside the surface of the earth – like today's hostage, for this reason the ferocious people did not have the heart to knock me over. I crawled here and there. My uncle and the monk preferred to stand at a lower place. The popcorn maker's face and chest were smeared dark with soot, except for the whites of his eyes, making him look like the chief witness at a wedding. The whites of his eyes proved his honesty and fair dealing. Evidently there was no deception in the popcorn. Uncle tested it with his fingers, then with his nose, finally with his soft lips and then everything was clear. He returned home. Then appeared some grave omens. While I was crawling among the crowd, I had already learned to detest the monk's cloth shoes. I attempted to climb to a higher place, after I grew up this became clearer. I moved slowly toward the popcorn maker. Showed him a small coin. On one side there were all odd numbers, on the other side all even numbers. The popcorn man grinned with puzzlement, I saw that besides the whites of his eyes, the inner edge of his lips near the gums was also white. I tossed the small coin into the air, it fell, and I pressed it in my hand. If the odd-numbered side was up, I would throw the coin into the popcorn machine, and pop it with the corn. The popcorn man knew my intention, he really was like the chief witness at a wedding, he showed me his kindest and most clever smile. When I grew up, I was taught that poetry should be written in lines. But at that time I did not know.

Zhou Yaping (1992), translated from the Chinese
by Jeff Twitchell

from *Short Talks*

Short Talk on Homo Sapiens

With small cuts Cro-Magnon man recorded the moon's phases on the handles of his tools, thinking about her as he worked. Animals. Horizon. Face in a pan of water. In every story I tell comes a point where I can see no further. I hate that point. It is why they call storytellers blind – a taunt.

Short Talk on the Total Collection

From childhood he dreamed of being able to keep with him all the objects in the world lined up on his shelves and bookcases. He denied lack, oblivion or even the likelihood of a missing piece. Order streamed from Noah in blue triangles and as the pure fury of his classifications rose around him, engulfing his life they came to be called waves by others, who drowned, a world of them.

Short Talk on the Truth to Be Had from Dreams

Seized by a sudden truth I started up at 4 a.m. The word *grip* pronounced 'gripe' is applied only to towns, cities and from *Short Talks*

inhabitations; the word *gripe* pronounced 'grip' can be used of human beings. In my dream I saw the two parts of this truth connected by a three-mile long rope of women's hair. And just at the moment all the questions of male and female soul murder, which were to be answered as soon as I pulled on the rope, broke away and fell in a chunk back down the rocky chasm where I had been asleep. We are the half and half again, we are the language stump.

Short Talk on the Sensation of Aeroplane Takeoff

Well you know I wonder, it could be love running towards my life with its arms up yelling let's buy it what a bargain!

Anne Carson (1992)

In Love with Raymond Chandler

An affair with Raymond Chandler, what a joy! Not because of the mangled bodies and the marinated cops and hints of eccentric sex, but because of his interest in furniture. He knew that furniture could breathe, could feel, not as we do but in a way more muffled, like the word *upholstery*, with its overtones of mustiness and dust, its bouquet of sunlight on aging cloth or of scuffed leather on the backs and seats of sleazy office chairs. I think of his sofas, stuffed to roundness, satin-covered, pale blue like the eyes of his cold blond unbodied murderous women, beating very slowly, like the hearts of hibernating crocodiles; of his chaises longues, with their malicious pillows. He knew about front lawns too, and greenhouses, and the interiors of cars.

This is how our love affair would go. We would meet at a hotel, or a motel, whether expensive or cheap it wouldn't matter. We would enter the room, lock the door, and begin to explore the furniture, fingering the curtains, running our hands along the spurious gilt frames of the pictures, over the real marble or the chipped enamel of the luxurious or tacky washroom sink, inhaling the odor of the carpets, old cigarette smoke and spilled gin and fast meaningless sex or else the rich abstract scent of the oval transparent soaps imported from England, it wouldn't matter to us; what would matter would be our response to the furniture, and the furniture's response to us. Only after we had sniffed, fingered, rubbed, rolled on, and absorbed the furniture of the room would we fall into each other's arms, and onto the bed (king-size? peach-colored? creaky? narrow? four-posted? pioneer-quilted? lime-green chenille-covered?), ready at last to do the same things to each other.

Margaret Atwood (1992)

Letters

Her mouth is but oil and she makes me see the little girl of it. How I wish it would hold, in the way of love an invention. This is the rosy iridescent silk suspended an inch off your breasts, how the waters do run in comparison. I wish in the way I clasped you I might *see* those groans the very walls come up with. Why must we even be restrained in madness.

I fear lest you see merely into this passage out of politeness. There is a judge of outrage but he does not open his mouth and so we do not know him. But I admit that I am made of granite and still waver. If I promise I can do nothing. Tighten yourself and stop seeing only what I present to you. You will coil that lace off your breast above your head as a greeting to me. You do have the liking for thick cloth as well?

My flesh will not come back to me without the placing of yours before me. And I would see your proof, as with a spoon. As spoons clasped we rise over the frightening texts of flesh habit scribed badly. I refer here to the white marble cask, as you know. Oh, hold me on my back and eat me like Shakespeare with vinegar. My writing must be as beautifully cast away as your strap that day on the grass. One must do it as in one flame well, from chocolate to amethyst, a thousand liquid breaks to the breasts. Do you fear so much the loudness of my room? I will be intoxicated before your slightest cry becomes melodic. May you bring yourself to pose in all the windows that I love.

Whatever the source of your name, I kiss you in that place. Adieu, my hand in bed, my dream of this world that hangs from the light of a dream, my sweet staring thickness, my hock.

Clark Coolidge (1991)

What No One Could Have Told Them

Once he comes to live on the outside of her, he will not sleep through the night or the next 400. He sleeps not, they sleep not. Ergo they steer gradually mad. The dog's head shifts another paw under the desk. Over a period of 400 nights.

You will see, she warns him. Life is full of television sets, invoices, organs of other animals thawing on counters.

In her first dream of him, she leaves him sleeping on Mamo's salt-bag quilt behind her alma mater. Leaves him to the Golden Goblins. Sleep, pretty one, sleep.

. . . the quilt that comforted her brother's youthful bed, the quilt he took to band camp.

Huh oh, he says, Huh oh. His word for many months. Merrily pouring a bottle of Pledge over the dog's dull coat. And with a round little belly that shakes like jelly.

Waiting out a shower in the Border Café; the bartender spoons a frozen strawberry into his palm-leaf basket while they lift their frosted mugs in a grateful click.

He sits up tall in his grandfather's lap, waving and waving to the Blue Bonnet truck. Bye, blue, bye.

In the next dream he stands on his toes, executes a flawless flip onto the braided rug. Resprings to crib.

The salt-bag quilt goes everywhere, the one the bitch Rosemary bore her litters on. The one they wrap around the mower, and bundle with black oak leaves.

How the bowl of Quick Quaker Oats fits his head.

He will have her milk at 1:42, 3:26, 4 a.m. Again at 6. Bent over the rail to settle his battling limbs down for an afternoon nap. Eyes shut, trying to picture what in the world she has on.

His nightlight – a snow-white pair of porcelain owls.

They remember him toothless, with one tooth, two tooths, five or seven scattered around in his head. They can see the day when he throws open his jaw to display several vicious rows.

Naked in a splash of sun, he pees into a paper plate the guest set down in the grass as she reached for potato chips.

Suppertime, the dog takes leave of the desk's cool cavity to patrol his highchair.

How patiently he pulls Kleenex from a box. Tissue by tissue. How quietly he stands at the door trailing the White Cloud; swabs his young hair with the toilet brush.

The dog inherits the salt-bag quilt. The one her Mamo made when she was seventeen – girlfriends stationed around a frame in black stockings sewing, talking about things their children would do;

He says: cereal, byebye, shoe, raisin, nobody. He hums.

She stands before the medicine chest, drawn. Swiftly he tumps discarded Tampax and hair from an old comb into her tub.

Wearily the man enters the house through the back. She isn't dressed. At the table there is weeping. Curses. Forking dried breasts of chicken.

while Little Sneed sat on the floor beneath the frame, pushing the needles back through.

One yawn followed by another yawn. Then little fists screwing little eyes. The wooden crib stuffed with bears and windup pillows wheeled in to receive him. Out in a twinkle. The powdered bottom airing the dark. The 400th night. When they give up their last honeyed morsel of love; the dog nestles in the batting of the salt-bag quilt commencing its long mope unto death.

C. D. Wright (1991)

An Anointing

Boys have to slash their fingers to become brothers. Girls trade their Kotex, me and Molly do it in the mall's public facility.

Me and Molly never remember each other's birthdays. On purpose. We don't like scores of any kind. We don't wear watches or weigh ourselves.

Me and Molly have tasted beer. We drank our shampoo. We went to the doctor together and lifted our specimen cups in a toast. We didn't drink that stuff. We just gargled.

When me and Molly get the urge, we are careful to put it back exactly as we found it. It looks untouched.

Between the two of us, me and Molly have 20/20 vision.

Me and Molly are in eighth grade for good. We like it there. We adore the view. We looked both ways and decided not to cross the street. Others who'd been to the other side didn't return. It was a trap.

Me and Molly don't double date. We don't multiply anything. We don't know our multiplication tables from a coffee table. We'll never be decent waitresses, indecent ones maybe.

Me and Molly do not believe in going ape or going bananas or going Dutch. We go as who we are. We go as what we are.

Me and Molly have wiped each other's asses with ferns. Made emergency tampons of our fingers. Me and Molly made do with what we have.

Me and Molly are in love with wiping the blackboard with each other's hair. The chalk gives me and Molly an idea of what old age is like; it is dusty and makes us sneeze. We are allergic to it.

Me and Molly, that's M and M, melt in your mouth.

What are we doing in your mouth? Me and Molly bet you'll never guess. Not in a million years. We plan to be around that long. Together that long. Even if we must freeze the moment and treat the photograph like the real thing.

Me and Molly don't care what people think. We're just glad that they do.

Me and Molly lick the dew off the morning grasses but taste no honey till we lick each other's tongues.

We wear full maternity sails. We boat upon my broken water. The katabatic action begins, Molly down my canal binnacle first, her water breaking in me like an anointing.

Thylias Moss (1991)

Man with a Mower

There is a man sitting on a tractor mowing circles in the park.

In the middle of the area he is mowing there is a group of people wandering about. Five of them. They move in a bunch. One of them holds a piece of paper which they all consult every so often. They stand for a while and look at the paper then they look up and around them and sometimes someone draws a line in the air with their finger and they all look at it, then look back at the paper again. Then one starts moving and the others follow. The grass is quite long and rather wet so they lift their legs high as they walk.

The men wear grey suits, the hems of which are getting damp from standing in the grass. They walk as though crossing a river, going from stone to stone. One of the men wears a lemon tie. One of the women has on a lemon outfit and red shoes. She and the man may be involved or it may merely be a coincidence. The women's legs are also getting wet as they move around in the grass in the park. They stand and look and study and point and look and move on. And all this time the man on the tractor is mowing his circles around them, getting closer and closer so the grass on the outside where he has been is short and the people stand in the long grass in the middle like an exhibit.

The tractor is noisy. The people in the grass must have to talk loudly when the mower passes on its way around them.

The man on the tractor wears ear muffs. He is thinking about a mince pie. He is thinking about Dolly Parton. He is thinking about the snake tattooed on his buttocks and the way it wriggles as he walks.

Jenny Bornholdt (1991)

Deer Dancer

Nearly everyone had left that bar in the middle of winter except the hardcore. It was the coldest night of the year, every place shut down, but not us. Of course we noticed when she came in. We were Indian ruins. She was the end of beauty. No one knew her, the stranger whose tribe we recognized, her family related to deer, if that's who she was, a people accustomed to hearing songs in pine trees, and making them hearts.

The woman inside the woman who was to dance naked in the bar of misfits blew deer magic. Henry Jack, who could not survive a sober day, thought she was Buffalo Calf Woman come back, passed out, his head by the toilet. All night he dreamed a dream he could not say. The next day he borrowed money, went home, and sent back the money I lent. Now that's a miracle. Some people see vision in a burned tortilla, some in the face of a woman.

This is the bar of broken survivors, the club of the shotgun, knife wound, of poison by culture. We who were taught not to stare drank our beer. The players gossiped down their cues. Someone put a quarter in the jukebox to relive despair. Richard's wife dove to kill her. We had to keep her still, while Richard secretly bought the beauty a drink.

How do I say it? In this language there are no words for how the real world collapses. I could say it in my own and the sacred mounds would come into focus, but I couldn't take it in this dingy envelope. So I look at the stars in this strange city, frozen to the back of the sky, the only promises that ever make sense.

My brother-in-law hung out with white people, went to law school with a perfect record, quit. Says you can keep your laws, your words. And practiced law on the street with his hands. He jimmied to the proverbial dream girl, the face of the moon, while the players racked a new game. He bragged to us, he told her magic words and that when she broke, became human.

But we all heard his bar voice crack:

What's a girl like you doing in a place like this?

That's what I'd like to know, what are we all doing in a place like this?

You would know she could hear only what she wanted to; don't we all? Left the drink of betrayal Richard bought her, at the bar. What was she on? We all wanted some. Put a quarter in the juke. We all take risks stepping into thin air. Our ceremonies didn't predict this. Or we expected more.

I had to tell you this, for the baby inside the girl sealed up with a lick of hope and swimming into the praise of nations. This is not a rooming house, but a dream of winter falls and the deer who portrayed the relatives of strangers. The way back is deer breath on icy windows.

The next dance none of us predicted. She borrowed a chair for the stairway to heaven and stood on a table of names. And danced in the room of children without shoes.

You picked a fine time to leave me, Lucille.
With four hungry children and a crop in the field.

And then she took off her clothes. She shook loose memory, waltzed with the empty lover we'd all become.

She was the myth slipped down through dreamtime. The promise of feast we all knew was coming. The deer who crossed through knots of a curse to find us. She was no slouch, and neither were we, watching.

The music ended. And so does the story. I wasn't there. But I imagined her like this, not a stained red dress with tape on her heels but the deer who entered our dream in white dawn, breathed mist into pine trees, her fawn a blessing of meat, the ancestors who never left.

Joy Harjo (1990)

from *The Stumbling Block Its Index*

The Stumbling Block is a graphite font. This black plinth was once a brush or similar terminal that was the lips of an intense electrical arc. Industries proud and violent need spoke through it to turn the wheel or smelt and cast the constructed challenge. Now abandoned it finds benediction in seclusion. It has softened its mouth to hold water, so that small animals and disjointed humans may drink or sign themselves in their passage.

The Stumbling Block has been used like an entrance step to sharpen knives on. Its fossil bristle of tight stone forcing the heavy blades down to a hiss along one edge. These are knives of gleaming hubris, long intentions honed for malice. They are magnetized and have been placed to construct a lectern. Each blade holding the next to form the platform. It may hold this index at its centre, hovering, placed outside in the aorta of streets. The removal of any of the blades from the assembled cluster will spill their fish bodies to the ground. The paper will drink any of the stains of their usage.

The Stumbling Block is an ark of extinction. A bouillon hive of the murdered past, frozen dry to a mass. Something has warmed its corner, the oxoed grit bleeds a vein of contagion, virulent in its passion to embrace and swim in human tides.

The Stumbling Block has become a pillow to the dispossessed. It can be moulded to the need of its companion, kneaded and pummelled so as not to lose its hunched purchase on the slippery pavement. They will warble and breathe into it, it becomes their mother as their alcoholic dribble writes a sad and caustic text in its interior. This wet laser chisel entwines their lineage with fine scrollwork into the intricate memory of the city. These are the inhabitants of the boundary, our necessary shadows that are being cast further from the warmth of their twins. The block gives itself completely to these and will fierce itself against the bright sneers and plastic credit blades that shave their humanity.

Without word or agreement, without plan or direction they have begun to sleep a line. In the gutters and elbows of curbs, in the approved architectural contrivances they have threaded themselves in a necklace cleated to ring a living, dreaming wall; a perimeter fence. Their expulsion has constructed a cage that concentrates the greed in its own bitter well.

The Stumbling Block is a night thing, that sits on the heart. It will sip from the ribs of guilt, to breathe luminous heat into flat shabby lungs elsewhere.

Brian Catling (1990)

Chekhov: A Sestina

Why him? He woke up and felt anxious. He was out of sorts,
out of character. If only it would go away. Ivashin loved Nadya
Vishnyevskaya and was afraid of his love. When the butler told
him the old lady had just gone out, but that the young lady was
at home, he fumbled in his fur coat and dresscoat pocket, found
his card, and said: 'Right.' But it was not right. Driving from his
house in the morning to pay a visit, he thought he was com-
pelled to it by the conventions of society which weighed heavily
upon him. But now it was clear that he went to pay calls only
because somewhere far away in the depths of his soul, as under
a veil, there lay hidden a hope that he would see Nadya, his
secret love. And he suddenly felt pitiful, sad, and not a little
anxious. In his soul, it seemed to him, it was snowing, and
everything was fading away. He was afraid to love Nadya,
because he thought he was too old for her, his appearance
unattractive, and did not believe that a young woman like her
could love a man for his mind or spiritual character. Every-
thing was dim, sharing, he felt, the same blank character. Still,
there would rise at times in him something like hope, a glimpse
of happiness, of things turning out all right. Then, just as
quickly, it would pass away. And he would wonder what had
come over him. Why should he, a retired councillor of state,
educated, liberal-minded, a well-traveled man; why should he,
in other words, be so anxious? Were there not other women

170

with whom he could fall in love? Surely, it was always possible to fall in love. It was possible, moreover, to fall in love without acting out of character. There was absolutely no need for him to be anxious. To be in love, to have a young pretty wife and children of his own, was not a crime or a deception, but his right. Clearly, there was something wrong with him. He wished he were far away . . . But suddenly he hears from somewhere in the house the young officer's spurs jingle and then die away. That instant marked the death of his timid love. And in its vanishing, he felt the seeds of a different sort of melancholy take root within him. Whatever happened now, whatever desolation might be his, it would build character. Yes, he thought, so it is only right. Yes, all is finished, and I'm glad, very glad, yes, and I'm not let down, no, nor am I in any way anxious. No, certainly not anxious. What he had to do now was to get away. But how could he make it look right? How could he have thought he was in love? How out of character! How very unlike him!

Mark Strand (1990)

Inflation

I stand on the edge of the place where I am expected to become invisible. I ask if this is all there is.

The fog lifts slightly and I walk towards an area slowly creasing into water. I look into the water and can just see a blur of grey. I do my hair, combing it carefully over the place where my scalp shines through.

When I look up, a young ferryman is standing in the shallows. Once, I would have caught him in my arms and pressed his body into mine. I would have fingered obsessively the small curls on the nape of his neck and pretended to read his soul. Now I feel nothing but hatred for him.

He grins mockingly and holds out his hand, making a deep bowl of the palm.

I lie that I have no change, not even two obols. He doesn't understand, or pretends he doesn't. His eyes still mock me.

When I have explained, he says he will not accept foreign coins. He mentions a three-figure sum, and demands a cheque, made out in sterling.

And it turns out he doesn't even go all the way to the underworld.

Carol Rumens (1989)

Quaker Oats

The grain elevators have stood empty for years. They used to feed an entire nation of children. Hunched in red leatherette breakfast-nooks, fingers dreaming, children let their spoons clack on the white sides of their bowls. They stare at the carton on the table, a miniature silo with a kindly face smiling under a stiff black hat.

They eat their oats with milk and butter and sugar. They eat their oats in their sleep, where horsedrawn carts jolt along miry roads, past cabins where other children wait, half-frozen under tattered counterpanes. The man with the black hat, a burlap sack tucked under his arm, steps down from the wagon whispering *come out, don't be afraid.*

And they come, the sick and the healthy; the red, the brown, the white; the ruddy and the sallow; the curly and the lank. They tumble from rafters and crawl out of trundles. He gives them to eat. He gives them prayers and a good start in the morning. He gives them free enterprise; he gives them the flag and PA systems and roller skates and citizenship. He gives them a tawny canoe to portage overland, through the woods, through the midwestern snow.

Rita Dove (1989)

from *The World Doesn't End*

My father loved the strange books of André Breton. He'd raise the wine glass and toast those far-off evenings 'when butterflies formed a single uncut ribbon.' Or we'd go out for a piss in the back alley and he'd say, 'Here are some binoculars for blindfolded eyes.' We lived in a rundown tenement that smelled of old people and their pets.

'Hovering on the edge of the abyss, permeated with the perfume of the forbidden,' we'd take turns cutting the smoked sausage on the table. 'I love America,' he'd tell us. We were going to make a million dollars manufacturing objects we had seen in dreams that night.

Charles Simic (1989)

Human Wishes

This morning the sun rose over the garden wall and a rare blue sky leaped from east to west. Man is altogether desire, say the Upanishads. Worth anything, a blue sky, says Mr. Acker, the Shelford gardener. Not altogether. In the end. Last night on television the ethnologist and the cameraman watched with hushed wonder while the chimpanzee carefully stripped a willow branch and inserted it into the anthill. He desired red ants. When they crawled slowly up the branch, he ate them, pinched between long fingers as the zoom lens enlarged his face. Sometimes he stopped to examine one, as if he were a judge at an ant beauty contest or God puzzled suddenly by the idea of suffering. There was an empty place in the universe where that branch wasn't and the chimp filled it, as Earlene, finding no back on an old Welsh cupboard she had bought in Saffron Walden, imagined one there and imagined both the cupboard and the imagined back against a kitchen wall in Berkeley, and went into town looking for a few boards of eighteenth-century tongue-in-groove pine to fill that empty space. I stayed home to write, or rather stayed home and stared at a blank piece of paper, waiting for her to come back, thinking tongue-in-groove, tongue-in-groove, as if language were a kind of moral cloud chamber through which the world passed and from which it emerged charged with desire. The man in the shop in Cambridge said he didn't have any old pine, but when

Earlene went back after thinking about it to say she was sure she had seen some, the man found it. Right under his feet, which was puzzling. Mr. Acker, hearing the story, explained. You know, he said, a lot of fiddling goes on in those places. The first time you went in, the governor was there, the second time he wasn't, so the chap sold you some scrap and he's four quid in pocket. No doubt he's having a good time now with his mates in the pub. Or he might have put it on the horses at Newmarket. He might parley it into a fortune.

Robert Hass (1989)

Burnt Hair

One night, under the cool sheets, I dreamt of grandmother. She came to me as in a shadow play, that ancient art of the south, her tiny figure fluttering into sight across my bedsheet. When her body sailed into full view I realized she sat on a stool, hands tied behind her, mouth stuffed with a gag.

Next, I saw the old fashioned sailing ship, the sort one sees on Lipton tea tins with three masts and a tottering deck. Her feet were tied to the foot of a mast, then knotted to the three-legged stool. Her profile was clear now, the high cheek bones, large firm mouth and beaked nose, all familiar from the photographs of my childhood. I beckoned in my dream, but she would not speak.

Then came the fat man, slowly, as if the shadow players were unwilling. Twice as large as she was. A broad brimmed hat, the cowboy kind thrust to his head, boots that came up to his knees. A whip in his right hand. A fat cigar in his mouth. A Britisher, without a doubt. He plucked it out.

Her arms moved up now, over the mast, still tied. By remote control, they moved up, inch by inch. I smelt the shock of singed hair, the fiery nib. I bit my tongue. I did not weep. How could I when she sat there, utterly still. She did not cringe, she did not twitch a lip, my grandmother.

The ship moved on. Water lapped against the deck in small pointy waves. The water touched her toes. She sat there holding the fire in her armpits. Finally he seemed to tire. He leant his hulk over the deck and vomited into water. The tiny men who scurried in bearing platters of peaches and pigs, turtle doves and duck eggs, knelt at the portholes and wept. They could not untie grandmother, their wrists too frail from malnutrition. They did not have metal hidden in their pockets.

She just sat there, my grandmother, as the ship sailed into darkness. Her arms were still lifted high. Did the moonlight cool her face? Did the ropes slip off, a cunning resolution the puppeteers sometimes allow? Was she lifted off the ship and carried in triumph? Did Gandhi greet her?

I did not ask consoling questions in my sleep. It was the stench of burnt hair that stayed with me.

Meena Alexander (1988)

The Hanoi Market

It smells of sea and earth, of things dying and newly born.
Duck eggs, pig feet, mandarin oranges. Wooden bins and metal
boxes of nails, screws, ratchets, balled copper wire, brass fit-
tings, jet and helicopter gadgets, lug wrenches, bolts of silk,
see-through paper, bamboo calligraphy pens, and curios ham-
mered out of artillery shells.

Faces painted on coconuts. Polished to a knife-edge or sealed in
layers of dust and grease, cogs and flywheels await secret mis-
sions. Aphrodisiacs for dream merchants. A silent storm moves
through this place. Someone's worked sweat into the sweet
loaves of bread lined up like coffins on a stone slab.

She tosses her blonde hair back and smiles down at everyone. Is
it the squid and shrimp we ate at lunch, am I seeing things? An
adjacent stall blooms with peacock feathers. The T-shirt wavers
like a pennant as a sluggish fan slices the humidity.

I remember her white dress billowing up in a blast of warm air
from a steel grate in New York City, reminding me of Miss Fire-
cracker flapping like a flag from an APC antenna. Did we kill
each other for this?

I stop at a table of figurines. What was meant to tear off a leg or arm twenty years ago, now is a child's toy I can't stop touching.

Maybe Marilyn thought she'd erase herself from our minds, but she's here when the fan flutters the T-shirt silkscreened with her face. The artist used five shades of red to get her smile right.

A door left ajar by a wedge of sunlight. Below the T-shirt, at the end of two rows of wooden bins, a chicken is tied directly across from a caged snake. Bright skin – deadly bite. I move from the chicken to the snake, caught in their hypnotic plea.

Yusef Komunyakaa (1988)

reading

there were so many books. she had to separate them to avoid being overwhelmed by the excessive implications of their words. she kept hundreds in a series of boxes inside a wire cage in a warehouse. and hundreds more on the shelves of her various rooms. when she changed houses she would pack some of the books into the boxes and exchange them for others that had been hibernating. these resurrected books were precious to her for a while. they had assumed the patinas of dusty chthonic wisdoms. and thus she would let them sit on the shelves admiring them from a distance. gathering time and air. she did not want to be intimate with their insides. the atmospherics suggested by the titles were enough. sometimes she would increase the psychic proximities between herself and the books and place a pile of them on the floor next to her bed. and quite possibly she absorbed their intentions while she slept.

if she intended travelling beyond a few hours she would occasionally remove a book from the shelves and place it in her bag. she carried 'the poetics of space' round india for three months and it returned to her shelves undamaged at the completion of the journey. every day of those three months she touched it and read some of the titles of its chapters to make sure it was there. and real. chapters called house and universe, nests, shells, intimate immensity, miniatures and, the significance of the hut. she had kept it in a pocket of her bag together with a coloured whistle and an acorn. she now kept this book in the darkness of her reference shelf. and she knew that one day she would have to admit to herself that this was the only book she had need of, that this was the book she would enter the pages of, that this was the book she was going to read

joanne burns (1988)

The First Week of Mourning

In memory of my daughters' mother's mother

Nearly home.

When, true to the habits of half a century, she bent down by the brook where she had washed her clothes as a child and discovered, much to her surprise, that she could not scoop up even half a drop of its refreshing clarity or see the slightest sign or shadow of her reflection in the mirror-like surface of the water, then, and only then, did she recall that because her son and daughter-in-law had followed the fashion of going to Church, no one had bothered to chant a Buddhist sutra to ease her soul into the next world, much less honour her in this world by giving her a spirit tablet in the family shrine.

As a peach petal floats through the fangs of the crescent moon, grandma almost bursts into tears. She has all but forgotten how she had just walked upon the waves of couch grass and walked upon the waves of rush flowers and walked upon the waves of the Formosa Strait and walked upon the waves of Dongting Lake and is nearly home.

Shang Qin (1987), translated from the Chinese
by Steve Bradbury

The Dogs

A country of mountains that are dogs, of valleys that are barks, of stones standing upright in the barking like dogs pulling at the end of their chains.

And in the leaps, the pantings, the fury, here is the open door, here is the hall. The fire is bright, the table set, the wine shines in the carafes.

Yves Bonnefoy (1987), translated from the French
by Richard Stamelman

from *My Life*

One begins as a student but becomes a friend of clouds

Back and backward, why, wide and wider. Such that art is inseparable from the search for reality. The continent is greater than the content. A river nets the peninsula. The garden rooster goes through the goldenrod. I watched a robin worming its way on the ridge, time on the uneven light ledge. There as in that's their truck there. Where it rested in the weather there it rusted. As one would say, my friends, meaning no possession, and don't harm my trees. Marigolds, nasturtiums, snapdragons, sweet William, forget-me-nots, replaced by chard, tomatoes, lettuce, garlic, peas, beans, carrots, radishes – but marigolds. The hum hurts. Still, I felt intuitively that this which was incomprehensible was expectant, increasing, was good. The greatest thrill was to be the one to 'tell.' All rivers' left banks remind me of Paris, not to see or sit upon but to hear spoken of. Cheese makes one thirsty but onions make a worse thirst. The Spanish make a little question frame. In the case, propped on a stand so as to beckon, was the hairy finger of St. Cecilia, covered with rings. The old dress is worn out, torn up, dumped. Erasures could not serve better authenticity. The years pass, years in which, I take it, events were not lacking. There are more colors in the great rose window of Chartres than in the rose. Beside a body, not a piece, of water. Serpentine is fool's jade. It is on a dressed stone. The previousness of plants in prior color – no dream can come up to the original, which in the common daylight is voluminous. Yet he insisted that his life had been full of happy chance, that he was luck's child. As a matter of fact, quite the obverse. After a 9-to-5 job he got to just go home. Do you have a compulsion to work and then did you have a good time. Now it is one o'clock on the dot, but that is only a coincidence and it has a bad name. Patriots drive larger cars. At the time the perpetual Latin of love kept things hidden. We might be late to the movies but *always* early for the kids. The women at the parents' meeting must wear rings, for continuity. More sheep than sleep. Paul was telling me a plot which involved time travel, I asked, 'How do they go into the future?' and he answered, 'What do you mean? – they wait and the future comes to them – of course!' so the problem was going into the past. I think my interests are much broader than those of people who have been saying the same thing for eight years, or so he said. Has the baby enough teeth for an apple. Juggle, jungle, chuckle. The hummingbird, for all we know, may be singing all day long. We had been in France where every word really was a bird, a thing singing. I laugh as if my pots were clean. The apple in the pie is the pie. An extremely pleasant and often comic satisfaction comes from conjunction, the fit, say, of comprehension in a reader's mind to content in a writer's work. But not bitter.

Lyn Hejinian (1987)

The Souvenir

The town where I was born, Radautz, in the county of Buko-
vina, threw me out when I was ten. On that day she forgot me,
as if I had died, and I forgot her too. We were both satisfied
with that.

Forty years later, all at once, she sent me a souvenir. Like an
unpleasant aunt whom you're supposed to love just because she
is a blood relative. It was a new photograph, her latest winter
portrait. A canopied wagon is waiting in the courtyard. The
horse, turning its head, gazes affectionately at an elderly man
who is busy closing some kind of gate. Ah, it's a funeral. There
are just two members left in the Burial Society: the grave-
digger and the horse.

But it's a splendid funeral; all around, in the strong wind, thou-
sands of snowflakes are crowding, each one a crystal star with
its own particular design. So there is still the same impulse to
be special, still the same illusions. Since all snow-stars have just
one pattern: six points, a Star of David in fact. In a minute they
will all start melting and turn into a mass of plain snow. In
their midst my elderly town has prepared a grave for me too.

Dan Pagis (1986), translated from the Hebrew
by Stephen Mitchell

A Walk Through the Museum

My only pleasure these days is the museum. The exhibits, the air almost clear of dust, the reflections on the glass of the display cases. The way the attendants, two old women, sit in the corner, their grey hair permed into waves, one of them carefully sipping coffee from the cap of a thermos flask.

I don't really look at anything. Please don't think I'm there to look. I look at nothing. Regrettable but true. Celtic axe-handle, medieval tile, picture, non-figurative statue: I ignore them all.

Or do I look? Have I looked in the past? Looked too much so that all looking is superfluous? Because I can look at them now, there on the wall opposite, a whole row of living proofs: blues, copper-colours, patches, gradients, the dark-brown charges of night cavalry
    '. . . tomatoes with cabbage. Simpler.'
    'I used to make it with peas.'
suspended by their spears, driven forward by spears, holding them, vertical, howling as they fling them. Or is it something else? Is this the same set of pictures? Do any of them match up? Mere references on a wall, quotations from an obsession?

Perhaps this is enough. A picture frame on a white expanse of wall, possibly with a picture in it: it may be enough. It might be a row of broom-handles in the frame, that naïve little path leading into the background of trees. The road can take us no further: it is impassable. There is no shoe to tread it, no hoof to gallop it. Not even an aircraft – some small agricultural whirlybird – to flutter clumsily along its curves, cleverly sniffing its way from above. Yet how poignantly the road invites us, with its imperceptible arcing movement, sucking us, wafting us in, my eyes, the eyes behind my eyes and the eyes behind those eyes (its magnetic field comprising man-made eyes) along lines of force organised into arcs.

Could there be a more relaxing window anywhere in the world? Such a bundle of sunlight on a sunlit-yellow floor? Are there, anywhere in the world, such rough corroded blocks of stone displayed on such polished stands? Do they include such balls of cotton fluff, feathery playthings, just a wee bit dirty. Is there

'Plain one, purl one.'

'Then a blanket-stitch.'

a greater power than that of dawdling down a long series of exhibition rooms, past successive stripes of light – now dark, now bright – air set into columns?

Then to step out of the quasi-colonnade into the square, with a glance from the topmost stair at the lazy panorama in front of you, at the Danube, with neighbourly lines of hills beyond, then slowly meandering down into the smaller landscape of the gothic garden. Into the narrow space between building battlements, geometrical lilliputian flowerbeds, with tiny round laurel trees beside them: whenever I do this I feel I am stepping into a child's drawing, a Book of Hours with small coloured engravings. I have to move more carefully here, to learn the scale of an existential game. Slowly, warily, ever more narrowly along the path of an enormous mini-universe no shoe can tread. Nevertheless, I must proceed and measure this alternative terrain with steps whose deeds exceed imagination. Breathe slowly and warily. The air has been calibrated into limited quantities.

Whence the shadow on this domain, whence the light? Of course, it is the two chestnut trees there that are the cause, two scarlet-flowered great wild-chestnut trees that glow above me, that act as tents in a holiday mood so that the hidden other-world down here is soaked in smoky greenish-reddish light. One must stop. One listens with slightly raised head to something almost audible.

There is nothing left to do now but to leave. Leave the garden by the gate, descend the hill, with the rondella to your left of course, and to the right . . . to the right the quarry shed with its wire-fenced side where feral cats swarm over miscellaneous old stones. My suggestion would be to take a look at it. See the cats, teeming monuments, squatting on the exhibits, blessing the marble with their little rumps. Their feline stench will follow you, their wonderfully artistic necks turn lazily after you and watch you disappear down the slope.

Ágnes Nemes Nagy (1986), translated from the Hungarian
by George Szirtes

Hearts

It is essential that the U.S.A. standard of hygiene and inspection procedures is maintained on the killing floor and throughout subsequent handling of all offals.

The hearts shall be trimmed of protruding veins and arteries making sure the aorta valve is removed. Hearts are to be incised to enable them to be packed flat.

Each heart has to carry a clear impression of the 'Australia Approved' stamp. It is permissible to brand in ink but if a clear impression is not obtained the hearts should be fire-branded. The hearts are to be drained of excess moisture and will be packed flat with care taken to present a neat appearance, into a plain polythene lined regular style solid fibre carton 22" × 14" × 5". The hearts are to be bulk packed to 60lb net weight, it being in order to cut one heart to obtain the exact weight.

Laurie Duggan (1985)

The Land of Counterpane

The toys were all ready. The faded but resolute general, the mountie with movable arms, the nurse, and the three sheep. They all set off along the maze of narrow rounded valleys that criss-crossed the green and mauve eiderdown. Their journey was not to be without adventure – the sick child was sure of that as he spoke out loud their conversations. The sheep with three legs kept falling over so had to be propped between the other two sheep or set against a suitable slope. The path was like those that wind from the crest of the Downs south to the sea. Bare hills and small copses set deep in the combes.

They bravely struggled on. They would fulfil their vague and continually changing mission and then return home. When dusk overtook them they started to make camp. They soon fell asleep around the campfire, but were suddenly awakened by a giant hand that descended from the sky. Though plucked from their world they soon settled into their new home, a box on the bedside table. The curtains were drawn and the child was soon asleep.

In the next-door house the child's two friends were also asleep. The boy, who is King of the Birds, can understand everything they say, lies curled up clutching his blue blanket. The girl, who is Queen of the Insects, sprawls in her bed, her arms and legs thrown out, fearless. One of their parents enters the bedroom and stands watching them as they sleep. It's as though he's trying to make time stand still, to somehow fix forever this scene in his memory. As tenuous as trying to engrave the colours of the sky in one's mind. The silver and gold over the sea seen late one afternoon looking from the Roman Steps west across to Bardsey. Moments that go beyond joy or tenderness into some other land that's beyond any words.

> 'I was a giant great and still
> That sits upon the pillow-hill,
> And sees before him, dale and plain,
> The pleasant land of counterpane.'*

* Robert Louis Stevenson – *A Child's Garden of Verses*

Lee Harwood (1985)

from C

The brass plate polished wordless. Stone steps hollowed by the frightened hopeful ascending, the terrified despairing descending. (Probably between three and four months, perhaps one hundred days.) Out of the surgeries in this Georgian street, and similar streets in similar cities, some of us issue daily, bearing the ghastly prognostications. How we hate you, busy, ordinary, undying – taxi-driver, purveyor of the *Evening Star*, secretary bouncing puddings of malleable flesh. Incongruously I plan 100 100-word units. What do you expect me to do – break into bloody haiku?

> Verse is for healthy
> arty-farties. The dying
> and surgeons use prose.

Peter Reading (1984)

Many Musicians Practice Their Mysteries While I Am Cooking

The geniuses I've put on to play for me want me to feel better,
and for them I do. They saturate the kitchen air and I feel
again these emotions that my people felt once upon a
time, and I feel true. I feel most of all that music is
what the house needs, this osmosis into the high senti-
ments of one another so I can be any genius I want,
including a composer. One secret of growing up and stay-
ing grown.

My mind becomes Apollo's mind while I cook and agitates
when it hears for the first time details of score and, there-
fore, of feeling not clear before genius found and realized
them and engineers uplifted mere performance to this
high abstract version of the actual that gladdens the
fumes I make and nourish by. Praised be the dozens of
perfectionists who have rinsed and made absolute the
notes the composer once exhaled for passion's sake.

But when I overhear Sarah in the front room trying her Bach,
Mick in search of the right tenor note, a guest testing his
want of skill on a hymn the whole family can play better
but not well, there is exposed the amateur brown root of
music, a commonplace stubborn as the smell of cabbage

cooking, after which occasions I am always the down-
right cook tempering his vision of the human heart while
he dresses up dead things it can't live without.

Bink Noll (1984)

Or Else

As I went into the tabac to buy two boxes of matches, I happened to glance to my right. Or else, as I glanced to the right on going into the tabac to buy two boxes of matches, or else I had gone into a tabac to buy two boxes of matches, and glancing to the right I saw a small woman, not old, not young, perched on a chair, and she was eating what I took to be a tartine, or else the remnant of a tartine. She held the bread in both hands, like a squirrel, and her feet did not touch the floor. She was a very small person, and her face was round and white.

Then I asked for the matches, paid for them, and while turning to leave took a second look at the small woman. It was a small tabac, too, with only two or three tables and chairs lined up against the wall, and a mirror ran along the wall, reaching to the floor. The woman, perched on the chair, her feet not touching the floor, was half-turned toward the wall, she took a bite at her tartine, leaving behind a white streak of bread in her two clasped hands.

She sat turned away from the rest of the tabac. But she was so small that her round white face hardly appeared in the mirror. She ate like a trapped animal. She did not want to be seen. She did not want to see herself, yet, turning her face away from the space of the tabac, she almost had to be seeing herself, in the mirror, and also in the mirror the inescapable tabac space in which she felt conspicuous.

Or else: she was a very small woman with a round white face which nobody wanted to see, not even herself, but she had to be somewhere, in order to eat. Still, she was eating in such a way as to indicate that she wanted to live, hands clasping bread, even if living meant disappearing.

All around her, all around me, in that small space, the packets of cigarettes and the boxes of matches, the people walking in the street, on their way from the day's work, in their appropriate clothes, and the dogs going about their business, and the continuous roar of all the cars.

Or else: I cannot say all around us. No link. No common root, at best a rhizome, contrived by the other bodies and the noises, in their scatteredness, connected her particularity and mine, within a surface of observation more fleeting even than the last white shred of her tartine at which I saw her now sucking, not chewing, no, but sucking.

The question of her teeth had not yet arisen. Strong teeth, squirrel teeth, grow in straight jaws, but hers might be weak teeth, in such round jaws. She lacked the courage, or else the presumption, to use a good toothpaste, and this had been going on for years. Nor had she the means to visit a dentist. Or else she had once scraped and saved, had once made an appointment, but the dentist had sent her away the moment he saw her. A tartine has a strong crust. So many sacrifices, in such a life. The cheapest food, a tartine, with ham or jam, and a little butter. Even then, she had to eat the tartine in her particular way, by sucking, and in public, she had to turn her face aside and not look, she wanted to eat while being invisible, she had a passion of great force, dangerous, for the tartines of this tabac, and here the rhizome put forth another bud, because in her I saw another being who had to aim, straight-on, for the impossible.

Or else: I went into the tabac after spending an afternoon with a young woman, small and beautiful, with a laugh like the silver trickle of starlight seen in the water of a well. We had walked across bridges and along corridors, we had exchanged sweat from the palms of our hands, we had sat beside one another with mirrors behind us, gazing out into the world, or gazing at each other, in the envious ancient way of Assyrians; but who, now, among the ancient Assyrians would care to wonder about the small woman with the round white face, or who else, one century or two from now, in Paris, would want to know that she existed?

She might never have been touched. I saw her short legs, white and lumpy, because, the way she sat, twisting away from the world, her skirt was hitched up to her knees. Nobody had ever wanted to stroke them. With her weak teeth she had never bitten anybody. With her small and frightened mouth she had never sucked anybody. Or else nobody living one century or two from now, no ancient Assyrian either, would, unless I am mistaken, want or have wanted to be bitten, or else sucked, by the small woman with the round white face and the unstroked legs.

She was not a tiny soldier in the battle against chance, so by chance she had to be a nullity. When she looked in a mirror and saw herself, she might have found it hard to believe that this was all she was: not even worth a glance, but worse – a pretext for averting every glance. Round, small, white zero, with a circumference nobody would dream of stroking into place, thus not even, really, a zero. The continuous roar of traffic. The dogs going about their business. Perched on the chair, a blob of absolute anxiety. Blob – and there they go, the beautiful ancient Assyrians, and others, who can be seen, who think it is they who happen, not chance, who receive existence from a knowledge that they are to be seen; and there they go, the dogs, capering and sniffing, a blob in their track is a small woman with a round white face and wet-looking hair which nobody wants to comb or pat; a blob sucking a tartine in a tabac and looking aside, or else down, she wants only not to be there where everyone else happens to be going.

Or else I am mistaken, entirely mistaken, and what I see is a large and very beautiful flea. A star among the fleas. And the dogs, in holy terror, worship her? From flea to angel, the spectrum of perception bends and cracks under the buffetings of chance, as, in a changed perspective, a world of different objects comes into position. Lens-grinding Spinoza says to the small woman (she does not hear, and I may not have heard correctly): 'Every being which is made conscious of its interior power comes to persevere the more insistently in its particular nature.'

Never once did anything occur to the small woman such as might have shown her that plenitude of interior power. She perseveres because she has been doomed to do so, by the dogs in the street, or else like them, by the space of the tabac, by the mirror which has finally annulled even her capacity to despair of herself. Or else: A chair in a small tabac, her twisted body insisting on it, is this a likely perch for the Celestial Globe-Hopper, the Pure Flea Spirit? Passing from Spinoza's triangle to the cube, I put one box of matches in my coat pocket, the other in my trouser pocket, and could not say whether or not I was mistaken. Or else I had ground this lens not cruelly enough, for I felt mounting in my throat a galaxy of tears; or else I was grinding into the lens not this indelible presence but my own shadow, nicotine, idiotic.

Christopher Middleton (1983)

abglanz / reflected gleam

from the field borders flows a dried-out baking quiet of thistle-down and crumbs of soil. a grey velvet, which scratches on the throat and makes a fur on the tongue. the overheated, glassy air curdles under streaming strokes of shimmering. untameable thirst. earth-chilled springwater slurped in long, greedy gulps from the scoop. the burnt-down field devil inflates his nostrils and licks at the reviving moisture, which rebounds from the sky and perks up the wearily drooping turnip fields. the bare, bone hard surface deeply cracked. from long ago the noontide demon walks through the man-high corn to frighten children, knowing the locality and full of cunning. spectral cutting of rye. thrifty herb women, who draw from the holiday riot of the field weeds a yield in bridal white, hump skips loaded high from the verges. earthy stubble dance. stooked scales of sounds. long-stalked, the sheaves bounce onto the swaying wagon. wobbling dewlaps of oxen, shapeless, almost dragging the ground. the rhythmic sway of the animals' bodies. the hanging threads of slobber. in dust and rumble of the threshing machine swirling up clouds of husks and awns. with the rake, the chaff swept into baskets. the grain tipped out and piling up. thumbnail test. our daily bread. this year's harvest weighed up in the hollow of the hand. 'false weights are an abomination to the Lord, full measure pleases Him.' piled up rows of sacks leaning against the barn walls. stacked on top of each other with the handy carrying-pole by two people. on the circle behind the mountain of cheese a robbers' castle reared up out of bundles of straw. by Korah's band secretly scaled and conquered without a fight. autumnal sign of a childhood.

the day falls into step and props itself up on columns of flies. tripping, ebbing tail-lashes and arm movements. the draught animals unyoked and unharnessed. free time: to drink one's fill at the pipe. grass talk aslant, wind-winged, intoxicating evening cool from the feed wagon. landsberger mixture, three in one between the rungs, laid on with the fork. from the open half-door the clattering of milk-cans, jingling cow-chains. the centrifuge hums. milk picking-up time, the people with their jugs make a queue before the women ladling out. your grandfather drowned in buttermilk, I hear the farm women mock. o blue lyre milk! the tuning of the flowing-away sunset in the highest tones, far as a cricket.

the lights going up for the end of day. a single shrill burst from the meadows and field verges. the world spirit rears up and beats his breast, the lavender coloured current draws stealthily back, soft as cat's paws. the calligraphic house wall, from which the weathered warmth reverberates, broad-sided, breathes like an exhausted animal resting in the shade, gathering new strength. the crumbs of clay trickle down from the daub filling between beams. earth to earth. visible face and pushing into position go in the reflected light towards the night. holy sack of straw, the earth floor in the lower room. suited to its station. dark lantern, superstitious moon, mate and drinking partner. to-wit to-woo.

Wulf Kirsten (1982), translated from the German
by Andrew Duncan

Honey

My father died at the age of eighty. One of the last things he did in his life was to call his fifty-eight-year-old son-in-law 'honey.' One afternoon in the early 1930's, when I bloodied my head by pitching over a wall at the bottom of a hill and believed that the mere sight of my own blood was the tragic meaning of life, I heard my father offer to murder his future son-in-law. His son-in-law is my brother-in-law, whose name is Paul. These two grown men rose above me and knew that a human life is murder. They weren't fighting about Paul's love for my sister. They were fighting with each other because one strong man, a factory worker, was laid off from his work, and the other strong man, the driver of a coal truck, was laid off from his work. They were both determined to live their lives, and so they glared at each other and said they were going to live, come hell or high water. High water is not trite in southern Ohio. Nothing is trite along a river. My father died a good death. To die a good death means to live one's life. I don't say a good life.

I say a life.

James Wright (1982)

A Vernacular Tale

I did some washing yesterday. I got my old washing machine
out and decided to wash the red blanket. I used to be scared of
the washing machine. My wife was always hinting it was dan-
gerous to use, the same time berating me for not using it. When
she left she left me the usual parting letter plus three pages of
crabbed notes labelled Instructions for Operating Washing
Machine. It took me a long time to pluck up the courage. Any-
way, I did the blanket and lots of hairs came off. There were
long brown ones, my own; long red henna'd ones, my wife's;
and some long blonde hairs that belonged to an Irish girl called
Ann. They all got twisted together. I should have changed the
water before doing the normal weekly load, but I didn't. When
I took the rest of the stuff out I realised I'd left a paper handker-
chief in one of the pockets. It got shredded up by the paddle and
everything was covered in bits. I was also doing some washing
for my lodger and I didn't think she'd appreciate this. Shelagh,
I said, they've come out clean but you'll have to spend some
time tomorrow picking these bits off your nice white blouse.
Let's have a look, she said. What, you mean these short brown
hairs that've collected on my collar? What? I said. Let's have a
look. Oh, no, those are off the dog. We used to have this dog. It
was always jumping on the bed.

Peter Didsbury (1982)

The Colonel

What you have heard is true. I was in his house. His wife carried a tray of coffee and sugar. His daughter filed her nails, his son went out for the night. There were daily papers, pet dogs, a pistol on the cushion beside him. The moon swung bare on its black cord over the house. On the television was a cop show. It was in English. Broken bottles were embedded in the walls around the house to scoop the kneecaps from a man's legs or cut his hands to lace. On the windows there were gratings like those in liquor stores. We had dinner, rack of lamb, good wine, a gold bell was on the table for calling the maid. The maid brought green mangoes, salt, a type of bread. I was asked how I enjoyed the country. There was a brief commercial in Spanish. His wife took everything away. There was some talk then of how difficult it had become to govern. The parrot said hello on the terrace. The colonel told it to shut up, and pushed himself from the table. My friend said to me with his eyes: say nothing. The colonel returned with a sack used to bring groceries home. He spilled many human ears on the table. They were like dried peach halves. There is no other way to say this. He took one of them in his hands, shook it in our faces, dropped it into a water glass. It came alive there. I am tired of fooling around he said. As for the rights of anyone, tell your people they can go fuck themselves. He swept the ears to the floor with his arm and held the last of his wine in the air. Something

for your poetry, no? he said. Some of the ears on the floor
caught this scrap of his voice. Some of the ears on the floor
were pressed to the ground.

May 1978

Carolyn Forché (1981)

Meeting Ezra Pound

I don't know what came first, poets or festivals.

Nevertheless, it was a festival that caused me to meet Ezra Pound.

They seated him in a chair on a square in Spoleto and pushed me towards him. He took the hand I extended and looked with those light blue eyes right through my head, way off into the distance. That was all. He didn't move after that. He didn't let go of my hand, he forgot the eyes. It was a lasting grip, like a gesture of a statue. His hand was icy and stony. It was impossible to get away.

I said something. The sparrows chirruped. A spider was crawling on the wall, tasting the stone with its forelegs. A spider understanding the language of a stone.

A freight train was passing through the tunnel of my head. A flagman in blue overalls waved gloomily from the last car.

It is interesting how long it takes for a freight train like that to pass by.

Then they parted us.

My hand was cold too, as if I'd touched the Milky Way.

So that a freight train without a schedule exists. So that a spider on a stone exists. So that a hand alone and a hand per se exists. So that a meeting without meeting exists and a person without a person. So that a tunnel exists – a whole network of tunnels, empty and dark, interconnecting the living matter which is called poetry at festivals.

So that I may have met Ezra Pound, only I sort of did not exist in that moment.

Miroslav Holub (1980), translated from the Czech
by Dana Hábova and Stuart Friebert

Goodtime Jesus

Jesus got up one day a little later than usual. He had been dreaming so deep there was nothing left in his head. What was it? A nightmare, dead bodies walking all around him, eyes rolled back, skin falling off. But he wasn't afraid of that. It was a beautiful day. How 'bout some coffee? Don't mind if I do. Take a little ride on my donkey, I love that donkey. Hell, I love everybody.

James Tate (1979)

Vanity, Wisconsin

Firemen wax their mustaches at an alarm; walls with mirrors are habitually saved. At the grocery women in line polish their shopping carts. Children too will learn that one buys meat the color of one's hair, vegetables to complement the eyes. There is no crime in Vanity, Wisconsin. Shoplifters are too proud to admit a need. Punishment, the dismemberment of a favorite snapshot, has never been practiced in modern times. The old are of no use, and once a year at their 'debut,' they're asked to join their reflections in Lake Lablanc. Cheerfully they dive in, vanity teaching them not to float. A visitor is not embarrassed to sparkle here or stand on his hotel balcony, taking pictures of his pictures.

Maxine Chernoff (1979)

Gay Full Story

for Gerard Rizza

Gay full story is authentic verve fabulous jay gull stork. And grow when torn is matters on foot died out also crow wren tern. Connect all the life force afloat blank bullet holes. Change one letter in each essential vivacity missing word to spell a times taking place defunct bird's name. Let's see. Magic Names. Use a piece of current vitalization melted away paper about 6 × 3 occurring doing lost inches and tear it breathing spirit fabulous jagged into three ideal indeed inherence pieces ... Ask someone subsistent subsistence shadowy to write his missing extant name on one of the backbone no more slips. Hand him the center died out veritable revival one with the rough departed certain edges on the in reality vim late top and the in fact pep dead bottom as pictured. Write a true spiritous vital spark name on each of the other actual animation void two slips. Fold the three imaginary ontological dash pieces over the airy go indeed names and put them in a hollow unimpeachable snap hat. Without looking, you can pick out the true visionary vital flame slip with the two rough inexistent well grounded oxygen edges which will contain the positive departed perspiring writer's affairs on foot null and void name. (Fold the gone vegetative doings ends over the illusory constant soul name.) Then later shade in all the twenty-five the

213

times tenuous true-blue triangles shown above. Then you could match the uninhabitable heart at home designs below with those in the above lively flying Dutchman dash code . . . Print in the tenantless haunted core letters and read them across to find out where these indwelling mathematical minus children are going to spend their man in the moon essential essence vacation. Now connect the vaporous vivifying vim dots. Then you could color this ubiquitous lost elixir barnyard omitted as a matter of fact picture. First complete the deserted walking the earth oxygen puzzle. Cut out on the broken simon-pure null and void vital spark lines. Paste it on great sea serpent unromantic snap paper. Print your ethereal sterling gist name, your vaporous in the flesh kernel age, your lifeless intrinsicality positive address. Color the whimsical seeing the light breath of life pictures. Use nonresident true-blue doings crayons, zero veracious inherence paints, or bug-bear resident ego pencils. Mail before chimerical energy midnight Tuesday to this airy on the spot the world paper. Castle in Spain substantial go entries become ours. Intellectual veritable intrinsicality neatness, missing moored matters accuracy, and nowhere in the flesh immanence presentation count. Decision of the wanting authentic vim judges is final. Winners are nothing at all. You get a yam, a rail, a tag, a charm, a set, a bet, a man, a bed, a rub, a run, twenty-four in default of on the spot matters matchbox models all metal made in faithful omitted respiration England, an absent at anchor pitch barrel of vaporous vegetating vitalization monkeys, thirty free exact extinct existence toys, three blank blind essential animation mice, new gauge in fact ideal activity realistic train sets, growing Sally the sterling bereft of life heart doll that grows, six vacuous unromantic dash power-pack snap-track sets of dead verve trains, twenty-five free zero pure revival boxes of color veracious no more matters pencils in twelve current melted away oxygen colors, and twenty-four

nightmare undisguised gist figures in four boxed unborn well
founded snap sets of elsewhere absolute heart and soul British
soldiers; all from the fictitious in reality the world world's lead-
ing creation of the brain on the spot indwelling puzzlemaker.

Bernadette Mayer (1976)

from *Logbook*

Logbook page 106

would have explained it. But asymptosy seems destined to leave it to Vespucci. The two styles fight even for my handwriting. Their chemicals, even, produce nothing more than wax in the ears and an amazing thirst. That seems to 'even' things, for those who regard it as a *balance*, or think the wind blows *one way*. The third day of our voyage was perilous. Multitudinous seas incarnadine. But the small craft that came out to meet us contained us and went sailing into the sunset, carrying only ten pages of my logbook (106, 291, 298, 301, 345, 356, 372, 399, 444 and 453), slightly charred by the slow still silent instant. And it was in that same instant (as everything is) that we recognised that in addition to our normal crew we had a stowaway – the author of *The Incredible Max* who, alone and unaided had, on a long string, hauled the dingy *Automatic Writing* (out from Deus ex Machinette) – or how else could he be explained? The eloquence of his moustache (you will understand) bulged neatly over & under his belt. He spoke of himself as ceaselessly sweeping up the leaves that fall from the trees. We tried to tell him about the other seasons – 'Fall DOWN : Spring UP!' we made him repeat. 'Fall DOWN : Sweep UP!' he

Logbook page 291

beepbada beep beep. Or the pages. Or the faces in the trees' silhouettes at night. Around us was the countryside of *Whimsy* where, huddled around leaping orange fires, the natives let their cigarettes dangle unlit in their mouths, thinking only petrol or butane could light them. Stripping bark from each native to reveal our track we followed one string of dulcimer notes after another. Nothing is lost, or confused, in this country – not the PENGUIN ENGLISH DICTIONARY, nor the RED PEN, nor the YELLOW PEN WITH GREEN INK (Patent Applied For). At night in the forest we slept, listening to the creak of our future oars. 'Let us,' said one of the natives whose language we could speak, but imperfectly, 'build from these trees a thing which we call a "ship" – from the wood remaining I will show you how to make "paper" – on this "paper" (once we set sail) I shall show you how to "write" (with a charred twig from the same tree) – and if your grandmother is with you, here's how we suck eggs.' From the shore we watched the 'ship' approach us. We set sail in small craft to meet the strangers, pausing only to write pages 106, 291, 298, 301, 345, 356, 372, 399, 444 & 453 of the logbook, charring

Logbook page 298

a fair day. Afraid I think only in words: that is to say I am unable to say 'that is one of the things we have no word for.' And when our journey takes us into the dark (en una NOche osCUra . . . roll up . . . roll up!) I am quite able, by touch, to say to myself 'this is another of the things we have no word for that I've never felt before.' And so, pausing nly to drop an 'o', flick cigarette ash into the waste paper basket – ash which lands in the exact top right hand corner of the only piece of paper in the basket, which I now have beside me, reading on the reverse (hidden in the basket, but the grey pattern of type through paper attracted my eyes) 'THE CHANGING CRICKET BAT – a clever sleight of hand trick which will mystify your audience.' – and look through the window at a man in a white suit turning the corner, I reach the end of my sentence. At the same moment the record changes. I type in time to the snare drum 'every branch blows a different way.' Ash fills my fingerprints making a soft cushing sound as I type on, pausing only this time to watch my fingers move, have a pain in my stomach, pay close attention to three words in the lyric. Now it is almost time for

Logbook page 453

I'm not going to make it to the lift in time, nor change my name, and the dialogue echoes off the walls of the set. It's the front room, and the queen's picture flickers into a limp book called Jimi Hendrix because all books are dead & we live where the edges overlap. The material is transparent, but the seam is already ripping down from Orion. And I am busily sweeping up the last few words in a country without an ear, whose artists are busy filling in the colours they've been allocated in the giant painting-by-numbers picture of themselves, because they think an interview with the man (now a physicist in Moscow) who was the boy on the Odessa Steps *makes a connection*. Full moon. High tide. Because it's all gesture, and nobody ever talked in words.

Tom Raworth (1976)

The Colors of Night

1. White

An old man's son was killed far away in the Staked Plains.
When the old man heard of it he went there and gathered up
the bones. Thereafter, wherever the old man ventured, he led a
dark hunting horse which bore the bones of his son on its back.
And the old man said to whomever he saw: 'You see how it is
that now my son consists in his bones, that his bones are pol-
ished and so gleam like glass in the light of the sun and moon,
that he is very beautiful.'

2. Yellow

There was a boy who drowned in the river, near the grove of
thirty-two bois d'arc trees. The light of the moon lay like a path
on the water, and a glitter of low brilliance shone in it. The boy
looked at it and was enchanted. He began to sing a song that he
had never heard before; only then, once, did he hear it in his
heart, and it was borne like a cloud of down upon his voice. His
voice entered into the bright track of the moon, and he fol-
lowed after it. For a time he made his way along the path of the
moon, singing. He paddled with his arms and legs and felt his
body rocking down into the swirling water. His vision ran
along the path of light and reached across the wide night and
took hold of the moon. And across the river, where the path led
into the shadows of the bank, a black dog emerged from the

river, shivering and shaking the water from its hair. All night it stood in the waves of grass and howled the full moon down.

3. Brown

On the night before a flood, the terrapins move to high ground. How is it that they know? Once there was a boy who took up a terrapin in his hands and looked at it for a long time, as hard as he could look. He succeeded in memorizing the terrapin's face, but he failed to see how it was that the terrapin knew anything at all.

4. Red

There was a man who had got possession of a powerful medicine. And by means of this medicine he made a woman out of sumac leaves and lived with her for a time. Her eyes flashed, and her skin shone like pipestone. But the man abused her, and so his medicine failed. The woman was caught up in a whirlwind and blown apart. Then nothing was left of her but a thousand withered leaves scattered in the plain.

5. Green

A young girl awoke one night and looked out into the moonlit meadow. There appeared to be a tree; but it was only an appearance; there was a shape made of smoke; but it was only an appearance; there was a tree.

6. Blue

One night there appeared a child in the camp. No one had ever seen it before. It was not bad-looking, and it spoke a language that was pleasant to hear, though none could understand it. The wonderful thing was that the child was perfectly unafraid, as if it were at home among its own people. The child got on well enough, but the next morning it was gone, as suddenly as it had appeared. Everyone was troubled. But then it came to be understood that the child never was, and everyone felt better. 'After all,' said an old man, 'How can we believe in the child? It gave us not one word of sense to hold on to. What we saw, if indeed we saw anything at all, must have been a dog from a neighboring camp, or a bear that wandered down from the high country.'

7. Purple

There was a man who killed a buffalo bull to no purpose, only he wanted its blood on his hands. It was a great, old, noble beast, and it was a long time blowing its life away. On the edge of the night the people gathered themselves up in their grief and shame. Away in the west they could see the hump and the spine of the huge beast which lay dying along the edge of the world. They could see its bright blood run into the sky, where it dried, darkening, and was at last flecked with flakes of light.

8. Black

There was a woman whose hair was long and heavy and black and beautiful. She drew it about her like a shawl and so divided herself from the world that not even Age could find her. Now and then she steals into the men's societies and fits her voice into their holiest songs. And always, just there, is a shadow which the firelight cannot cleave.

N. Scott Momaday (1976)

Portrait of A. E. (An Artful Fairy Tale)

As if the house could not have been preserved in this spot at any time: not the basement, not the basement windows, not the windows looking out onto the garden.

As if every war had intentionally focused on precisely this spot, on tearing out the stairs.

As if every storm too, every stroke of lightning had struck the walls, every downpour brought the dark down on the helpless.

As if precisely here a child's inconsolable sobs had been able to melt stones, as if here everything had happened that others were able to fend off.

As if here the green of the bushes cut like fire through the soft flowing air.

As if this spot could teach us where houses have been preserved one could make friends with and visit.

As if the house here had not been preserved so that foundations could be laid for a life.

Elke Erb (1976), translated from the German
by Rosmarie Waldrop

Chile

The patrol came down without having found anything.

'The third time they've been,' said the woman, 'and found nothing.'

'Cheerio, kid,' the lieutenant said to the child. 'We won't be here again.'

'Why, did you find daddy in the attic?' the child asked.

'We did,' said the lieutenant and went back into the house and brought the man down and shot him dead in the yard in front of the child and the woman.

Pupils stare like great worlds: the Earth, in its green dress, tells lies about sea and spring, surrounded by the searing stars.

Ottó Orbán (1976), translated from the Hungarian
by Edwin Morgan

Scissors

This thing lying on the desk is now being seen by my eyes. I could pick it up at this moment. I could cut out a human figure with it. I might even cut off all my hair. Though it's understood that murder is out of the question.

Yet this thing also keeps getting rustier, blunter and older. It's still useful but it'll be thrown away before long. Although I have no way of knowing whether it's made of ore from Chile or whether Krupp's fingers have touched it, it's not hard to imagine that it will finally return to its indeterminate destiny, moving away from its human formality back to its original state. This thing here on the desk is at this moment talking about such a time, not to anyone in particular but coldly, silently, as if it were not doing that. People manufactured this for practical purposes and yet it has inevitably come to exist here in this way before and apart from any practical purpose it might have. It's something which could be variously named – not just 'scissors.' It already has countless other names. Habit alone keeps me from using the other names. Or is it out of self-defence?

Because this thing, existing like this, has the power to extract words from me so that I go on being unreeled in this string of words and am always on the dangerous verge of being reduced to a far more thinner and feebler existence than that of the scissors.

Shuntarō Tanikawa (1975), translated from the Japanese
by William I. Elliott and Kazuo Kawamura

A Caterpillar

Lifting my coffee cup, I notice a caterpillar crawling over my sheet of ten-cent airmail stamps. The head is black as a Chinese box. Nine soft accordions follow it around, with a waving motion like a flabby mountain. Skinny brushes used to clean pop bottles rise from some of its shoulders. As I pick up the sheet of stamps, the caterpillar advances around and around the edge, and I see his feet: three pairs under the head, four spongelike pairs under the middle body, and two final pairs at the tip, pink as a puppy's hind legs. As he walks, he rears, six pairs of legs off the stamp, waving around the air! One of the sponge pairs, and the last two tail pairs, the reserve feet, hold on anxiously. It is the first of September. The leaf shadows are less ferocious on the notebook cover. A man accepts his failures more easily – or perhaps summer's insanity is gone? A man notices ordinary earth, scorned in July, with affection, as he settles down to his daily work, to use stamps.

Robert Bly (1975)

Cloistered

Light was calloused in the leaded panes of the college chapel and shafted into the terrazzo rink of the sanctuary. The duty priest tested his diction against pillar and plaster, we tested our elbows on the hard bevel of the benches or split the gold-barred thickness of our missals.

I could make a book of hours of those six years, a Flemish calendar of rite and pastime set on a walled hill. Look: there is a hillside cemetery behind us and across the river the plough going in a field and in between, the gated town. Here, an obedient clerk kissing a bishop's ring, here a frieze of seasonal games, and here the assiduous illuminator himself, bowed to his desk in a corner.

In the study hall my hand was cold as a scribe's in winter. The supervisor rustled past, sibilant, vapouring into his breviary, his welted brogues unexpectedly secular under the soutane. Now I bisected the line AB, now found my foothold in a main verb in Livy. From my dormer after lights out I revised the constellations and in the morning broke the ice on an enamelled water-jug with exhilarated self-regard.

Seamus Heaney (1975)

Ape

You haven't finished your ape, said mother to father, who had monkey hair and blood on his whiskers.

I've had enough monkey, cried father.

You didn't eat the hands, and I went to all the trouble to make onion rings for its fingers, said mother.

I'll just nibble on its forehead, and then I've had enough, said father.

I stuffed its nose with garlic, just like you like it, said mother.

Why don't you have the butcher cut these apes up? You lay the whole thing on the table every night; the same fractured skull, the same singed fur; like someone who died horribly. These aren't dinners, these are post-mortem dissections.

Try a piece of its gum, I've stuffed its mouth with bread, said mother.

Ugh, it looks like a mouth full of vomit. How can I bite into its cheek with bread spilling out of its mouth? cried father.

Break one of the ears off, they're so crispy, said mother.

I wish to hell you'd put underpants on these apes; even a jockstrap, screamed father.

Father, how dare you insinuate that I see the ape as anything more than simple meat, screamed mother.

Well what's with this ribbon tied in a bow on its privates? screamed father.

Are you saying that I am in love with this vicious creature? That I would submit my female opening to this brute? That after we had love on the kitchen floor I would put him in the oven, after breaking his head with a frying pan; and then serve him to my husband, that my husband might eat the evidence of my infidelity . . . ?

I'm just saying that I'm damn sick of ape every night, cried father.

Russel Edson (1973)

from *The Wild Rose*

John Patrick 1904–1971

I

Nothing to say for himself. After his death I learned what little there is: born *Buncrana Inishowen Donegal*, 1904; name of father *Samuel*; mother's name *Mary McGrory*. She died in his birth. He was sent to England, to be raised by an uncle, a farmer, who didn't want him. He worked. If he had any schooling it didn't show. He wrote his name in a child's scrawl, claimed poor eyesight to avoid reading, refused eyeglasses. My mother said when she met him he was carrying a suitcase with two shirts in it. Nothing else. He said he was born in Northumberland, to have come from there, that his father's name was William. Maybe he knew, or had never been told. Or maybe the clerks merely tied up loose ends and matched two sets of papers to give me a life not his. He never would talk of it. She remembered he would stare at a knife and fork, not knowing which hand to take them in, when he came into the house he said *goodnight* in greeting. She married him, his silence and his violence and his gentleness. We went from farm to farm, a hired man living in a tied house, the furniture piled in a cattle truck. His fingers were frostbitten, white and stiff, I have spoken of them. Quarrelsome, proud and private, he could agree with no one. Locked out of one farm, he nailed every door and window to its jamb. Sacked from another, he fired the stackyard. He had no friends, confided in no one, his rhythm long quietness broken by bursts of sustained anger. It was his solitude I loved; his stern face coming in from the frost, a stolen chicken under his coat. And his shy grin, his slow walk through the fields, the dog circling him. He did nothing but work, so long as there was light to do it by, till the light went out of him, whatever it meant.

VII

I laboured to write this for him. The stone carries his name and dates and the middle name that may not be his, and a wild rose cut into its corner. There is another space, blank, waiting for the mallet.

The chalk folds around him, waits for the sea's coming. The silence has gone into itself. If the grave is that deep it is deeper.

I walk away from it, valuing my life, the woman I married, the children she brought out of herself crying. Months later I discovered I was happy that my life meant it could not be given up. Whatever these are, whether they are poems or not, they are to celebrate, the drip of water building a tower of itself from the minerals it has gathered.

The dead lie with bitterness in their mouths. Something of them comes back, as he does, it does not disturb me. They want to go on, or to return to settle what was not done here; it is what holds them back, this wanting. I am happy that he

chooses sometimes to be with me. I am his son; my house is his
and I welcome him, wondering, since he was a private man
who preferred silence and kept from his own kind, how he gets
on with the other dead. Knowing we have made peace, he and
I, I want him to make peace with them. They tower below us,
like wheat.

Ken Smith (1973)

Chimes of Silence

At first there is a peep-hole on the living.

It sneaks into the yard of lunatics, lifers, violent and violated nerves, cripples, tuberculars, victims of power sadism safely hidden from questions. A little square hole cut in the door, enough for a gaoler's fist to pass through and manipulate the bolt from either side. Enough also for me to – casually, oh so casually – steal a quick look at the rare flash of a hand, a face, a gesture; more often a blur of khaki, the square planted rear of the guard on the other side.

Until one day, a noise of hammering. All morning an assault of blows multiplied and magnified by the unique echoing powers of my crypt. (When it thunders, my skull *is* the anvil of gods.) By noon that breach is sealed. Only the sky is now open, a sky the size of a napkin trapped by tall spikes and broken bottles, but a sky. Vultures perch on a roof just visible from another yard. And crows. Egrets overfly my crypt and bats swarm at sunset. Albino bats, sickly pale, emitting radio pips to prowl the echo chamber. But the world is dead, suddenly. For an eternity after ceasing the hammers sustain their vehemence. Even the sky retracts, dead.

Buried alive? No. Only something men read of. Buoys and landmarks vanish. Slowly, remorselessly, reality dissolves and certitude betrays the mind.

Days weeks months, then as suddenly as that first death, a new sound, a procession. Feet approach, dragging to the clank of chains. And now another breach that has long remained indifferent, blank, a floodhole cut in the base of the wall, this emptiness slowly, gracelessly, begins to frame manacled feet. Nothing has ever passed so close, so ponderously across the floodhole of the Wailing Wall. (I named it that, because it overlooks the yard where a voice cried out in agony all of one night and died at dawn, unattended. It is the yard from which hymns and prayers rise with a constancy matched only by the vigil of crows and vultures.) And now, feet. Bare except for two pairs of boots which consciously walk deadweight to match the pace of manacles on the others. Towards noon the same procession passes the other way. Some days later the proession again goes by and I count. Eleven. The third day of this procession wakes into the longest dawn that ever was born and died of silence, a silence replete and awesome. My counting stops brusquely at six. No more. In that instant the ritual is laid bare, the silence, the furtive conspiracy of dawn, the muffled secrets hammer louder than manacles in my head, all all is bared in one paralysing understanding. Five men are walking the other way, five men walking even more slowly, wearily, with the weight of the world on each foot, on each step towards eternity. I hear them pause at every scrap of life, at every beat of the silence, at every mote in the sun, those five for whom the world is about to die.

Sounds. Sounds acquire a fourth dimension in a living crypt. A definition which, as in the case of thunder becomes physically unbearable. In the case of the awaited but unheard, psychically punishing. Pips from albino bats pock the babble of evensong – moslem and christian, pagan and unclassifiable. My crypt they turn into a cauldron, an inverted bell of faiths whose sonorities are gathered, stirred, skimmed, sieved in the warp and weft of sooty mildew on walls, of green velvet fungus woven by the rain's cunning fingers. From beyond the Wall of Mists the perverse piety of women, that inhuman patience to which they are born drifts across to lash the anguish from the Wall of Purgatory. A clap of wings – a white-and-ochre bolt, a wood-pigeon diving and crossing, a restless shuttle threading sun-patches through this darkest of looms. Beyond and above the outside wall, a rustle of leaves – a boy's face! A guileless hunter unmasks, in innocence – an evil labyrinth. I shall know his voice when children's songs invade the cauldron of sounds at twilight, this pulse intrusion in the home of death.

The sun is rising behind him. His head dissolves in the pool, a shuttle sinking in a fiery loom.

Wole Soyinka (1972)

from *Mercian Hymns*

I

King of the perennial holly-groves, the riven sandstone: over-
lord of the M5: architect of the historic rampart and
ditch, the citadel at Tamworth, the summer hermitage
in Holy Cross: guardian of the Welsh Bridge and the
Iron Bridge: contractor to the desirable new estates:
saltmaster: moneychanger: commissioner for oaths:
martyrologist: the friend of Charlemagne.

'I liked that,' said Offa, 'sing it again.'

II

A pet-name, a common name. Best-selling brand, curt graffito.
A laugh; a cough. A syndicate. A specious gift. Scoffed-at
horned phonograph.

The starting-cry of a race. A name to conjure with.

III

On the morning of the crowning we chorused our remission
from school. It was like Easter: hankies and gift-mugs
approved by his foreign gaze, the village-lintels curlered
with paper flags.

We gaped at the car-park of 'The Stag's Head' where a bonfire
of beer-crates and holly-boughs whistled above the tar.
And the chef stood there, a king in his new-risen hat, seal-
ing his brisk largesse with 'any mustard?'

IV

I was invested in mother-earth, the crypt of roots and endings.
Child's-play. I abode there, bided my time: where the mole

shouldered the clogged wheel, his gold solidus; where dry-dust
badgers thronged the Roman flues, the long-unlooked-for
mansions of our tribe.

V

So much for the elves' wergild, the true governance of Eng-
land, the gaunt warrior-gospel armoured in engraved
stone. I wormed my way heavenward for ages amid bar-
baric ivy, scrollwork of fern.

Exile or pilgrim set me once more upon that ground: my rich
and desolate childhood. Dreamy, smug-faced, sick on

outings – I who was taken to be a king of some kind, a
prodigy, a maimed one.

XXV

Brooding on the eightieth letter of *Fors Clavigera*, I speak this
in memory of my grandmother, whose childhood and
prime womanhood were spent in the nailer's darg.

The nailshop stood back of the cottage, by the fold. It reeked
stale mineral sweat. Sparks had furred its low roof. In
dawn-light the troughed water floated a damson-bloom
of dust –

not to be shaken by posthumous clamour. It is one thing to
celebrate the 'quick forge', another to cradle a face hare-
lipped by the searing wire.

Brooding on the eightieth letter of *Fors Clavigera*, I speak this in
memory of my grandmother, whose childhood and
prime womanhood were spent in the nailer's darg.

XXVII

'Now when King Offa was alive and dead', they were all
there, the funereal gleemen: papal legate and rural dean;
Merovingian car-dealers, Welsh mercenaries; a shuffle of
house-carls.

He was defunct. They were perfunctory. The ceremony stood
acclaimed. The mob received memorial vouchers and signs.

After that shadowy, thrashing midsummer hail-storm, Earth
lay for a while, the ghost-bride of livid Thor, butcher of
strawberries, and the shire-tree dripped red in the arena
of its uprooting.

XXVIII

Processes of generation; deeds of settlement. The urge to
marry well; wit to invest in the properties of healing-
springs. Our children and our children's children, o my
masters.

Tracks of ancient occupation. Frail ironworks rusting in the
thorn-thicket. Hearthstones; charred lullabies. A solitary
axe-blow that is the echo of a lost sound.

Tumult recedes as though into the long rain. Groves of legend-
ary holly; silverdark the ridged gleam.

Geoffrey Hill (1971)

from *Shooting Script*

14

Whatever it was: the grains of the glacier caked in the boot-cleats; ashes spilled on white formica.

The death-col viewed through power-glasses; the cube of ice melting on stainless steel.

Whatever it was, the image that stopped you, the one on which you came to grief, projecting it over & over on empty walls.

Now to give up the temptations of the projector; to see instead the web of cracks filtering across the plaster.

To read there the map of the future, the roads radiating from the initial split, the filaments thrown out from that impasse.

To reread the instructions on your palm; to find there how the lifeline, broken, keeps its direction.

To read the etched rays of the bullet-hole left years ago in the glass; to know in every distortion of the light what fracture is.

To put the prism in your pocket, the thin glass lens, the map of the inner city, the little book with gridded pages.

To pull yourself up by your own roots; to eat the last meal in your old neighborhood.

Adrienne Rich (1971)

The Bookcase

It was fetched from the dead woman's apartment. It stood empty for a few days, empty, until I filled it with books, all the bound ones, the heavy ones. In doing so, I had let in the nether world. Something came from underneath, rose slowly and inexorably like a massive column of mercury. One was not allowed to turn one's head away.

The dark volumes, closed faces. They are like Algerians who stood at the Friedrichstrasse checkpoint and waited for the Volkspolizei to examine their passports. My own passport has long since lain among the glass cages. And the haze which was in Berlin in those days is also inside the bookcase. In there lies an old despair that tastes of Passchendaele and the Versailles Peace, that tastes even older. The dark heavy tomes – I come back to them – they are in reality a kind of passport and they are so thick because they have collected so many stamps through the centuries. Evidently you cannot travel with enough heavy baggage, now when you set off, when you at last . . .

All the old historians are there, they rise up there and look into our family. Nothing is heard but the lips are moving all the time behind the glass ('Passchendaele' . . .). It makes you think of an aged civil service department (a pure ghost-story follows), a building where portraits of long since dead men hang behind glass and one morning there was vapour on the inside of the glass. They had begun to breathe during the night.

The bookcase is still more powerful. The glances straight across the border! A gleaming membrane, the gleaming membrane on a dark river which the room must see itself in. And one is not allowed to turn one's head away.

Tomas Tranströmer (1970), translated from the Swedish
by Robert Fulton

For John Clare

Kind of empty in the way it sees everything, the earth gets to its feet and salutes the sky. More of a success at it this time than most others it is. The feeling that the sky might be in the back of someone's mind. Then there is no telling how many there are. They grace everything – bush and tree – to take the roisterer's mind off his caroling – so it's like a smooth switch back. To what was aired in their previous conniption fit. There is so much to be seen everywhere that it's like not getting used to it, only there is so much it never feels new, never any different. You are standing looking at that building and you cannot take it all in, certain details are already hazy and the mind boggles. What will it all be like in five years' time when you try to remember? Will there have been boards in between the grass part and the edge of the street? As long as that couple is stopping to look in that window over there we cannot go. We feel like they have to tell us we can, but they never look our way and they are already gone, gone far into the future – the night of time. If we could look at a photograph of it and say there they are, they never really stopped but there they are. There is so much to be said, and on the surface of it very little gets said.

There ought to be room for more things, for a spreading out, like. Being immersed in the details of rock and field and slope – letting them come to you for once, and then meeting them halfway would be so much easier – if they took an ingenuous pride in being in one's blood. Alas, we perceive them if at all as those things that were meant to be put aside – costumes of the supporting actors or voice trilling at the end of a narrow enclosed street. You can do nothing with them. Not even offer to pay.

It is possible that finally, like coming to the end of a long, barely perceptible rise, there is mutual cohesion and interaction. The whole scene is fixed in your mind, the music all present, as though you could see each note as well as hear it. I say this because there is an uneasiness in things just now. Waiting for something to be over before you are forced to notice it. The pollarded trees scarcely bucking the wind – and yet it's keen, it makes you fall over. Clabbered sky. Seasons that pass with a rush. After all it's their time too – nothing says they aren't to make something of it. As for Jenny Wren, she cares, hopping about on her little twig like she was tryin' to tell us somethin', but that's just it, she couldn't even if she wanted to – dumb bird. But the others – and they in some way must know too – it would never occur to them to want to, even if they could take the first step of the terrible journey toward feeling somebody should act, that ends in utter confusion and hopelessness, east of the sun and west of the moon. So their comment is: 'No comment.' Meanwhile the whole history of probabilities is coming to life, starting in the upper left-hand corner, like a sail.

John Ashbery (1969)

Milk

Milk used to come in tall glass, heavy and uncrystalline as frozen melted snow. It rose direct and thick as horse-chestnut tree trunks that do not spread out upon the ground even a little: a shaft of white drink narrowing at the cream and rounded off in a thick-lipped grin. Empty and unrinsed, a diluted milk ghost entrapped and dulled light and vision.

Then things got a little worse: squared, high-shouldered and rounded off in the wrong places, a milk replica of a handmade Danish wooden milk bat. But that was only the beginning. Things got worse than that.

Milk came in waxed paper that swelled and spilled and oozed flat pieces of milk. It had a little lid that didn't close properly or resisted when pulled so that when it did give way milk jumped out.

Things are getting better now. Milk is bigger – half-a-gallon, at least – in thin milky plastic with a handle, a jug founded on an oblong. Pick it up and the milk moves, rising enthusiastically in the neck as it shifts its center of weight. Heavy as a breast, but lighter, shaping itself without much changing shape: like bringing home the milk in a bandana, a neckerchief or a scarf, strong as canvas water wings whose strength was only felt dragged under water.

On the highway this morning at the go-round, about where you leave New Hampshire, there had been an accident. Milk was sloshed on the gray-blue-black so much like a sheet of early winter ice you drove over it slowly, no matter what the temperature of the weather that eddied in through the shatterproof glass gills. There were milk-skins all around, the way dessert plates look after everyone has left the table in the Concord grape season. Only bigger, unpigmented though pretty opaque, not squashed but no less empty.

Trembling, milk is coming into its own.

James Schuyler (1969)

from *it*

I

On the first day they invented sand. And the sand settled into
itself, just as they thought it would. After the sand had settled,
they tried it out to see if it could be walked on. It could. When
they walked they sank in a little, but not enough to worry about.
And they saw that they left marks in the sand. Every step they
took left marks in the sand. They called them footprints. Now it
was easier to see where they had walked. That was good. And
they hadn't invented wind and rain, so the footprints stayed
where they were. That way others could follow them. If any
others should want to. And that would be good. So on the very
first day they made a lot of footprints in the sand. The whole
first day they walked around and made footprints in the sand.
When they really had made a lot of footprints in the sand, they
sat down to rest and to enjoy the results of their efforts. They
looked over the endless expanse and described it to each other.
And when they were through describing it to each other and
had no more to say to each other, either about the sand or about
the many footprints they had made in the endless expanse, they
saw that something was missing. And one of them said: I go in
and out of this desert whenever I want

2

On the second day they invented light. And the light spread by itself, as they had thought it would. When the light was through spreading and there was light everywhere, they saw that they could see the sand. And they immediately began to describe what they saw. Yellow and brown, they said. And green and blue and red, they said. And black and white, they said. And gray, they said. And they said it a lot of times. Finally they really felt that they were all seeing the same thing. And that was good. A little later they saw that they could also see each other. We can see each other, they said. Just like that. And because they had said it just like that, they felt that they were all seeing the same thing. And that was good. In the middle of the day, when the light was very strong, they realized the light was very strong, and they closed their eyes and sat down in the sand to rest and to keep from getting lost. They had never imagined that the light would be so strong. It's taken over, they said. And while they sat there in the sand with their eyes closed, they really did suffer in the heat of all the light they had invented. They hadn't invented wind and rain, remember. So there was no coolness at all. Let's look away from it all for a moment, one of them said. So they did. And they really felt that they were all seeing the same thing. I can visualize the light, they said. That was how they suddenly understood that they had loved each other all along.

3

On the third day they invented water. If they hadn't, the water might have appeared by itself. It looks like it appeared by itself, they said. And they tried it out, to see if it could be walked on. It couldn't. They kept falling through. And when they went back to the sand their feet were wet, and the sand stuck to them. So they sat down and brushed the sand from their feet. At first it was hard because the sand was wet. Little by little it got easier because the sand dried. So they talked together about the sand and the water and their effects on each other. And they realized that they had felt the sand back on the first day. It had vanished between their fingers. So they felt the water. It vanished between their fingers. Finally they felt the light. It was as if our fingers were vanishing, they said. And they felt that now they had proof of their love.

Inger Christensen (1969), translated from the Danish
by Susanna Nied

A Case

They call me that we have a case at the hospital. It is a fine night, not late, only a little after eleven. When I arrive, they tell me, 'Mr H— is going to operate. The patient is in the first bed on the left in the men's ward.' I go in.

It is dark but some light comes from a wall fixture above the bed. He is a man in early life. I begin to ask the usual questions. I explain that I will give the anaesthetic for the operation. He says, 'My name is Pisgah.' I nod and go on with my questions and examination. He appears tired and in some distress. The exact nature of his condition is still in doubt.

It is true, when he tells me his name, I have a momentary surprise, which I suppress. The name is that of the mountain mentioned in the Bible from which Moses is said to have viewed the Promised Land. As a child, the name had intrigued me. It also occurs in a hymn, as if it were a man's name: Pisgah's Mount. I had often thought, singing the verse: who was Pisgah? I had used the name later, rather at random, for a person who existed in a story I was writing.

It was a story upon which I had exerted myself and then, in one sense, abandoned. Pisgah, in fact, was the person in that story with whom I was most concerned. I had written two extended versions, and others more fragmentary, without being able to bring them to any satisfaction.

That I had not finished those pieces did not mean that I had abandoned the work. To abandon a piece of writing is one thing. To abandon a work, is another. A particular piece of writing is a means, for a writer, which may not always finally serve the work. Thus, I write this, which also serves, for the moment.

I give the anaesthetic while my friend Mr H— does the surgery. The details of the case are of no consequence. It goes well. Towards the end, when my attention is not too pressed with technical details, I have the chance to look more closely at Pisgah's face.

It is the face of a man asleep. As he sleeps, he is remote, both from himself and from us. Yet he sleeps by my will. I check his pulse, his blood pressure, his colour, his muscle tone, and gently assist each breath.

In the story I had often had the experience that Pisgah was difficult to lay hold upon. His character seemed to change. Even the details of what he did or said. I had wanted to discover who exactly he was. So that I could, in some way, come to terms with him, to finish the story. Now, suddenly, I felt him alive against my hand. And that life dependent upon my attention. If my attention should fail, I might lose him for ever.

I speak occasionally with Mr H—. Sometimes about the details of what he is doing. Sometimes about other things entirely. Neither of us speaks of the man with whom, in our several ways, we are involved.

Later, before leaving the hospital, I make a last routine visit to Pisgah's bed. He is now partly awake and responds to a touch on the face or a simple question. I look again into that face, somewhat firmer now, and occasionally tightened by the first twinges of pain from the incision.

'Who are you?' I ask. He smiles faintly, out of his half sleep, as if amused that after all this time I should not know.

Gael Turnbull (1968)

An Old-fashioned Traveller on the Trade Routes

I was sitting upstairs in a bus, cursing the waste of time, and pouring my life away on one of those insane journeys across London – while gradually the wavering motion of this precarious glass salon, that flung us about softly like trusses of wheat or Judo Lords, began its medicinal work inside the magnetic landscape of London.

The bus, with its transparent decks of people, trembled. And was as uniquely ceremonious in propelling itself as an eminent Jellyfish with an iron will, by expulsions, valves, hisses, steams, and emotional respirations. A militant, elementary, caparisoned Jellyfish, of the feminine sex, systematically eating and drinking the sea.

I began to feel as battered as though I had been making love all night! My limbs distilled the same interesting wide-awake weariness.

We went forward at a swimmer's pace, gazing through the walls that rocked the weather about like a cloudy drink from a chemist's shop – with the depth and sting of the Baltic. The air-shocks, the sulphur dioxides, the gelatin ignitions! We were all of us parcelled up in mud-coloured clothes, dreaming, while the rich perishable ensemble – as stuffy and exclusive as a bag of fish and chips, or as an Eskimo's bed in a glass drift – cautiously advanced as though on an exercise from a naval college.

The jogging was consistently idiotic, it induced a feeling of complete security. I gave up my complicated life on the spot; and lay screwed up like an old handkerchief screwed up in a pocket, suspended in time, ready to go to the ends of the earth. O trans-Siberian railways! Balloons! Astronauts!

Rosemary Tonks (1967)

Strayed Crab

This is not my home. How did I get so far from water? It must be over that way somewhere.

I am the color of wine, of *tinta*. The inside of my powerful right claw is saffron-yellow. See, I see it now; I wave it like a flag. I am dapper and elegant; I move with great precision, cleverly managing all my smaller yellow claws. I believe in the oblique, the indirect approach, and I keep my feelings to myself.

But on this strange, smooth surface I am making too much noise. I wasn't meant for this. If I maneuver a bit and keep a sharp lookout, I shall find my pool again. Watch out for my right claw, all passersby! This place is too hard. The rain has stopped, and it is damp, but still not wet enough to please me.

My eyes are good, though small; my shell is tough and tight. In my own pool are many small gray fish. I see right through them. Only their large eyes are opaque, and twitch at me. They are hard to catch but I, I catch them quickly in my arms and eat them up.

What is that big soft monster, like a yellow cloud, stifling and warm? What is it doing? It pats my back. Out, claw. There, I have frightened it away. It's sitting down, pretending nothing's happened. I'll skirt it. It's still pretending not to see me. Out of my way, O monster. I own a pool, all the little fish that swim in it, and all the skittering waterbugs that smell like rotten apples.

Cheer up, O grievous snail. I tap your shell, encouragingly, not that you will ever know about it.

And I want nothing to do with you, either, sulking toad. Imagine, at least four times my size and yet so vulnerable . . . I could open your belly with my claw. You glare and bulge, a watchdog near my pool; you make a loud and hollow noise. I do not care for such stupidity. I admire compression, lightness, and agility, all rare in this loose world.

Elizabeth Bishop (1967)

The Flag

My flag is blue and sports a fish rampant, locked in and let loose by two bracelets. In winter, when the wind blows hard and there's no one about in these out-of-the-way places, I like to hear the flag crack like a whip with the fish swimming in the sky as if it were alive.

And why this fish, I'm asked. Is it mystical? Yes, I say, it is the ichthyous symbol, the prechristic, the luminocratic, the friddled, the true, the fried, the fried fish.

– And nothing else?

– Nothing else.

But in high winter, the flag thrashes up there with its fish in the air, trembling with cold, wind and sky.

Pablo Neruda (1966), translated from the Spanish
by Nathaniel Tarn

Vocabulary

'*La Pologne? La Pologne?* Isn't it terribly cold there?' she asked, and then sighed with relief. So many countries have been turning up lately that the safest thing to talk about is climate.

'Madame,' I want to reply, 'my people's poets do all their writing in mittens. I don't mean to imply that they never remove them; they do, indeed, if the moon is warm enough. In stanzas composed of raucous whooping, for only such can drown the windstorms' constant roar, they glorify the simple lives of our walrus herders. Our Classicists engrave their odes with inky icicles on trampled snowdrifts. The rest, our Decadents, bewail their fate with snowflakes instead of tears. He who wishes to drown himself must have an ax at hand to cut the ice. Oh, madame, dearest madame.'

That's what I mean to say. But I've forgotten the word for walrus in French. And I'm not sure of icicle and ax.

'*La Pologne? La Pologne?* Isn't it terribly cold there?'

'*Pas du tout,*' I answer icily.

Wisława Szymborska (1962), translated from the Polish
by Stanisław Barańczak and Clare Cavanagh

Catherine of Siena

Bridges. Ways over and ways to wait. Place for a stance or a stillness. Places, too, for violence. Bridges are blown and a war starts.

And in the water you can see the fish – if you watch carefully, if you side-step your own shadow, if you gaze deeper than self-love or arrogance.

Many have paused here. Have noted the faint sky reflected, the full moon falling, it seems, in the water. Have fallen in love with the dark.

For her, they were ways merely. Bridges meant building, meant the creak of planks, the delicate balance where wood is articulate, where men move as one, where the water is conquered.

Where prayer is most painful, she sought for an image. Others learnt light, air, steps, birds (the dove as a pretext or omen). All insubstantial for her. She needed the passion, the building, something to cleave – and connect.

Not standing there, letting the night drown in the water, watching the dear shadows that hold off the mountain. For her, the poise before the moment's abandon, all the reprisals of pain.

Pope, people, kings, confessors came to her. Proud professions passed over her bridges. Only Siena – round hill-city, seething with feud and friendship – was the safe place, solid ground, sweet summit where winds meet. Only here were bridges redundant.

Can light heal? Can the fountain surrender? Dare the fisherman pause? Her bridges were built for a journey. The unconcerned waters flowed on.

Elizabeth Jennings (1961)

from *City*

Walking through the suburb at night, as I pass the dentist's house I hear a clock chime a quarter, a desolate brassy sound. I know where it stands, on the mantelpiece in the still surgery. The chime falls back into the house, and beyond it, without end. Peace.

I sense the simple nakedness of these tiers of sleeping men and women beneath whose windows I pass. I imagine it in its own setting, a mean bathroom in a house no longer new, a bathroom with plank panelling, painted a peculiar shade of green by an amateur, and badly preserved. It is full of steam, so much as to obscure the yellow light and hide the high, patched ceiling. In this dream, standing quiet, the private image of the householder or his wife, damp and clean.

I see this as it might be floating in the dark, as if the twinkling point of a distant street-lamp had blown in closer, swelling and softening to a foggy oval. I can call up a series of such glimpses that need have no end, for they are all the bodies of strangers. Some are deformed or diseased, some are ashamed, but the peace of humility and weakness is there in them all.

I have often felt myself to be vicious, in living so much by the eye, yet among so many people. I can be afraid that the egg of light through which I see these bodies might present itself as a keyhole. Yet I can find no sadism in the way I see them now. They are warmfleshed, yet their shapes have the minuscule, remote morality of some mediaeval woodcut of the Expulsion: an eternally startled Adam, a permanently bemused Eve. I see them as homunculi, moving privately each in a softly lit fruit in a nocturnal tree. I can consider without scorn or envy the well-found bedrooms I pass, walnut and rose-pink, altars of tidy, dark-haired women, bare-backed, wifely. Even in these I can see order.

I come quite often now upon a sort of ecstasy, a rag of light blowing among the things I know, making me feel I am not the one for whom it was intended, that I have inadvertently been looking through another's eyes and have seen what I cannot receive.

I want to believe I live in a single world. That is why I am keeping my eyes at home while I can. The light keeps on separating the world like a table knife: it sweeps across what I see and suggests what I do not. The imaginary comes to me with as much force as the real, the remembered with as much force as the immediate. The countries on the map divide and pile up like ice-floes: what is strange is that I feel no stress, no grating discomfort among the confusion, no loss; only a belief that I should not be here. I see the iron fences and the shallow ditches of the countryside the mild wind has travelled over. I cannot enter that countryside; nor can I escape it. I cannot join together the mild wind and the shallow ditches, I cannot lay the light across the world and then watch it slide away. Each thought is at once translucent and icily capricious. A polytheism without gods.

Roy Fisher (1961)

Borges and I

The other one, the one called Borges, is the one things happen to. I walk through the streets of Buenos Aires and stop for a moment, perhaps mechanically now, to look at the arch of an entrance hall and the grillwork on the gate; I know of Borges from the mail and see his name on a list of professors or in a biographical dictionary. I like hourglasses, maps, eighteenth-century typography, the taste of coffee and the prose of Stevenson; he shares these preferences, but in a vain way that turns them into the attributes of an actor. It would be an exaggeration to say that ours is a hostile relationship; I live, let myself go on living, so that Borges may contrive his literature, and this literature justifies me. It is no effort for me to confess that he has achieved some valid pages, but those pages cannot save me, perhaps because what is good belongs to no one, not even to him, but rather to the language and to tradition. Besides, I am destined to perish, definitively, and only some instant of myself can survive in him. Little by little, I am giving over everything to him, though I am quite aware of his perverse custom of falsifying and magnifying things. Spinoza knew that all things long to persist in their being; the stone eternally wants to be a stone and the tiger a tiger. I shall remain in Borges, not in myself (if it is true that I am someone), but I recognize myself less in his books than in many others or in the laborious strumming of a guitar. Years ago I tried to free myself from him and went from the mythologies of the outskirts to the games with time and infinity, but those games belong to Borges now and I shall have to imagine other things. Thus my life is a flight and I lose everything and everything belongs to oblivion, or to him.

I do not know which of us has written this page.

Jorge Luis Borges (1960), translated from the Spanish
by James E. Irby

from *Letters to James Alexander*

Dear James

It is absolutely clear and absolutely sunny as if neither a cloud nor a moon had ever been invented. I am lying here on the grass of the University of California, a slave state but one which today seems peculiarly beneficent. I have not had a letter from you in weeks.

I read them all (your letters and mine) to the poets assembled for the occasion last Wednesday. Ebbe was annoyed since he thought that letters should remain letters (unless they were essays) and poems poems (a black butterfly just flew past my leg) and that the universe of the personal and the impersonal should be kept in order. George Stanley thought that I was robbing Jim to pay James. They sounded beautiful all of them.

Things cannot die in such a spring (unless the old men of the world commit suicide (our suicide) over the question of whether East Germans be called East Germans in diplomatic notes) and every leaf and flower of this red-hot February asks me to remember this. Though it is on the other side of poetry, spring, thank whatever created both of them, is spring. And I am not sure on a day like this that the living and dying world does not have something analogous to poetry in it. That every flower and every leaf (properly read) is not a James as well as a Jim.

Things cannot die in such a spring and yet your silence (for the spring itself proclaims that there are such things as clouds and moons) frightens me when I close my eyes or begin to write a poem.

I wish you were with me now on this grass and could be with me like the leaves and the flowers and the grass a part of this spring. Jim and James.

Love,
Jack

Jack Spicer (1959)

Hermes, Dog and Star

Hermes is going along in the world. He meets a dog.

– I'm a god – Hermes introduces himself politely.

The dog sniffs his feet.

– I feel lonely. People betray the gods. But mortal animals without self-consciousness, that's what we want. In the evening after traveling all day we'll sit down under an oak. Then I'll tell you I feel old and want to die. It'll be a lie necessary to get you to lick my hands.

– Sure – the dog replies casually – I'll lick your hands. They're cold and they smell strange.

They go along and after a while they meet a star.

– I'm Hermes – the god says – and produces one of his most handsome faces. – Would you by any chance feel like coming with us to the end of the world? I'll try to work it so that it's scary there and you have to lean your head on my arm.

– OK – says the star in a glassy voice. I don't care where I go. But your saying the end of the world is pure naïveté. Sadly, there is no end of the world.

They go along. The dog, Hermes, and the star. Holding hands. Hermes thinks to himself: the next time he goes out looking for friends, he won't be so sincere.

Zbigniew Herbert (1957), translated from the Polish
by Alissa Valles

Where the Tennis Court Was . . .

Where the tennis court once was, enclosed by the small rectangle down by the railroad tracks where the wild pines grow, the couch-weed now runs matted over the ground, and the rabbits scratch in the tall grass in those hours when it is safe to come out.

One day here two sisters came to play, two white butterflies, in the early hours of the afternoon. Toward the east the view was (and still is) open – and the damp rocks of the Corone still ripen the strong grapes for the *'sciacchetra'*. It is curious to think that each of us has a country like this one, even if altogether different, which must always remain *his* landscape, unchanging; it is curious that the physical order of things is so slow to filter down into us, and then so impossible to drain back out. But what of the rest? Actually, to ask the how and why of the interrupted game is like asking the how and why of that scarf of vapor rising from the loaded cargo ship anchored down there at the docks of Palmaria. Soon they will light, in the gulf, the first lamps.

Around, as far as the eye can see, the iniquity of objects persists, intangibly. The grotto encrusted with shells should be unchanged in the dense and heavy-planted garden under the tennis court; but the fanatical uncle will come no more with his tripod camera and magnesium lamp to photograph the single flower, unrepeatable, risen from the spiny cactus, and predestined to live only the shortest of lives. Even the villas of the South Americans seem deserted. And there haven't always been the heirs and heiresses ready to squander their sumptuously shoddy goods that came always side-by-side with the rattle of pesos and milreis. Or maybe the sarabande of the newly arrived tells us of passings on to other regions: surely we here are perfectly sheltered and out of the line of fire. It is almost as though life could not be ignited here except by lightning; as though it feeds only on such inert things as it can safely accumulate; as though it quickly cankers in such deserted zones.

'Del salon en angulo oscuro – silenciosa y cubierta de polvo – veiase el arpa . . .' Oh, yes, the museum would be impressive if one were able to uncover this ex-paradise of Victoriana. And no one was ever seen again on the seashell-inlayed terrace, supported by the giant Neptune (now scraped clean) after the Lion of Callao lost the election, and died; but there, by the outrageous bay window, frescoed in pears, apples and the serpents of the earthly paradise, the good-hearted Señora Paquita thought, in vain, to carry out her serene old age, comforted by her wily needles and the smile of posterity. But one day the husbands of the daughters arrived (Brazilian sons-in-law), and, the mask having been ripped away, carried these good things off. Of the duenna, and the others, not a word more was ever heard – one of the descendants came back later and performed miracles, it is said. By then, however, it was, more or less, the time of the Tripolitan hymns. And these objects, these houses, stayed inside the living circle so long as it lasted. For few felt from the start that the cold was actually coming; and among these, perhaps, was my father who, even during the hottest days of

August, supper out on the terrace over (carried on amidst moths and more persistent insects), and after having thrown a wool shawl around his shoulders, would repeat, always in French for who knows what reason, *'il fait bien froid, bien froid'*; then he would go off immediately into his room and lie down on the bed and smoke his 7 centime Cavour.

Eugenio Montale (1956), translated from the Italian
by Charles Wright

A Supermarket in California

What thoughts I have of you tonight, Walt Whitman, for I walked down the sidestreets under the trees with a headache self-conscious looking at the full moon.

In my hungry fatigue, and shopping for images, I went into the neon fruit supermarket, dreaming of your enumerations!

What peaches and what penumbras! Whole families shopping at night! Aisles full of husbands! Wives in the avocados, babies in the tomatoes!—and you, García Lorca, what were you doing down by the watermelons?

I saw you, Walt Whitman, childless, lonely old grubber, poking among the meats in the refrigerator and eyeing the grocery boys.

I heard you asking questions of each: Who killed the pork chops? What price bananas? Are you my Angel?

I wandered in and out of the brilliant stacks of cans following you, and followed in my imagination by the store detective.

We strode down the open corridors together in our solitary fancy tasting artichokes, possessing every frozen delicacy, and never passing the cashier.

Where are we going, Walt Whitman? The doors close in an hour. Which way does your beard point tonight?

(I touch your book and dream of our odyssey in the supermarket and feel absurd.)

Will we walk all night through solitary streets? The trees add shade to shade, lights out in the houses, we'll both be lonely.

Will we stroll dreaming of the lost America of love past blue automobiles in driveways, home to our silent cottage?

Ah, dear father, graybeard, lonely old courage-teacher, what America did you have when Charon quit poling his ferry and you got out on a smoking bank and stood watching the boat disappear on the black waters of Lethe?

Berkeley, 1955

Allen Ginsberg (1956)

Clock

In the warm air of the ceiling the footlights of dreams turn on.

The white walls have curved. The burdened chest breathes confused words. In the mirror, the wind from the south spins, carrying leaves and feathers. The window is blocked. The heart is almost extinguished among the already cold ashes of the moon – the hands are without shelter – as all the trees lying down. In the wind from the desert the needles bend and my hour is past.

Pierre Reverdy (1955), translated from the French
by Lydia Davis

Meditations in an Emergency

Am I to become profligate as if I were a blonde? Or religious as if I were French?

Each time my heart is broken it makes me feel more adventurous (and how the same names keep recurring on that interminable list!), but one of these days there'll be nothing left with which to venture forth.

Why should I share you? Why don't you get rid of someone else for a change?

I am the least difficult of men. All I want is boundless love.

Even trees understand me! Good heavens, I lie under them, too, don't I? I'm just like a pile of leaves.

However, I have never clogged myself with the praises of pastoral life, nor with nostalgia for an innocent past of perverted acts in pastures. No. One need never leave the confines of New York to get all the greenery one wishes – I can't even enjoy a blade of grass unless I know there's a subway handy, or a record store or some other sign that people do not totally *regret* life. It is more important to affirm the least sincere; the clouds get enough attention as it is and even they continue to pass. Do they know what they're missing? Uh huh.

My eyes are vague blue, like the sky, and change all the time; they are indiscriminate but fleeting, entirely specific and disloyal, so that no one trusts me. I am always looking away. Or again at something after it has given me up. It makes me restless and that makes me unhappy, but I cannot keep them still. If only I had grey, green, black, brown, yellow eyes; I would stay at home and do something. It's not that I am curious. On the contrary, I am bored but it's my duty to be attentive, I am needed by things as the sky must be above the earth. And lately, so great has *their* anxiety become, I can spare myself little sleep.

Now there is only one man I love to kiss when he is unshaven. Heterosexuality! you are inexorably approaching. (How discourage her?)

St. Serapion, I wrap myself in the robes of your whiteness which is like midnight in Dostoevsky. How am I to become a legend, my dear? I've tried love, but that hides you in the bosom of another and I am always springing forth from it like the lotus – the ecstasy of always bursting forth! (but one must not be distracted by it!) or like a hyacinth, 'to keep the filth of life away,' yes, there, even in the heart, where the filth is pumped in and slanders and pollutes and determines. I will my will, though I may become famous for a mysterious vacancy in that department, that greenhouse.

Destroy yourself, if you don't know!

It is easy to be beautiful; it is difficult to appear so. I admire you, beloved, for the trap you've set. It's like a final chapter no one reads because the plot is over.

'Fanny Brown is run away – scampered off with a Cornet of Horse; I do love that little Minx, & hope She may be happy, tho' She has vexed me by this Exploit a little too. – Poor silly Cecchina! or F:B: as we used to call her. – I wish She had a good Whipping and 10,000 pounds.' – Mrs. Thrale.

I've got to get out of here. I choose a piece of shawl and my dirtiest suntans. I'll be back, I'll re-emerge, defeated, from the valley; you don't want me to go where you go, so I go where you don't want me to. It's only afternoon, there's a lot ahead. There won't be any mail downstairs. Turning, I spit in the lock and the knob turns.

Frank O'Hara (1954)

Love Letter to King Tutankhamun

Young King Tutankhamun:

Yesterday afternoon in the museum I saw a small ivory column painted blue, pink and yellow.

For that one simple column, which is utterly useless and meaningless to our modern lives, for that simple little column of ivory painted by your tender hands – like autumn leaves – I would have given the ten most beautiful years of my life, ten years of love and faith, each year equally useless and meaningless.

Next to the small column I also saw, young Tutankhamun, yesterday afternoon I also saw – it was one of those clear afternoons of your beloved Egypt – I also saw your heart enclosed in a golden chest.

For that small heart of dust, for that small heart kept in a gold, enamel box, I would have given my young, warm, and still pure heart.

Because yesterday afternoon, my King full of Death, my heart beat full of life for you, and my life embraced your death and seemed to melt into it.

The hard death that sticks to your bones melted under the heat of my breath and the blood of my dream, and from so much mixing of love and death I'm still intoxicated from so much dying and loving.

Yesterday afternoon, an Egyptian afternoon speckled with white ibises, I loved your impossible eyes through the glass.

And in some other distant Egyptian afternoon not unlike this one – the light broken up by birds – your eyes were immense, two long slits stretching to your trembling temples.

A long time ago on an afternoon like this one your eyes lay down on the earth, and they opened on it like your country's two mysterious lotuses.

They were crimson eyes refreshed by twilights and high rivers in the month of September.

Your eyes were the owners of a kingdom that boasted cities in full bloom, giant stones that had already been there for millions of years, lands sown to the horizon, armies that conquered territories extending beyond the sandy wastelands of the Nubian desert, and those renowned archers and intrepid charioteers who have remained in profile forever, as still as hieroglyphics and monoliths.

Everything fit in your eyes, tender, most powerful King. Everything was destined for you before you had time to gaze on it. And you certainly had no time.

Now your eyes are shut and there is a gray dust on your eyelids. They have nothing now but this gray dust, this ash of long-consumed dreams, and now, between your eyes and mine, there is an impenetrable glass.

For those eyes of yours, which I couldn't half-open with my kisses, I would give my own two eyes to whoever wants them, my own two eyes, so avid for landscapes, and like two thieves that steal from your sky, like masters of the world's sun.

I would give away my living eyes just to feel your gaze come to me through three thousand nine hundred years, to feel it upon me, to feel it come, vaguely terrifying, bearing the pale halo of Isis.

Young King Tutankhamun, dead at nineteen years of age, let me tell you these absurd words that perhaps no one ever told you, let me tell them to you in the solitude of my hotel room, in the frigidity of walls shared with strangers, walls colder than those of the tomb you didn't want to share with anyone.

I tell them to you, adolescent King, you who were left in the stillness of your youthful profile, left in your crystalline grace, left in the gesture that prohibited the sacrifice of innocent doves in the temple of the terrible Ammon-Ra.

This is how I will go on seeing you when I am faraway, standing tall before suspicious priests and circled by a flurry of white wings taking flight.

I will have nothing of you, nothing but this dream, because everything that is you is now reserved, prohibited, and infinitely impossible. For hundreds of years your gods held a vigil for you, hanging to the last hair on your head.

I think your hair must have been straight like the rain that falls in the night. For your hair and your doves and your nineteen years so close to death, I would have been what I will never be: a fragment of love.

But you didn't wait for me. You walked along the edge of a crescent moon. You left me and went to the kingdom of the dead the way a child goes to a park, followed by your shimmering gazelles and your ivory carriage full of toys that still entertained you.

If the crowds of sensible people wouldn't have become indignant, I would have kissed your toys one by one, your heavy gold and silver toys, your strange exotic toys that children of today, who box and play soccer, would never know how to use.

If the crowds of sensible people wouldn't have become scandalized, I would have taken you out of your sarcophagus, which itself was inside three wooden sarcophagi, which were themselves inside a great granite sarcophagus. I would have lifted you out of the sinister depths, the sinister depths in which you grow more dead, more dead before my emboldened heart, which beats for you alone. For you alone, Sweetest of All Kings, my heart beats on this clear Egyptian afternoon on the Nile's luminous arm!

If the crowds of sensible people wouldn't have become furious, I would have taken you out of your five different sarcophagi, I would have loosed you from the bindings that press too heavily on your indelible body and I would have gently wrapped you in my silk shawl.

I would have held you to my chest like a sick little boy and I would have sung to you the most beautiful, the most tender, of my tropical songs. I would have sung to you, sweet King, the shortest of all my poems.

Dulce María Loynaz (1953), translated from the Spanish
by James O'Connor

The Clerk's Vision

And to fill all these white pages that are left for me with the same monotonous question: at what hour do the hours end? And the anterooms, the memorials, the intrigues, the negotiations with the Janitor, the Rotating Chairman, the Secretary, the Associate, the Delegate. To glimpse the Influential from afar and to send my card each year to remind – who? – that in some corner, devoted, steady, plodding, although not very sure of my existence, I too await the coming of my hour, I too exist. No. I quit.

Yes, I know, I could settle down in an idea, in a custom, in an obsession. Or stretch out on the coals of a pain or some hope and wait there, not making much noise. Of course it's not so bad: I eat, drink, sleep, make love, observe the marked holidays and go to the beach in summer. People like me and I like them. I take my condition lightly: sickness, insomnia, nightmares, social gatherings, the idea of death, the little worm that burrows into the heart or the liver (the little worm that leaves its eggs in the brain and at night pierces the deepest sleep), the future at the expense of today – the today that never comes on time, that always loses its bets. No. I renounce my ration card, my I.D., my birth certificate, voter's registration, passport, code number, countersign, credentials, safe conduct pass, insignia, tattoo, brand.

The world stretches out before me, the vast world of the big, the little, and the medium. Universe of kings and presidents and jailors, of mandarins and pariahs and liberators and liberated, of judges and witnesses and the condemned: stars of the first, second, third and nth magnitudes, planets, comets, bodies errant and eccentric or routine and domesticated by the laws of gravity, the subtle laws of falling, all keeping step, all turning slowly or rapidly around a void. Where they claim the central sun lies, the solar being, the hot beam made out of every human gaze, there is nothing but a hole and less than a hole: the eye of a dead fish, the giddy cavity of the eye that falls into itself and looks at itself without seeing. There is nothing with which to fill the hollow center of the whirlwind. The springs are smashed, the foundations collapsed, the visible or invisible bonds that joined one star to another, one body to another, one man to another, are nothing but a tangle of wires and thorns, a jungle of claws and teeth that twist us and chew us and spit us out and chew us again. No one hangs himself by the rope of a physical law. The equations fall tirelessly into themselves.

And in regard to the present matter, if the present matters: I do not belong to the masters. I don't wash my hands of it, but I am not a judge, nor a witness for the prosecution, nor an executioner. I do not torture, interrogate, or suffer interrogation. I do not loudly plead for leniency, nor wish to save myself or anyone else. And for all that I don't do and for all that they do to us, I neither ask forgiveness nor forgive. Their piety is as abject as their justice. Am I innocent? I'm guilty. Am I guilty? I'm innocent. (I'm innocent when I'm guilty, guilty when I'm innocent. I'm guilty when . . . but that is another song. Another song? It's all the same song.) Guilty innocent, innocent guilty, the fact is I quit.

I remember my loves, my conversation, my friendships. I remember it all, see it all, see them all. With melancholy, but without nostalgia. And above all, without hope. I know that it is immortal, and that, if we are anything, we are the hope of something. For me, expectation has spent itself. I quit the nevertheless, the even, the in spite of everything, the moratoriums, the excuses and forgiving. I know the mechanism of the trap of morality and the drowsiness of certain words. I have lost faith in all those constructions of stone, ideas, ciphers. I quit. I no longer defend this broken tower. And, in silence, I await the event.

A light breeze, slightly chilly, will start to blow. The newspapers will talk of a cold wave. The people will shrug their shoulders and continue life as always. The first deaths will barely swell the daily count, and no one in the statistics bureau will notice that extra zero. But after a while everyone will begin to look at each other and ask: what's happening? Because for months doors and windows are going to rattle, furniture and trees will creak. For years there will be a shivering in the bones and a chattering of teeth, chills and goose bumps. For years the chimneys, prophets, and chiefs will howl. The mist that hangs over stagnant ponds will drift into the city. And at noon beneath the equivocal sun, the breeze will drag the smell of dry blood from a slaughterhouse abandoned even by flies.

No use going out or staying at home. No use erecting walls against the impalpable. A mouth will extinguish all the fires, a doubt will root up all the decisions. It will be everywhere without being anywhere. It will blur all the mirrors. Penetrating walls and convictions, vestments and well-tempered souls, it will install itself in the marrow of everyone. Whistling between body and body, crouching between soul and soul. And all the wounds will open because, with expert and delicate, although somewhat cold, hands, it will irritate sores and pimples, will burst pustules and swellings and dig into the old, badly healed wounds. Oh fountain of blood, forever inexhaustible! Life will be a knife, a gray and agile and cutting and exact and arbitrary blade that falls and slashes and divides. To crack, to claw, to quarter, the verbs that move with giant steps against us!

It is not the sword that shines in the confusion of what will be. It is not the saber, but fear and the whip. I speak of what is already among us. Everywhere there are trembling and whispers, insinuations and murmurs. Everywhere the light wind blows, the breeze that provokes the immense whiplash each time it unwinds in the air. Already many carry the purple insignia in their flesh. The light wind rises from the meadows of the past, and hurries closer to our time.

Octavio Paz (1951), translated from the Spanish
by Eliot Weinberger

Around the Star's Throne

A sea of feathers billows. It billows with happy billows. It billows with hilarious, happy billows of white, red and yellow feathers. It chirps, crows, pipes, flirts and trills around the star's throne. But how are we to imagine the throne of the star? Deep, formless, blue, unending, green, terrifying.

Hans Arp (1951), translated from the German
by Bethany Schneider

The God of War

I saw the old god of war standing on a stump, on one side an abyss, on the other a cliff wall.

He smelled of free beer and carbolic and he showed off his gonads to the teenagers, the while some professors had rejuvenated him.

In his hoarse wolf's voice he declared his love for all that is young. And there was a pregnant woman standing by, and she shivered.

And he continued without shame, presenting himself as a great champion of order. And he described how he created order in the barns, by emptying them.

As a man may scatter crumbs for the sparrows, so he fed poor people with crusts of bread he had taken from poor people. His voice was sometimes loud, sometimes quiet, but always hoarse.

In a loud voice he spoke of the great times to come, and in a quiet voice he taught the women how to boil crows and seagulls.

All the while he was uneasy in himself, and he looked over his shoulder time and again as if in fear of a stab in the back.

And every five minutes he assured his public that he was minded to make his entrance brief.

Bertolt Brecht (1949), translated from the German
by Thomas Kuhn

The Swift

Swift with wings too wide, wheeling and shrieking his joy around the house. Such is the heart.

He dries up thunder. He sows in the serene sky. If he touches ground, he tears himself apart.

His response is the swallow, the familiar, whom he detests. What value has lace from the tower?

His pause is in the most somber hollow. No one lives in space more narrow than he.

Through the summer of long brightness, he will streak his way in shadows, by the blinds of midnight.

No eyes can hold him. He shrieks for his only presence. A slight gun is about to fell him. Such is the heart.

René Char (1948), translated from the French
by Mary Ann Caws

Phrase

And why not the hedge of geysers the obelisks of hours the
　　　smooth cry of clouds the quartered sea pale green bedunged
　　　by good-for-nothing birds and hope playing marbles on
　　　the beams and for-the-time-beings of houses and the sea
　　　bream rips of banana tree suckers

in the top branches of the sun on the stubbed heart of morn-
　　　ings on the acrid canvas of the sky a day of chalk of falcon
　　　of rain and acacia on a portulan of primeval islands shak-
　　　ing their salt hair interposed by fingers of masts in every
　　　hand to every purpose beneath the batting of an eyelash
　　　of chance with its shadow sung delights an assassin clad
　　　in rich and calm muslins like a chant of hard wine

　　　　　　　　　　Aimé Césaire (1946), translated from the French
　　　　　　　　　　　　by Clayton Eshleman and A. James Arnold

The Modern Prose Poem

The Modern Prose Poem

Street Cries

They were three street cries.

One when spring had come, late in the afternoon, the balconies open, and floating up to them on the breeze a sharp aroma, rough and hard, that almost tickled your nose. People went by: women dressed in light, sheer fabrics; men, some in black wool or yellowish suits, and others in discolored white linen jackets and carrying wicker lunch trays, empty, on their way home from work. Then, a few streets over, the cry went up – 'Carnations! Carnations!' – a slightly muffled cry, whose sound that sharp aroma, that same rough, scratchy scent that rose on the breeze to the opened balconies, converged with and merged in the scent of carnations. Dissolved in the air it had floated nameless, bathing the afternoon, until the cry betrayed it, giving it a voice and a sound, plunging it deep in your chest, like a knife whose scar time will never heal.

The second street cry was at noon, in summer. The awning was unfurled over the patio, keeping the house cool and shady. The door to the street scarcely allowed an echo of light to penetrate the entryway. Water sounded in the drowsy fountain under its corona of green leaves. What a pleasure it was in the laziness of the summer noon, in that sleepy atmosphere, to rock in the wicker rocker. Everything was light, afloat; the world turned slowly, like a soap bubble, delicate, iridescent, unreal. And suddenly, from outside the doors, from the street flooded with sunlight, came the wild cry, like a moan of pleasure, 'Mackerel!' The same as when you're stirred from sleep in the middle of the night and that vague awakening brings with it just enough awareness that you can feel the surrounding calm and quiet, and you turn and fall back to sleep. There was in that cry a sudden bolt of gold and scarlet light, like lightning flashing through the darkness of an aquarium, that sent a sudden chill through your flesh. The world, having stopped for a moment, resumed its smooth turning, turning.

The third cry was at nightfall, in autumn. The lamplighter had already passed, with his long hook on his shoulder, at whose far end flickered the little blue flame like a soul, lighting the street-lamps. The paving stones, damp from the first rains, shone under the bluish gas light. A balcony here, a door there, began to be lit up along the opposite wall, so close together in the narrow street. Then you could hear the blinds being lowered, the shutters closing. Through the balcony's sheer curtain, his forehead pressed against the cold window, the little boy watched the street for a moment, waiting. Then came the voice of the old peddler, filling the dusk with his hoarse cry, 'Fresh lavender!' – the vowels closed in on themselves like the ululating call of an owl. He could be guessed at more than seen, dragging one foot behind him, stormcloud face beneath the hat brim fallen on him like a roof tile, moving, with his sack of lavender over his shoulder, to close the cycle of the year and of life itself.

The first cry was the voice, the pure voice; the second the song, the melody; the third the memory and the echo, voice and melody now vanished.

Luis Cernuda (1943), translated from the Spanish
by Stephen Kessler

Rain

The rain, in the courtyard where I watch it fall, comes down at very different speeds. In the centre, it is a fine discontinuous curtain (or mesh), falling implacably but relatively slowly, a drizzle, a never-ending languid precipitation, an intense dose of pure meteor. Not far from the right and left walls heavier drops fall more noisily, separately. Here they seem to be about the size of a grain of wheat, there of a pea, elsewhere nearly a marble. On the moulding, on the window ledges, the rain runs horizontally while on the undersides of these same obstacles it is suspended, plump as a humbug. It streams across the entire surface of a little zinc roof the peephole looks down on, in a thin moiré sheet due to the different currents set in motion by the imperceptible undulations and bumps in the roofing. From the adjoining gutter, where it runs with the restraint of a brook in a nearly level bed, it suddenly plunges in a perfectly vertical, coarsely braided stream to the ground, where it splatters and springs up again flashing like needles.

Each of its forms has a particular speed: each responds with a particular sound. The whole lives as intensely as a complicated mechanism, as precise as it is chancy, a clockwork whose spring is the weight of a given mass of precipitate vapour.

The chiming of the vertical streams on the ground, the gurgling of the gutters, the tiny gong beats multiply and resound all at once in a concert without monotony, not without delicacy.

When the spring is unwound, certain gears continue to function for a while, gradually slowing down, until the whole mechanism grinds to a halt. Then, if the sun comes out, everything is erased, the brilliant apparatus evaporates: it has rained.

Francis Ponge (1942), translated from the French
by Beverley Bie Brahic

The Pleasures of the Door

Kings never touch doors.

They're not familiar with this happiness: to push, gently or roughly before you one of these great friendly panels, to turn towards it to put it back in place – to hold a door in your arms.

The happiness of seizing one of these tall barriers to a room by the porcelain knob of its belly; this quick hand-to-hand, during which your progress slows for a moment, your eye opens up and your whole body adapts to its new apartment.

With a friendly hand you hold on a bit longer, before firmly pushing it back and shutting yourself in – of which you are agreeably assured by the click of the powerful, well-oiled latch.

Francis Ponge (1942), translated from the French
by C. K. Williams

Crate

Halfway between *crib* and *cage* the French language places *crate*, a simple slatted box for transporting those fruits that fall ill at the least lack of air.

Built in such a way that it can be broken down effortlessly after use, it is never used twice. It is really more perishable than the deliquescing foodstuffs that it carries.

On the corners of streets that lead to the markets, it gleams like white wood without wood's vanity. Still very new, and slightly surprised to find itself in this awkward position, having been thrown into the gutter without hope of retrieval, it remains a most likable object on whose fate we will not dwell for long.

Francis Ponge (1942), translated from the French
by Joshua Corey and Jean-Luc Garneau

from *Vigils*

I

At dawn the throb of the bombers coming home.

Pull back the curtains, and see how the noiseless fire of sunrise eats down the chestnut trees. The still chestnut trees with their feet bathed with dew.

There is work to be done, there are friends to be met; today is for laughter, and feet firmly planted on earth, as the dew quivers up into mid-day. The plate-glass river has caught and transposed the blue of the sky like a theme in music.

Across the morning papers the metal-breasted squadrons engage, the furious tanks articulate with flame and the cannon charge in their hundreds, are burst in a rain of shells. There are voices proclaiming that heroes have died, that factories roar, that an abracadabra of figures makes triumph certain. A gruesome sensation: sharks follow a raft of torpedoed seamen for nine days and nights.

Searching among the letters by the coffee-cup for one that still delays. There are three more posts today.

A strange dream last night about the troop-train. Was I on my way to some distant front, or returning from the battle? What country was that half-lit ruined station in? How clearly I remember those friends of old days, my two companions. Their warm lips parted they tried to explain to me – what was it? And yet they are a thousand miles away, perhaps in other armies; and if alive, who knows?

But if death comes to me? Could happen any moment, any night of bombs and fire.

Forget that darkness. Danger quickens the tide in the veins. Look, the summer-laden trees, the yellow irises along the wall, are more precious for the thought. Look with what style the young airmen march the street, and sailors fling the foam of their living into the smiles that greet them. Being is everything.

There is work to be done. Telephones will be answered, letters posted, new problems faced like rivers, crossing improvised, achieved. Skill of hand or eye adorns triumphantly like flowers or medals.

The tide of the day is at the full. Over the festivals of meat and wine, among the jostling tables, the chances of battle are debated; a new film that opened last night is appraised: a witty story told about a minister. Repulse, endurance, victory, the hero's death, all glitter like mist that pearls above a fountain.

But if this is only the scarf with which we hide despair? But if the pounding of the guns, the plunging of the massed bomb-racks rubs out, not just this house or that, but the whole monument of love and history? Sands have covered cities, every stone lost and skulls forgotten.

Scattering of yesterday's friends. Where are the words of love by the window, all the bubble and excitement round the fire? Does the web still hold we wove then? So frail it seems now, stretched to the edge of language by otherness of place and otherness of meaning.

Across the evening paper the squadrons engage, the warships rock in the violent birth of their broadsides. There are prophets shouting in the wings, a grand transformation scene. Prophets, magicians, schemers: but the text is blurred. Is this the promised revolution that will atone for all? The last rung into sunlight? Or only an error, the miscarriage of machines?

Does it matter? Changing is living. Music seduces, breaking from behind the curtain of a bar. We are one now, blood flows between us, meeting and parting, the brief exchange of fondness, is music, is singing, in the lights as we crowd by the piano in the bar. Goodnight, then, goodbye and God bless you.

Let your latchkey into the door, look down eagerly among the scattered letters, the postman's final visit for the day. Stamps, inks, envelopes, so many voices speaking up from them; but the longed for accents do not answer. Silence.

A great wind is blowing from the centre. Hearths that were red yesterday are now dead ashes, and the wind blowing through the burst-open windows. If we hold on: but how much longer?

The bells begin to chime the hour all over the town, recalling the sweetness of centuries, hope stored like honey in the clustered towers. There was a room once above the street, and your name over the door, and the bells chiming. But that is already like another life.

Come back. There were dreams, there was faith. We must build. Come back from the white skulls and sandstorms of Africa, from the murderous teeth of the sea. Without your laughter confident beside me, without your answering and warm-veined hand, my feet, stepping for the solid earth, find only air.

At dusk, the throb of the bombers going out.

John Lehmann (1942)

Nijinski

He appeared as I was staring at the lighted coals in my fire-place. He held in his hands a large box of red matches which he displayed to me like a conjuror taking an egg out of the nose of the person in the next seat. He struck a match, set fire to the box, disappeared behind an enormous flame, and then stood before me. I recall his crimson smile and his vitreous eyes. A hurdy-gurdy in the street went on repeating the same note. I don't know how to describe what he was wearing, but he kept making me think of a purple cypress. Gradually his arms began to separate from his taut body and to form a cross. Where did so many birds come from? It was as if he'd had them hidden under his wings. They flew clumsily, madly, violently, knocking against the walls of the narrow room, against the window-panes, then covered the floor as though wounded. I felt a warm layer of down and pulsations growing at my feet. I gazed at him, a strange fever possessed my body like a current coursing through it. When he'd finished raising his arms and his palms were together, he gave a sudden leap, as if the spring of a watch had broken in front of me. He knocked against the ceiling, making it echo with the sound of a cymbal, extended his right arm, seized the wire of the lamp, moved slightly, relaxed, then began to describe with his body a figure of eight against the darkness. The sight made me dizzy and I covered my face with both hands, crushing the darkness against my

eyelids, while the hurdy-gurdy went on repeating the same
note and then stopped abruptly. A sudden icy wind struck me;
I felt my legs go numb. Now I also heard the low velvety sound
of a flute, followed immediately by a heavy and regular beat-
ing. I opened my eyes and again saw him, standing tiptoe on a
crystal sphere in the middle of the room, in his mouth a strange
green flute over which he was running his fingers as though
there were thousands of them. The birds now came back to life
in an extraordinary order, rose up, mingled, formed into a cor-
tège as wide as my outspread arms, and went out into the night
through the window that was somehow open. When the last
flutter had died away and only a suffocating smell of hunting
was left, I decided to look him in the face. There was no face:
above the purple body, seemingly headless, he sported a golden
mask, of the kind found in Mycenaean tombs, with a pointed
beard reaching down to the throat. I tried to get up, but
I'd hardly made the first movement when a cataclysmic sound,
like a pile of kettledrums collapsing in a funeral march, rooted
me to the spot. It was the mask. His face appeared again as
I'd originally seen it – the eyes, the smile, and something which
I now remarked for the first time: the white skin suspended
from two black curls that pinned it into place at the temples. He
tried to leap but no longer possessed his initial agility. I think
he even stumbled against a book fallen there by accident, and
he knelt down on one knee. Now I could observe him carefully.
I saw the pores of his skin oozing fine beads of sweat. Some-
thing like breathlessness came over me. I tried to discover why
his eyes had seemed so strange. He closed them and began to
get up; but it must have been terribly difficult, for he seemed to
concentrate all his strength without being able to do anything.
He even knelt now on the other knee as well. The white skin
seemed terribly pale, like yellow ivory, and his black hair was
lifeless. Though I was witnessing an agonizing struggle, I had

the feeling that I was better, that I'd triumphed over something.

Before I could draw breath I saw him, fallen full length now, plunge into a green pagoda portrayed on my carpet.

George Seferis (1940), translated from the Greek
by Edmund Keeley and Phillip Sherrard

The Right Meaning

'Mother, you know there is a place somewhere called Paris. It's a huge place and a long way off and it really is huge.'

My mother turns up my coat collar, not because it's starting to snow, but in order that it may start.

My father's wife is in love with me, walking up, always keeping her back to my birth, and her face toward my death. Because I am hers twice: by my goodbye and by my coming home. When I return home, I close her. That is why her eyes gave me so much, pronounced innocent of me, caught in the act of me, everything occurs through finished arrangements, through covenants carried out.

Has my mother confessed me, has she been named publicly? Why doesn't she give so much to my other brothers? To Victor, for example, the oldest, who is so old now that people say, 'He looked like his father's youngest brother!' It must be because I have travelled so much! It must be because I have lived more!

My mother gives me illuminated permissions to explore my coming-home tales. Face to face with my returning-home life, remembering that I journeyed for two whole hearts through her womb, she blushes and goes deathly pale when I say in the discourse of the soul: 'That night I was happy!' But she grows more sad, she grew more sad.

'How old you're getting, son!'

And she walks firmly through the color yellow to cry, because I seem to her to be getting old, on the blade of a sword, in the delta of my face. Weeps with me, grows sad with me. Why should my youth be necessary, if I will always be her son? Why do mothers feel pain when their sons get old, if their age will never equal anyway the age of the mothers? And why, if the sons, the more they get on, merely come nearer to the age of the fathers? My mother cries because I am old in my time and because I will never get old enough to be old in hers!

My goodbyes left from a point in her being more toward the outside than the point in her being to which I come back. I am, because I am so overdue coming back, more the man to my mother than the son to my mother. The purity that lights us both now with three flames lies precisely in that. I say then until I finally fall silent:

'Mother, you know there is this place somewhere called Paris. It's a huge place and a long way off and it really is huge.'

The wife of my father, hearing my voice, goes on eating her lunch, and her eyes that will die descend gently along my arms.

César Vallejo (1939), translated from the Spanish
by Robert Bly

Blue Notebook, No. 10

There once lived a red-headed man who had no eyes or ears. He also had no hair, so he was only in a manner of speaking called red-haired.

He couldn't speak, since he had no mouth. He had no nose either.

He didn't even have arms or legs. And he had no stomach, and he had no back, and he had no spine, and he had no innards at all. He had nothing at all! So there's no knowing who we are talking about.

We'd better not talk about him any more.

Daniil Kharms (1937), translated from the Russian
by Robert Chandler

Bourgeois News

Floods are frequent because the rivers of Britain have been neglected for a century. Positive movements of transgression carry the sea and its deposits over the lands, drowning them and their features under tens or hundreds of fathoms of water. Efforts to advance the prosperity of the country should be directed towards building on the foundations already laid by the native himself, rather than to hazardous introductions or innovations. Commercial possibilities are not clearly and courageously visualized, and the new ventures are often the product and concern of individuals facing the traditional difficulties of lonely pioneers. The indoor staff remains comparatively small. The vigour of mountain building, of volcanoes, and of other manifestations of unrest, has shown no sign of senility or lack of energy. An operator received concussion and a wound on the head from a cast-iron cover blown off a 60A switch-fuse box.

Geodesists have welcomed escape from the rising and sinking of the crust. To follow their food from over-grazed or sun-scorched regions they required to be able to migrate easily and quickly. Today you cannot fight summer-heat with haphazard measures. The fermenting mass is turned three times. Nevertheless the gates are not kept locked and there is a considerable freedom to the public provided no fires are lighted and respect is shown for the plantations.

Colonel Popham, who began work as a tea planter, murmured, 'They say a man is too old at forty. Or is it fifty? I think it must be seventy or eighty. I speak four different Chinese dialects fluently. It helped a lot. Then the slump came and trade went stagnant. I have lost all my money, but I can always earn more. As soon as I have saved up enough I shall put it all into another show. What is money for? If it is to be spent it finds work for a lot of people and keeps in circulation. Our seventy-eight-year-old customer said he had taken the umbrella with him round the world, through jungles and across prairies. He boasted that he had never lost it because he would never lend it. He brought it to us to be re-covered. That was less than five years ago. We now occupy three floors of the building where we began, and have overflowed into an adjoining building. No company such as this with a fine tradition for honest dealing with native peoples can remain in a depressed condition for an indefinite period. A reorganization scheme has been delayed owing to some difference of opinion with the American (Guggenheim) interests. That has now been settled, and the way is clear for the reorganization plan. London could be reached in twenty minutes. Rows of imposing neon-lighted shops erected. Super-cinemas built.'

*   *   *

The mountains heaved up like a rough sea for twelve miles, and the hamlet with its 200 inhabitants disappeared. Two mail-coaches arrived safely at their destination, but with the drivers frozen dead in their seats. Trains were buried for three days. London awoke to chaos on the 19th. The snow lay a uniform solid three feet thick and fifteen feet in drifts. Many boats careered wildly along the road, crashing into houses and other buildings on the river bank. The crew of the Strathrye soaked their beds in paraffin and ignited them to attract attention. Days were passed in making shrouds, in farewells, in drinking holy thin soup. The schools were empty so that the whole family could die together, and no debts were paid.

Shortly after midnight a great light was seen to be appearing on the high hills a little way off. As the light became brighter they shrieked and lamented and wrapped themselves in white cloth. The light, however, turned out to be the primitive acetylene lights of an early motorcar. The aborigines immediately proceeded to take the carburettor to bits with a great deal of interested chatter that thoroughly frightened the traveller. To his amazement they then put the pieces together again, after which the engine worked perfectly and the boat went on its way.

★ ★ ★

A man of fifty-nine will sit next Sunday on a divan of cloth of gold and precious stones. Ten million people in all parts of the East will give thanks. He looks beautiful. His neck has grown straight and supple. He swings his head about more than usual, as if he enjoys the movement. Fir bushes grow around, the path has been kept weeded, but no one visits this strange, empty mausoleum. Mrs King has resolutely refused to allow the body to be taken out of her home. 'She still regards him as living.'

He was interested in the stock market. But in New York the market closes at 3 p.m., which is noon in Hollywood. The rest of the day was empty. He had no hobbies. He went from one extreme to the other. He tore his nervous system to shreds worrying over grievances, more often imaginary than real. Then suddenly he would thrust his worries from him and be the most gay, charming, high-spirited companion in the world, full of a vaulting optimism as little justified as his depths of gloom. He had said that he made his wife an annual allowance up to 1917, when he gave her two factories. Then he was in poor circumstances and could not do any more.

'At last I found what it was,' he said. 'I wanted to see my wife. I wanted her to grumble at me for eating the wrong food and wearing the wrong clothes. Pretty bunches of evenly sized bright pink and yellow sticks may attract her and increase the sales of rhubarb, which have been declining for some years.'

* * *

This is an interesting Government. And a strange one. It is big. Very big. It is strong. Very strong. Yet all the three leaders of it are discredited. Far from being extinguished the antelope has become a menace, since it is roaming the south-west of the province in herds, and farmers are imploring the Government to protect them from it. Even the most thorough-going rogues have enjoyed such popularity that thousands of admirers have refused to believe any ill of them, in spite of all the evidence to the contrary. Japan, for instance, has had her representatives in special training for weeks at a camp near the old Shogun city of Kamakura. What we have to do is to listen to the tiny voice of conscience and not smother it. In the past two or three weeks I have been visiting armaments works. The net result of my conclusions is that I do not think the country can afford to allow valuable men like Sir Charles Craven to be wasting their time giving evidence before armaments commissions. It takes around eight months to make a 4.7-inch gun. It does seem to me a poor kind of compliment to the intelligence of the councillors to suggest that they do not know their own minds from one day to the next. As they must not leave their room during the deliberation, which will be long, twelve beds have been installed for them. In the course of yesterday, the successive bulletins were of a more reassuring nature: 'The most probable cause is the present state of flux in native life, the disappearance of tribal discipline, and the results of undigested education. It is possible to change some factors; it is not possible to change geography.' These reassurances did not everywhere produce the desired effect.

On the third day, using wire ropes, the wreck was lifted to the surface, but a swell on the sea made it impossible to get it onto the lighter. The ropes snapped, and the flying-boat drifted for 100 ft., and sank in 60 ft. of water, where it remained. As the day wore on, and the anticyclone began to withdraw to the Continent, three quarters of those present made for the door. There was no panic. They could go on their way peacefully, because they were strong.

Charles Madge (1937)

Lozanne

It was seven, it was nine o'clock, the doors were closing, the windows were screaming. You bent over the shadow that lay on the floor and saw its eyes dissolving. The band about your forehead began to turn. The band of fever.

The armchair turned into a palace, the carpet became a bank of withered flowers, *and then it was time to go.* Every semblance of that which had gone before became the means by which you ascended the great staircase. And took your place among the stars.

For it is significant, is it not, that the *blemish* about which you were so insistent was nothing less than that interminable voice which haunted you in your dreams, saying 'I love you' over and over again. And the panelling of the room where they asked you questions was made of exactly the same wood as the mallet which you had to hate.

The dusty and ashen residue of a passion that now raged elsewhere, but still raged, rose slowly upwards to the surface of the lake as your blood sank slowly through it. And the other returned to ice. Oh, I can see through your eyes now and I can see what flame it was that melted everything before it! (Though the obstinate sod refused to become softened by the rain of thaw.) But you were spared passing through that black box where a masked man kisses his victim before her death. I ask the glass again: Who gave the victims right to refuse life to those who refuse to be victimized?

Those who damned shall be damned.

David Gascoyne (1936)

In Praise of Glass

Glass, Buddhistic glass, full of images yet lacking one of its own: the one that receives my profile and returns it: that takes in reckless sunsets but doesn't absorb them into its blood: the one the rain washes – the eternal rain and the sensual earth – and yet that remains marvelously dry.

The glass that gathers and relinquishes forms: glass with a coastline, glass with the whole forest refracted through its gorgeousness, in the windows of the poor; glass of the goblets where the wine believes it is alone, rising straight up in the air like a miracle, in which the water thinks of itself as a brimless fountain. Glass that holds the lamp's flame and whose cheek doesn't burn. The glass, always as happy as the righteous, without stains of its own, without tears of its own, though burdened by others' tears, innocent as an Abel of the earth.

The glass without veins for blood or joints like wrists; the unanimous glass: the glass that doesn't thicken or endure anything superfluous: sufficient, like something perfect.

The glass, my soul's only envy.

The glass that helped water in its desire to remain, to lie in the hollow of the hand without treachery, to be loyal to the eye that watches and loved it, like a loyal woman: that gave the water a second body, one that doesn't escape like an arrow, crazed with its own modest restraint.

The glass of our windows, where night rests its hands like a great ivy, so that it can be seen and so that we don't completely forget it.

The glass of my desire: the glass that sits still in the midst of the ferment of creatures; that will never boil; that will never belong to anyone but itself.

The glass, fresh as a temple is always fresh, preserved from old age since its earliest day, with its enduring childhood, with no pretty growth and no ugly growth.

The glass discovered with joy, like a Christ, by men who have never since been able to find anything better than that discovery.

The glass that always emerges as something of a surprise, something unexpected, from the hands of the workers, who always feel a bit abashed that it comes out resembling the soul, as it leaves their black and knotted hands.

The workers who made glass all their lives arrived in heaven and found that it resembled what they had made on earth: a glass purified of distance, of large and small dimensions: in which God was so far away and so close that it frightened them. Without knowing it, they had been trapped in a glass reproduced with their faces, their shoulders, their feet, and they saw their second shoulders and their feet freed from corruption.

They still experience the shock of learning that they too were made of glass material as they moved through their workshop casting hard shadows against the walls. The glassworkers compensated with their hands, which went through the fire like the salamander straightening and calming the crucibles.

The metalworkers came to a violent copper heaven; they are happy in their violent joy. The woodworkers came to a heaven that smelled of maritime pines, a heaven echoless, still, and dry as old age. The glassworkers in their heaven watch the others: the copper heaven, the pine heaven, and the others too.

Gabriela Mistral (1933), translated from the Spanish
by Stephen Tapscott

from *The Orators*

Argument: I

Lo, I a skull show you, exuded from dyke when no pick was by pressure of bulbs: at Dalehead a light moving, lanterns for lambing. Before the forenoon of discussion, as the dawn-gust wrinkles the pools, I waken with an idea of building.

Speak the name only with meaning only for us, meaning Him, a call to our clearing. Secret the meeting in time and place, the time of the off-shore wind, the place where the loyalty is divided. Meeting of seven, each with a talent.

On the concrete banks of baths, in the grassy squares of exercise, we are joined, brave in the long body, under His eye. (Their annual games under the auspices of the dead.) Our bond, friend, is a third party.

Smile inwardly on their day handing round tea. (Their women have the faces of birds.) Walking in the mountains we were persons unknown to our parents, awarded them little, had a word of our own for our better shadow. Crossing ourselves under the arch of a bridge we crucified fear.

Crofter, leader of hay, working in sweat and weathers, tin-streamer, heckler, blow-room major, we are within a vein's distance of your prisoned blood. Stranger who cannot read our letters, you are remembered.

Rooks argue in the clump of elms to the left. Expect what dream above the indented heel, end-on to traffic, down the laurelled drive?

At the frontier getting down, at railhead drinking hot tea waiting for pack-mules, at the box with the three levers watching the swallows. Choosing of guides for the passage through gorges.

The young mother in the red kerchief suckling her child in the doorway, and the dog fleaing itself in the hot dust. Clatter of nails on the inn's flagged floor. The hare-lipped girl sent with as far as the second turning. Talk of generals in a panelled room translated into a bayonet thrust at a sunbrowned throat, wounds among wheat fields. Grit from the robbers' track on goggles, a present from aunts. Interrogation of villagers before a folding table, a verbal trap. Execution of a spy in the nettled patch at the back of the byre. A tale of sexual prowess told at a brazier and followed by a maternal song. The fatty smell of drying clothes, smell of cordite in a wood, and the new moon seen along the barrel of a gun. Establishment of a torpedo base at the head of the loch; where the bye-roads meet, a depot for tractors, with sliding doors. Visit to a tannery in the hill-village where the stream runs under the houses; to the mine with obsolete machinery, an undershot wheel, steam pipes in the open, swaddled in sacking. Designs for the flow sheet of a mill. Sound of our hammers in the solemn beat of a quarry, and the packing of labelled specimens in japanned boxes. Theories inter-relating the system of feudal tenure with metabolic gradients, and arguments from the other side of the lake on the formation of hanging valleys, interrupted by the daughter of the house with a broken doll. Writing reports for Him in the copper-green evenings. (Trunks caught by the grapnel dragged inert towards the spurting saw, ewers of warm milk, the sugary layer under the rind, and pipe-lines clamped to the rock) and at the tiny post-office, His word waiting.

If it were possible, yes, now certain. To meet Him alone on the narrow path, forcing a question, would show our unique knowledge. Would hide Him wounded in a cave, kneeling all night by His bed of bracken, bringing hourly an infusion of bitter herbs; wearing His cloak receive the mistaken stab, deliver His message, fall at His feet, He gripping our moribund hands, smiling. But never for us with notebooks there, a league of two or three waiting for low water to execute His will. The tripod shadow falls on the dunes. World of the Spider, not Him.

Rook shadows cross to the right. A schoolmaster cleanses himself at half-term with a vegetable offering; on the north side of the hill, one writes with his penis in a patch of snow 'Resurgam'.

Going abroad to-day? Under a creaking sign, one yellow leg drawn up, he crows, the cock. The dew-wet hare hangs smoking, garotted by gin. The emmet looks at sky through lenses of fallen water. Sound of horns in the moist spring weather, and the women tender. I feel sorry for you I do.

Girls, it is His will just now that we get up early. But watching the morning dredger, picking the afternoon fruit, wait; do not falsify our obedience. When we shuffle at night late round up-country stoves, although in waders, a dance of males, it is your hour; remember. It is your art just now against the inner life. Parting by hangars we are sorry but reborn.

Wrap gifts in clothes, prepare a present for a simpler nation. A heliograph seen from below, a camera with smuggled lenses: a soured drink for the tongue, a douche for the unpopular member, a dream dirt-cheap for the man of action. Leave the corks behind as warning of wires, let the shafts be fenced as before, leave ordinary kindness.

Going abroad to-night? The face lit up by the booking-clerk's window. Poetry of the waiting-room. Is it wise, the short adventure on the narrow ship? The boat-train dives accomplished for the hoop of the tunnel; over the derne cutting lingering, its white excreta. Too late: smelling the first sea-weed we may not linger. The waving handkerchiefs recede and the gulls wheel after screaming for scraps. Throb of turbines below water, passing the mud islands, the recurrent light. Past. Handrail, funnel, oilskins, them, His will. The lasting sky.

W. H. Auden (1932)

My Occupations

I can rarely see anyone without fighting him. Others prefer the internal monologue. Not me. I like fighting best.

There are people who sit down in front of me at the restaurant and say nothing, they stay on a while, for they have decided to eat.

Here is one of them.

See how I grab him, boom!

See how I re-grab him, boom!

I hang him on the coat hook.

I unhook him.

I hang him up again.

I re-unhook him.

I put him on the table, I push him together and choke him.

I foul him up, I flood him.

He revives.

I rinse him off, I stretch him out (I'm beginning to get worked up, I must finish off), I bunch him together, I squeeze him, I sum him up and introduce him into my glass, and ostentatiously throw the contents on the ground, and say to the waiter: 'Let me have a cleaner glass.'

But I feel ill, I pay the check quickly and go off.

Henri Michaux (1930), translated from the French
by Richard Ellmann

Force of Habit

The table is placed in the dining-room; the taps give out clear water, soft water, tepid water, scented water. The bed is as large for two as for one. After the bud will come the leaf and after the leaf the flower and after rain fine weather. Because it is time, the eyes open, the body stands up, the hand stretches out, the fire is lit, the smile contends with night's wrinkles for their unmalicious curve. And they are the clock's hands that open, that stand up, that stretch out, that set light to themselves and mark the hour of the smile. The sun's ray goes about the house in a white blouse. It's going to snow again, a few drops of blood are going to fall again at about five o'clock, but that'll be nothing. Oh! I was frightened, I suddenly thought there was no longer any street outside the window, but it is there just the same as ever. The chemist is even raising his metal shutters. There will soon be more people at the wheel than at the mill. Work is sharpened, hammered, thinned down, reckoned out. Once more the hand takes pleasure in finding the security of sleep in the familiar implement.

Provided that it lasts!

The mirror is a marvellous witness, changing all the time. It gives evidence calmly and with power, but when it has finished speaking you can see that it has been caught out again over everything. It is the current personification of verity.

On the hairpin-bend road obstinately tied to the legs of him who assesses today as he will assess tomorrow, on the light bearings of carelessness, a thousand steps each day espouse the steps of the vigil. They have come already and they will come again without being invited. Each one has passed that way, going from his joy to his sorrow. It is a little refuge with an enormous gas-jet. You put one foot in front of the other and then you are gone.

The walls cover themselves with pictures, the holidays sift themselves with bouquets, the mirror covers itself with vapour. As many light-houses on a stream and the stream is in the vessel of the river. Two eyes the same, for the use of your single face – two eyes covered with the same ants. Green is almost uniformly spread over the plants, the wind follows the birds, no one risks seeing the stones die. The result is not a broken-in animal but an animal trainer. Bah! It is the indefeasible order of a ceremony already, on the whole, so very gorgeous! It is the repeating pistol which makes flowers appear in vases and smoke in the mouth.

Love, in the end, is well satisfied with seeing night clearly.

When you are no longer there, your perfume is there to search for me. I only come to get back the oracle of your weakness. My hand in your hand is so little like your hand in mine. Unhappiness, you see, unhappiness itself profits from being known. I let you share my lot, you cannot not be there, you are the proof that I exist. And everything conforms with that life which I have made to assure myself of you.

What are you thinking about?

Nothing.

André Breton and Paul Eluard (1930),
translated from the French by David Gascoyne

Sunflowers Are Already Black Gunpowder

Grass seed floated in this evening's soup. One thousand islands. The great majority of marksmen, for some unknown reason, have long, unkempt moustaches. On thinking about that it must provide 'some form of resistance.' (Smiles.)

Try writing 'we' a number of times and it looks like children skipping. WeWeWeWeWeWeWe.

She (she being a domestic pet) has gentle creases in the corners of her eyes like Chekhov. Instead of a ribbon I shall give her a bone.

An autumn butterfly has settled on the towel I put inside the glass.

– Sunflowers are already black gunpowder.

Anzai Fuye (1929), translated from the Japanese
by Dennis Keene

The Dog's Retort

I dreamed I was walking in a narrow lane, my clothes in rags, like a beggar.

A dog started barking behind me.

I looked back contemptuously and shouted at him:

'Bah! Shut up! Lick-spittle cur!'

He sniggered.

'Oh no!' he said. 'I'm not up to man in that respect.'

'What!' Quite outraged, I felt that this was the supreme insult.

'I'm ashamed to say I still don't know how to distinguish between copper and silver, between silk and cloth, between officials and common citizens, between masters and their slaves, between . . .'

I turned and fled.

'Wait a bit! Let us talk some more . . .' From behind he urged me loudly to stay.

But I ran straight on as fast as I could, until I had run right out of my dream and was back in my own bed.

April 23, 1925

Lu Xun (1927), translated from the Chinese
by Yang Xianyi and Gladys Yang

Snow

The rain of the south has never congealed into icy, glittering snowflakes. Men who have seen the world consider this humdrum; does the rain, too, think it unfortunate? The snow south of the Yangtze is extremely moist and pretty, like the first indefinable intimation of spring, or the bloom of a young girl radiant with health. In the snowy wilderness are blood-red camellias, pale, white plum blossom tinged with green, and the golden, bell-shaped flowers of the winter plum; while beneath the snow lurk cold green weeds. Butterflies there are certainly none, and whether or no bees come to gather honey from the camellias and plum blossom I cannot clearly remember. But before my eyes I can see the wintry flowers in the snowy wilderness, with bees flying busily to and fro – I can hear their humming and droning.

Seven or eight children, who have gathered to build a snow Buddha, are breathing on their little red fingers, frozen like crimson shoots of ginger. When they are not successful, somebody's father comes to help. The Buddha is higher than the children; and though it is only a pear-shaped mass which might be a gourd or might be a Buddha, it is beautifully white and dazzling. Held together by its own moisture, the whole figure glitters and sparkles. The children use fruit stones for its eyes, and steal rouge from some mother's vanity-case for its lips. So now it is really a respectable Buddha. With gleaming eyes and scarlet lips, it sits on the snowy ground.

Some children come to visit it the next day. Clapping their hands before it, they nod their heads and laugh. The Buddha just sits there alone. A fine day melts its skin, but a cold night gives it another coat of ice, till it looks like opaque crystal. Then a series of fine days makes it unrecognisable, and the rouge on its lips disappears.

But the snowflakes that fall in the north remain to the last like powder or sand and never bond together, whether scattered on roofs, the ground or the withered grass. The warmth from the stoves inside has melted some of the snow on the roofs. As for the rest, when a whirlwind springs up under a clear sky, it flies up wildly, glittering in the sunlight like thick mist around a flame, revolving and rising till it fills the sky, and the whole sky glitters as it whirls and rises.

On the boundless wilderness, under heaven's chilly vault, this glittering, spiralling wraith is the ghost of rain . . .

Yes, it is lonely snow, dead rain, the ghost of rain.

January 18, 1925

Lu Xun (1927), translated from the Chinese by
Yang Xianyi and Gladys Yang

Song

Under the bronze leaves a colt was foaled. Came such an one
who laid bitter fruit in our hands. Stranger. Who passed. Here
comes news of other provinces to my liking. – 'Hail, daughter!
under the tallest tree of the year.'

        ★   ★   ★

For the Sun enters the sign of the Lion and the Stranger has laid
his finger on the mouth of the Dead. Stranger. Who laughed.
And tells us of an herb. O from the provinces blow many winds.
What ease to our way! how the trumpet rejoices my heart and
the feather revels in the scandal of the wing! 'My Soul, great
girl, you had your ways which are not ours.'

        ★   ★   ★

Under the bronze leaves a colt had been foaled. Came such an
one who laid this bitter fruit in our hands. Stranger. Who
passed. Out of the bronze tree comes a great bruit of voices.
Roses and bitumen, gift of song, thunder and fluting in the
rooms. O what ease in our ways, how many tales to the year,
and by the roads of all the earth the Stranger to his ways . . .
'Hail, daughter! robed in the loveliest robe of the year.'

St-John Perse (1924), translated from the French
by T. S. Eliot

Hell Is Graduated

When I was employed at Cooperative Fashions, in spite of the dark, ugly old maid, I tried to steal some garters. I was pursued down the superb staircases, not for the theft, but for my laziness at work and for my hatred of the innocent finery. Descend, you are pursued. The staircases are less beautiful in the offices than in the part open to the public. The staircases are less beautiful in the 'service' quarters than in the offices. The staircases are still less beautiful in the cellar! But what can I say of the marsh where I arrived? What can I say of the laughter? Of the animals that brushed by me, and of the whisperings of unseen creatures? Water gave place to fire, to fear, to unconsciousness; when I came to myself I was in the hands of silent and nameless surgeons.

Max Jacob (1924), translated from the French
by Elizabeth Bishop

A Day

That afternoon comes back to my mind. From time to time the downpour grows feeble; then, suddenly, a gust of wind whips it to fury.

The room has darkened and I have no mind for work. I take in my hand the *setar* and play on it a melody of the rains.

From the next room she comes to the doorway and retires again. Then she enters silently and sits down. In her hand she has a piece of needlework – with bowed head she begins to sew. After a while she ceases and, through the window, looks out into the trees shrouded in mist.

The rain has stopped and my playing has ended. She rises and retires to do her hair.

Nothing has happened; just that one afternoon made up of rain and music, darkness and indolence.

History is littered with tales of emperors, accounts of wars and revolutions. But the tiny incident of one afternoon remains hidden like a rare jewel in the casket of Time. Only two people have heard it.

Rabindranath Tagore (1921), translated from the Bengali
by Aurobindo Bose

from *Kora in Hell: Improvisations*

I

Why go further? One might conceivably rectify the rhythm, study all out and arrive at the perfection of a tiger lily or a china doorknob. One might lift all out of the ruck, be a worthy successor to – the man in the moon. Instead of breaking the back of a willing phrase why not try to follow the wheel through – approach death at a walk, take in all the scenery. There's as much reason one way as the other and then – one never knows – perhaps we'll bring back Eurydice – this time!

Between two contending forces there may at all times arrive that moment when the stress is equal on both sides so that with a great pushing a great stability results giving a picture of perfect rest. And so it may be that once upon the way the end drives back upon the beginning and a stoppage will occur. At such a time the poet shrinks from the doom that is calling him forgetting the delicate rhythms of perfect beauty, preferring in his mind the gross buffetings of good and evil fortune.

2

Ay dio! I could say so much were it not for the tunes changing, changing, darting so many ways. One step and the cart's left you sprawling. Here's the way! and you're – hip bogged. And there's blame of the light too: when eyes are humming birds who'll tie them with a lead string? But it's the tunes they want most, – send them skipping out at the tree tops. Whistle then! Who'd stop the leaves swarming; curving down the east in their braided jackets? Well enough – but there's small comfort in naked branches when the heart's not set that way.

_____

A man's desire is to win his way to some hilltop. But against him seem to swarm a hundred jumping devils. These are his constant companions, these are the friendly images which he has invented out of his mind and which are inviting him to rest and to disport himself according to hidden reasons. The man being half a poet is cast down and longs to rid himself of his torment and his tormentors.

3

When you hang your clothes on the line you do not expect to see the line broken and them trailing in the mud. Nor would you expect to keep your hands clean by putting them in a dirty pocket. However and of course if you are a market man, fish, cheeses and the like going under your fingers every minute in the hour you would not leave off the business and expect to handle a basket of fine laces without at least mopping yourself on a towel, soiled as it may be. Then how will you expect a fine trickle of words to follow you through the intimacies of this dance without – oh, come let us walk together into the air awhile first. One must be watchman to much secret arrogance before his ways are tuned to these measures. You see there is a dip of the ground between us. You think you can leap up from your gross caresses of these creatures and at a gesture fling it all off and step out in silver to my finger tips. Ah, it is not that I do not wait for you, always! But my sweet fellow – you have broken yourself without purpose, you are – Hark! it is the music! Whence does it come? What! Out of the ground? Is it this that you have been preparing for me? Ha, goodbye, I have a rendezvous in the tips of three birch sisters. *Encouragez vos musiciens!* Ask them to play faster. I will return – later. Ah you are kind – and I? must dance with the wind, make my own snowflakes, whistle a contrapuntal melody to my own fugue! Huzza then, this is the dance of the blue moss bank! Huzza then, this is the mazurka of the hollow log! Huzza then, this is the dance of rain in the cold trees.

William Carlos Williams (1920)

Tired

I am tired of work; I am tired of building up somebody else's
civilization.

Let us take a rest, M'Lissy Jane.

I will go down to the Last Chance Saloon, drink a gallon or two
of gin, shoot a game or two of dice and sleep the rest of
the night on one of Mike's barrels.

You will let the old shanty go to rot, the white people's clothes
turn to dust, and the Calvary Baptist Church sink to the
bottomless pit.

You will spend your days forgetting you married me and your
nights hunting the warm gin Mike serves the ladies in the
rear of the Last Chance Saloon.

Throw the children into the river; civilization has given us too
many. It is better to die than it is to grow up and find out
that you are colored.

Pluck the stars out of the heavens. The stars mark our destiny.
    The stars marked my destiny.

I am tired of civilization.

Fenton Johnson (1919)

Pulmonary Tuberculosis

The man in the room next to mine has the same complaint as I. When I wake in the night I hear him turning. And then he coughs. And I cough. And after a silence I cough. And he coughs again. This goes on for a long time. Until I feel we are like two roosters calling to each other at false dawn. From far-away hidden farms.

Katherine Mansfield (1918)

Hysteria

As she laughed I was aware of becoming involved in her laughter and being part of it, until her teeth were only accidental stars with a talent for squad-drill. I was drawn in by short gasps, inhaled at each momentary recovery, lost finally in the dark caverns of her throat, bruised by the ripple of unseen muscles. An elderly waiter with trembling hands was hurriedly spreading a pink and white checked cloth over the rusty green iron table, saying: 'If the lady and gentleman wish to take their tea in the garden, if the lady and gentleman wish to take their tea in the garden . . .' I decided that if the shaking of her breasts could be stopped, some of the fragments of the afternoon might be collected, and I concentrated my attention with careful subtlety to this end.

T. S. Eliot (1917)

Spring Day

Bath

The day is fresh-washed and fair, and there is a smell of tulips and narcissus in the air.

The sunshine pours in at the bath-room window and bores through the water in the bath-tub in lathes and planes of greenish-white. It cleaves the water into flaws like a jewel, and cracks it to bright light.

Little spots of sunshine lie on the surface of the water and dance, dance, and their reflections wobble deliciously over the ceiling; a stir of my finger sets them whirring, reeling. I move a foot, and the planes of light in the water jar. I lie back and laugh, and let the green-white water, the sun-flawed beryl water, flow over me. The day is almost too bright to bear, the green water covers me from the too bright day. I will lie here awhile and play with the water and the sun spots.

The sky is blue and high. A crow flaps by the window, and there is a whiff of tulips and narcissus in the air.

Breakfast Table

In the fresh-washed sunlight, the breakfast table is decked and white. It offers itself in flat surrender, tendering tastes, and smells, and colours, and metals, and grains, and the white cloth falls over its side, draped and wide. Wheels of white glitter in the silver coffee-pot, hot and spinning like catherine-wheels, they whirl, and twirl – and my eyes begin to smart, the little white, dazzling wheels prick them like darts. Placid and peaceful, the rolls of bread spread themselves in the sun to bask. A stack of butter-pats, pyramidal, shout orange through the white, scream, flutter, call: 'Yellow! Yellow! Yellow!' Coffee steam rises in a stream, clouds the silver tea-service with mist, and twists up into the sunlight, revolved, involuted, suspiring higher and higher, fluting in a thin spiral up the high blue sky. A crow flies by and croaks at the coffee steam. The day is new and fair with good smells in the air.

Walk

Over the street the white clouds meet, and sheer away without touching.

On the sidewalks, boys are playing marbles. Glass marbles, with amber and blue hearts, roll together and part with a sweet clashing noise. The boys strike them with black and red striped agates. The glass marbles spit crimson when they are hit, and slip into the gutters under rushing brown water. I smell tulips and narcissus in the air, but there are no flowers anywhere, only white dust whipping up the street, and a girl with a gay Spring hat and blowing skirts. The dust and the wind flirt at her ankles and her neat, high-heeled patent leather shoes. Tap, tap, the little heels pat the pavement, and the wind rustles among the flowers on her hat.

A water-cart crawls slowly on the other side of the way. It is green and gay with new paint, and rumbles contentedly, sprinkling clear water over the white dust. Clear zigzagging water, which smells of tulips and narcissus.

The thickening branches make a pink *grisaille* against the blue sky.

Whoop! The clouds go dashing at each other and sheer away just in time. Whoop! And a man's hat careers down the street in front of the white dust, leaps into the branches of a tree, veers away and trundles ahead of the wind, jarring the sunlight into spokes of rose-colour and green.

A motor-car cuts a swathe through the bright air, sharp-beaked, irresistible, shouting to the wind to make way. A glare of dust and sunshine tosses together behind it, and settles down. The sky is quiet and high, and the morning is fair with fresh-washed air.

Midday and Afternoon

Swirl of crowded streets. Shock and recoil of traffic. The stock-still brick façade of an old church, against which the waves of people lurch and withdraw. Flare of sunshine down side-streets. Eddies of light in the windows of chemists' shops, with their blue, gold, purple jars, darting colours far into the crowd. Loud bangs and tremors, murmurings out of high windows, whirring of machine belts, blurring of horses and motors. A quick spin and shudder of brakes on an electric car, and the jar of a church-bell knocking against the metal blue of the sky. I am a piece of the town, a bit of blown dust, thrust along with the crowd. Proud to feel the pavement under me, reeling with feet. Feet tripping, skipping, lagging, dragging, plodding doggedly, or springing up and advancing on firm elastic insteps. A boy is selling papers, I smell them clean and new from the press. They are fresh like the air, and pungent as tulips and narcissus.

The blue sky pales to lemon, and great tongues of gold blind the shop-windows, putting out their contents in a flood of flame.

Night and Sleep

The day takes her ease in slippered yellow. Electric signs gleam out along the shop fronts, following each other. They grow, and grow, and blow into patterns of fire-flowers as the sky fades. Trades scream in spots of light at the unruffled night. Twinkle, jab, snap, that means a new play; and over the way: plop, drop, quiver, is the sidelong sliver of a watchmaker's sign with its length on another street. A gigantic mug of beer effervesces to the atmosphere over a tall building, but the sky is high and has her own stars, why should she heed ours?

I leave the city with speed. Wheels whirl to take me back to my trees and my quietness. The breeze which blows with me is fresh-washed and clean, it has come but recently from the high sky. There are no flowers in bloom yet, but the earth of my garden smells of tulips and narcissus.

My room is tranquil and friendly. Out of the window I can see the distant city, a band of twinkling gems, little flower-heads with no stems. I cannot see the beer-glass, nor the letters of the restaurants and shops I passed, now the signs blur and all together make the city, glowing on a night of fine weather, like a garden stirring and blowing for the Spring.

The night is fresh-washed and fair and there is a whiff of flowers in the air.

Wrap me close, sheets of lavender. Pour your blue and purple dreams into my ears. The breeze whispers at the shutters and mutters queer tales of old days, and cobbled streets, and youths leaping their horses down marble stairways. Pale blue lavender, you are the colour of the sky when it is fresh-washed and fair . . . I smell the stars . . . they are like tulips and narcissus . . . I smell them in the air.

Amy Lowell (1916)

The Moon

New York, April 23
To Alfonso Reyes

Broadway. Evening. Signs in the sky that make one dizzy with color. New constellations: The Pig, all green, dancing and waving greetings to the left and right with his straw hat, the Bottle which pops its ruddy cork with a muted detonation against a sun with eyes and a mouth, the Electric Stocking which dances madly by itself like a tail separated from a salamander, the Scotchman who displays and pours his whiskey with its white reflections, the Fountain of mallow-pink and orange water through whose shower, like a snake, pass hills and valleys of wavering sun and shade, links of gold and iron (that braid a shower of light and another darkness . . .), the Book which illuminates and extinguishes the successive imbecilities of its owner, the Ship which every moment, as it lights up, sails pitching toward its prison, to run aground immediately in the darkness . . . and . . .

The moon! Let's see! Look at it between those two tall buildings over there, above the river, over the red octave beneath, don't you see it? Wait, let's see! No . . . is it the moon or just an advertisement of the moon?

Juan Ramón Jiménez (1916), translated from the Spanish
by H. R. Hays

London Notes

In Park Lane

Long necked feminine structures support almost without grimacing the elegant discomfort of restricted elbows.

Hyde Park

Commonplace, titanic figures with a splendid motion stride across the parched plateau of grass, little London houses only a foot high huddle at their heels.

Under trees all the morning women sit sewing and knitting, their monotonous occupation accompanying the agreeable muddle of their thoughts.

In the Row. Vitality civilized to a needle's-point; highly-bred men and horses pass swiftly in useless delightful motion; women walk enamoured of their own accomplished movements.

British Museum

Gigantic cubes of iron rock are set in a parallelogram of orange sand.

Ranks of black columns of immense weight and immobility are threaded by a stream of angular volatile shapes. Their trunks shrink quickly in retreat towards the cavernous roof.

Innumerable pigeons fret the stone steps with delicate restlessness.

Egyptian Gallery

In a rectangular channel of space light drops in oblique layers upon rows of polished cubes sustaining gods and fragments.

Monstrous human heads without backs protrude lips satisfied with the taste of pride.

Seductive goddesses, cat-faced and maiden-breasted sit eternally stroking smooth knees.

Reading-Room

This colossal globe of achievement presses upon two hundred cosmopolitan foreheads, respectfully inclined.

Piccadilly

The embankment of brick and stone is fancifully devised and stuck with flowers and flags.

Towers of scaffolding draw their criss-cross pattern of bars upon the sky, a monstrous tartan.

Delicate fingers of cranes describe beneficent motions in space.

Glazed cases contain curious human specimens.

Nature with a brush of green pigment paints rural landscape up to the edge of the frame.

Pseudo-romantic hollows and hillocks are peopled by reality prostrate and hostile.

Fleet Street

Precious slips of houses, packed like books on a shelf, are littered all over with signs and letters.

A dark, agitated stream straggles turbulently along the channel bottom; clouds race overhead.

Curiously exciting are so many perspective lines, withdrawing, converging; they indicate evidently something of importance beyond the limits of sight.

Jessie Dismorr (1915)

Street Circus

In the middle of that crowd there is a child who is dancing, a man lifting weights. His arms with blue tattoos call on the sky to witness their useless strength.

The child dances, lightly, in tights too big for him, lighter than the balls he's balancing himself on. And when he passes the hat, no one gives anything. No one gives for fear of making it too heavy. He is so thin.

Pierre Reverdy (1915), translated from the French
by Ron Padgett

from *Tender Buttons*

A Carafe, That Is a Blind Glass.

A kind in glass and a cousin, a spectacle and nothing strange a single hurt color and an arrangement in a system to pointing. All this and not ordinary, not unordered in not resembling. The difference is spreading.

Dirt and Not Copper.

Dirt and not copper makes a color darker. It makes the shape so heavy and makes no melody harder. It makes mercy and relaxation and even a strength to spread a table fuller. There are more places not empty. They see cover.

A New Cup and Saucer.

Enthusiastically hurting a clouded yellow bud and saucer, enthusiastically so is the bite in the ribbon.

A Little Bit of a Tumbler.

A shining indication of yellow consists in there having been more of the same color than could have been expected when all four were bought. This was the hope which made the six and seven have no use for any more places and this necessarily spread into nothing. Spread into nothing.

Red Roses.

A cool red rose and a pink cut pink, a collapse and a sold hole, a little less hot.

In Between.

In between a place and candy is a narrow foot-path that shows more mounting than anything, so much really that a calling meaning a bolster measured a whole thing with that. A virgin a whole virgin is judged made and so between curves and out-lines and real seasons and more out glasses and a perfectly unprecedented arrangement between old ladies and mild colds there is no satin wood shining.

A Sound.

Elephant beaten with candy and little pops and chews all bolts and reckless reckless rats, this is this.

Roastbeef.

In the inside there is sleeping, in the outside there is reddening, in the morning there is meaning, in the evening there is feeling. In the evening there is feeling. In feeling anything is resting, in feeling anything is mounting, in feeling there is resignation, in feeling there is recognition, in feeling there is recurrence and entirely mistaken there is pinching. All the standards have steamers and all the curtains have bed linen and all the yellow has discrimination and all the circle has circling. This makes sand.

Very well. Certainly the length is thinner and the rest, the round rest has a longer summer. To shine, why not shine, to shine, to station, to enlarge, to hurry the measure all this means nothing if there is singing, if there is singing then there is the resumption.

The change the dirt, not to change dirt means that there is no beefsteak and not to have that is no obstruction, it is so easy to exchange meaning, it is so easy to see the difference. The difference is that a plain resource is not entangled with thickness and it does not mean that thickness shows such cutting, it does mean that a meadow is useful and a cow absurd. It does not mean that there are tears, it does not mean that exudation is cumbersome, it means no more than a memory, a choice and a reestablishment, it means more than any escape from a surrounding extra. All the time that there is use there is use and any time there is a surface there is a surface, and every time there is an exception there is an exception and every time there is a division there is a dividing. Any time there is a surface there is a surface and every time there is a suggestion there is a suggestion and every time there is silence there is silence and every time that is languid there is that there then and not oftener, not always, not particular, tender and changing and external and central and surrounded and singular and simple and the same and the surface and the circle and the shine and the succor and the white and the same and the better and the red and the same and the centre and the yellow and the tender and the better, and altogether.

Considering the circumstances there is no occasion for a reduction, considering that there is no pealing there is no occasion for an obligation, considering that there is no outrage there is no necessity for any reparation, considering that there is no particle sodden there is no occasion for deliberation. Considering everything and which way the turn is tending, considering everything why is there no restraint, considering everything what makes the place settle and the plate distinguish some specialties. The whole thing is not understood and this is not strange considering that there is no education, this is not strange because having that certainly does show the difference in cutting, it shows that when there is turning there is no distress.

In kind, in a control, in a period, in the alteration of pigeons, in kind cuts and thick and thin spaces, in kind ham and different colors, the length of leaning a strong thing outside not to make a sound but to suggest a crust, the principal taste is when there is a whole chance to be reasonable, this does not mean that there is overtaking, this means nothing precious, this means clearly that the chance to exercise is a social success. So then the sound is not obtrusive. Suppose it is obtrusive, suppose it is. What is certainly the desertion is not a reduced description, a description is not a birthday.

Lovely snipe and tender turn, excellent vapor and slender butter, all the splinter and the trunk, all the poisonous darkning drunk, all the joy in weak success, all the joyful tenderness, all the section and the tea, all the stouter symmetry.

Around the size that is small, inside the stern that is the middle, besides the remains that are praying, inside the between that is turning, all the region is measuring and melting is exaggerating.

Rectangular ribbon does not mean that there is no eruption it means that if there is no place to hold there is no place to spread. Kindness is not earnest, it is not assiduous it is not revered.

Room to comb chickens and feathers and ripe purple, room to curve single plates and large sets and second silver, room to send everything away, room to save heat and distemper, room to search a light that is simpler, all room has no shadow.

There is no use there is no use at all in smell, in taste, in teeth, in toast, in anything, there is no use at all and the respect is mutual.

Why should that which is uneven, that which is resumed, that which is tolerable why should all this resemble a smell, a thing is there, it whistles, it is not narrower, why is there no obligation to stay away and yet courage, courage is everywhere and the best remains to stay.

If there could be that which is contained in that which is felt there would be a chair where there are chairs and there would be no more denial about a clatter. A clatter is not a smell. All this is good.

The Saturday evening which is Sunday is every week day. What choice is there when there is a difference. A regulation is not active. Thirstiness is not equal division.

Anyway, to be older and ageder is not a surfeit nor a suction, it is not dated and careful, it is not dirty. Any little thing is clean, rubbing is black. Why should ancient lambs be goats and young colts and never beef, why should they, they should because there is so much difference in age.

A sound, a whole sound is not separation, a whole sound is in an order.

Suppose there is a pigeon, suppose there is.

Looseness, why is there a shadow in a kitchen, there is a shadow in a kitchen because every little thing is bigger.

The time when there are four choices and there are four choices in a difference, the time when there are four choices there is a kind and there is a kind. There is a kind. There is a kind. Supposing there is a bone, there is a bone. Supposing there are bones. There are bones. When there are bones there is no supposing there are bones. There are bones and there is that consuming. The kindly way to feel separating is to have a space between. This shows a likeness.

Hope in gates, hope in spoons, hope in doors, hope in tables, no hope in daintiness and determination. Hope in dates.

Tin is not a can and a stove is hardly. Tin is not necessary and neither is a stretcher. Tin is never narrow and thick.

Color is in coal. Coal is outlasting roasting and a spoonful, a whole spoon that is full is not spilling. Coal any coal is copper.

Claiming nothing, not claiming anything, not a claim in everything, collecting claiming, all this makes a harmony, it even makes a succession.

Sincerely gracious one morning, sincerely graciously trembling, sincere in gracious eloping, all this makes a furnace and a blanket. All this shows quantity.

Like an eye, not so much more, not any searching, no compliments.

Please be the beef, please beef, pleasure is not wailing. Please beef, please be carved clear, please be a case of consideration.

Search a neglect. A sale, any greatness is a stall and there is no memory, there is no clear collection.

A satin sight, what is a trick, no trick is mountainous and the color, all the rush is in the blood.

Bargaining for a little, bargain for a touch, a liberty, an estrangement, a characteristic turkey.

Please spice, please no name, place a whole weight, sink into a standard rising, raise a circle, choose a right around, make the resonance accounted and gather green any collar.

To bury a slender chicken, to raise an old feather, to surround a garland and to bake a pole splinter, to suggest a repose and to settle simply, to surrender one another, to succeed saving simpler, to satisfy a singularity and not to be blinder, to sugar nothing darker and to read redder, to have the color better, to sort out dinner, to remain together, to surprise no sinner, to curve nothing sweeter, to continue thinner, to increase in resting recreation to design string not dimmer.

Cloudiness what is cloudiness, is it a lining, is it a roll, is it melting.

The sooner there is jerking, the sooner freshness is tender, the sooner the round it is not round the sooner it is withdrawn in cutting, the sooner the measure means service, the sooner there is chinking, the sooner there is sadder than salad, the sooner there is none do her, the sooner there is no choice, the sooner there is a gloom freer, the same sooner and more sooner, this is no error in hurry and in pressure and in opposition to consideration.

A recital, what is a recital, it is an organ and use does not strengthen valor, it soothes medicine.

A transfer, a large transfer, a little transfer, some transfer, clouds and tracks do transfer, a transfer is not neglected.

Pride, when is there perfect pretence, there is no more than yesterday and ordinary.

A sentence of a vagueness that is violence is authority and a mission and stumbling and also certainly also a prison. Calmness, calm is beside the plate and in way in. There is no turn in terror. There is no volume in sound.

There is coagulation in cold and there is none in prudence. Something is preserved and the evening is long and the colder spring has sudden shadows in a sun. All the stain is tender and lilacs really lilacs are disturbed. Why is the perfect reestablishment practiced and prized, why is it composed. The result the pure result is juice and size and baking and exhibition and nonchalance and sacrifice and volume and a section in division and the surrounding recognition and horticulture and no murmur. This is a result. There is no superposition and circumstance, there is hardness and a reason and the rest and remainder. There is no delight and no mathematics.

Custard.

Custard is this. It has aches, aches when. Not to be. Not to be narrowly. This makes a whole little hill.

It is better than a little thing that has mellow real mellow. It is better than lakes whole lakes, it is better than seeding.

Potatoes.

Real potatoes cut in between.

Potatoes.

In the preparation of cheese, in the preparation of crackers, in the preparation of butter, in it.

Roast Potatoes.

Roast potatoes for.

Gertrude Stein (1914)

Winter Night

It has been snowing. Past midnight, drunk on purple wine, you leave the gloomy shelters of men, and the red fire of their fireplaces. Oh the darkness of night.

Black frost. The ground is hard, the air has a bitter taste. Your stars make unlucky figures.

With a stiff walk, you tramp along the railroad embankment with huge eyes, like a soldier charging a dark machinegun nest. Onward!

Bitter snow and moon.

A red wolf, that an angel is strangling. Your trouser legs rustle, as you walk, like blue ice, and a smile full of suffering and pride petrifies your face, and your forehead is white before the ripe desire of the frost;

or else it bends down silently over the doze of the night watch-man, slumped down in his wooden shack.

Frost and smoke. A white shirt of stars burns on your clothed shoulders, and the hawk of God strips flesh out of your hard heart.

Oh the stony hill. The cool body, forgotten and silent, is melting away in the silver snow.

Sleep is black. For a long time the ear follows the motion of the stars deep down in the ice.

When you woke, the churchbells were ringing in the town. Out of the door in the east the rose-colored day walked with silver light.

Georg Trakl (1914), translated from the German
by James Wright

from *Scented Leaves – from a Chinese Jar*

The Bitter Purple Willows

Meditating on the glory of illustrious lineage I lifted up my eyes and beheld the bitter purple willows growing round the tombs of the exalted Mings.

The Marigold

Even as the seed of the marigold, carried by the wind, lodges on the roofs of palaces, and lights the air with flame-coloured blossoms, so may the child-like words of the insignificant poet confer honour on lofty and disdainful mandarins.

The Milky Way

My mother taught me that every night a procession of junks carrying lanterns moves silently across the sky, and the water sprinkled from their paddles falls to the earth in the form of dew. I no longer believe that the stars are junks carrying lanterns, no longer that the dew is shaken from their oars.

Allen Upward (1913)

Menagerie

to Vyacheslav Ivanov

Zoo! Zoo!

Where the iron of the cages is like a father, reminding brothers that they are brothers, and stopping their bloody skirmish.

Where Germans come to drink beer.

And pretty ladies sell their bodies.

Where eagles sit like centuries, defined by a present day that still hasn't reached its evening.

Where the camel, whose high hump is denied a rider, knows the mystery of Buddhism and has concealed the smirk of China.

Where a deer is nothing but terror, flowering like a wide stone.

Where the people's costumes are terribly fancy.

Where people go about frowning and trying to be clever.

And Germans blossom with health.

Where the black gaze of the swan, who exactly resembles winter but whose yellow-black beak is a little grove in autumn, is slightly guarded and mistrustful even for the swan itself.

Where the dark-blue pretty peacock, pretteacock, drops a tail that is like Siberia seen from the rock of Pavda, when over the gold leaves and the green forest is thrown a blue net of clouds, and all this takes on various shades from the soil's unevenness.

Where you feel the desire to pull out the Australian lyre-birds' tail-feathers and pluck them like guitar strings and sing of Russian exploits.

Where we clench our fists as if holding a sword and whisper an oath: to keep the Russian species separate, at the price of life, at the price of death, at any price.

Where the monkeys get angry in different ways and show off their various extremities and are always annoyed at the presence of people, apart from the sad ones and the mild ones.

Where the elephants, twisting like mountains twist in an earthquake, beg children for food, adding their ancient meaning to the more general truth: 'I wanna eat! Gimme something to eat!' – and then they slump to the ground as if to beg for mercy.

Where the agile bears climb up and look down, and wait for
their keeper's command.

Where the pipistrelles hang overturned, like the heart of a
modern Russian.

Where the falcon's breast reminds us of the feathery clouds
before a storm.

Where the low-slung pheasant drags a golden sunset after
itself, and all the coals of its fire.

Where in the tiger's face, framed by a white beard and with the
eyes of an elderly Muslim, we honour the Prophet's first
follower and read the essence of Islam.

Where we start to think that faiths are the retreating waves
whose advance is the various species.

And that there are so many beasts on the earth because they
see God in different ways.

Where the beasts, tired of roaring, stand up and look at the sky.

Where the torments of sinners are vividly recalled in the seal,
howling as it drags itself round its cage.

Where the ridiculous fish-wing penguins care for each other
with the tenderness of Gogol's Old World landowners.

Zoo, Zoo, where the gaze of a beast means more than books
learned by heart.

Zoo.

Where the eagle complains about something, complaining like
a tired child.

Where the husky kicks up the Siberian dust, completing the
ancient ritual of enmity under the gaze of a cat that is
licking itself clean.

Where the goats beg by sticking their cloven hooves through
the wires, and wave them, their eyes taking on a self-
satisfied or happy expression once they've got what they
wanted.

Where a too-tall giraffe stands and stares.

Where the noon cannon makes the eagles stare up at the sky in
expectation of a storm.

Where the eagles fall from their tall perches like idols during
an earthquake from the roofs of temples and houses.

Where one eagle, tousled as a little girl, looks up at the sky and
then down at its foot.

Where we see a wooden totem in the face of the motionless
stag.

Where an eagle sits with its back to the people and looks at the
wall, holding its wings strangely wide. Does it think that
it is hovering high over the mountains? Or is it praying?
Or is it too hot?

Where an elk kisses the smooth-horned buffalo through a
fence.

Where the deer lick the cold iron.

Where a black seal slides along the floor leaning on its long
flippers, with the movements of a man tied up in a sack,
like a cast-iron monument caught by a fit of the giggles.

Where the lion, shaggy-haired 'Vyacheslav Ivanov', rushes
around and beats its paw angrily against the iron when-
ever the keeper calls it 'comrade'.

Where all the lions dream with their faces against their paws.

Where the deer unwearyingly knock against the wire with
their horns and beat it with their heads.

Where all the ducks of one particular species in their dry cage
cry out in unison after a brief shower of rain, as if offering
a prayer – does it have feet and a beak? – a prayer of thanks
to their deity.

Where the guineafowl are sometimes loud gentlewomen with
naked stripped necks and an ashy-silver body made to
measure by the same tailor who caters to the night sky.

Where I refuse to recognize a fellow northerner in the honey
bear and instead discover the Mongol hidden within him,
and want to take revenge on him for Port Arthur.

Where the wolves show compliance and devotion in their
twisted attentive eyes.

Where, as I enter their stuffy house where it is difficult to stay
for long, I am showered with a unanimous cry of
'prrrrick!' and the husks of seeds by the idle parrots, who
chatter fluently.

Where the fat and shining walrus waves its black slippery fan-
shaped foot like a tired coquette and then falls into the
water, and when it drags itself up onto the ramp once
more, its powerful greasy body is topped by the mous-
tachioed spiny head and smooth brow of Nietzsche.

Where the jaws of the white, tall, black-eyed llama and that of
the smooth, short buffalo, and those of all other rum-
inants move evenly to the right and to the left, just like
the life of the country.

Where the rhinoceros holds in his red-white eyes the unquench-
able fury of a deposed tsar and alone of all the beasts does
not hide his contempt for mankind, like contempt for a
slave rebellion. He conceals Ivan the Terrible within
himself.

Where the gulls with their long beaks and their cold ice-blue
eyes that seem to exist inside round spectacles look like
international businessmen, something we find confirmed
in the innate skill with which they steal on the wing the
food that is meant for the seals.

Where, remembering that Russians used to call their great
chieftains 'falcon', and remembering also that the eye of
the Cossack, sunk deep beneath a brooding brow, and of
this bird – the race of royal birds – are identical, we begin
to know who it was who taught the Russians the art of

war. O hawks, piercing the breasts of herons! And the heron's sharp beak pointed to the sky! And the pin where that rare person – endowed with honesty, truthfulness and a sense of duty – mounts his insects!

Where the red duck who stands on his webbed feet reminds you of the skulls of Russians who have fallen for their motherland, in whose bones his ancestors built their nests.

Where, in the golden forelock of one breed of bird, dwells the flame of that strength that is only characterized by a vow of celibacy.

Where Russia pronounces the name 'Cossack' like an eagle's screech.

Where the elephants have forgotten their trumpet calls and make a sound that seems to mourn their condition. Could it be that, seeing us so insignificant, they have started to consider it a sign of good taste to make such insignificant sounds themselves? I do not know. O grey wrinkled mountains! Covered with lichen and with grass growing in your ravines!

Where in the beasts some kinds of beautiful possibilities are dying, like – written in a Book of Hours – the *Lay of Igor's Campaign* during the fire of Moscow.

Velimir Khlebnikov (1911), translated from the Russian
by James Womack

Painting

Let some one fasten this piece of silk by the four corners for me, and I shall not put the sky upon it. The sea and its shores, the forest and the mountains, do not tempt my art. But from the top to the bottom and from one side to the other, as between new horizons, with an artless hand I shall paint the Earth. The limits of communities, the divisions of fields, will be exactly outlined, – those that are already plowed, those where the battalions of sheaves still stand. I shall not fail to count each tree. The smallest house will be represented with an ingenuous industry. Looking closely, you may distinguish the people; he who crosses an arched bridge of stone, parasol in hand; he who washes buckets at a pond; the litter traveling on the shoulders of two porters, and the patient laborer who plows a new furrow the length of the old. A long road bordered with a double row of skiffs crosses the picture from one corner to the other, and in one of the circular moats can be seen, in a scrap of azure for water, three quarters of a slightly yellow moon.

Paul Claudel (1900), translated from the French
by Teresa Frances and William Rose Benét

Absinthia Taetra

Green changed to white, emerald to an opal: nothing was changed.

The man let the water trickle gently into his glass, and as the green clouded, a mist fell from his mind.

Then he drank opaline.

Memories and terrors beset him. The past tore after him like a panther and through the blackness of the present he saw the luminous tiger eyes of the things to be.

But he drank opaline.

And that obscure night of the soul, and the valley of humiliation, through which he stumbled were forgotten. He saw blue vistas of undiscovered countries, high prospects and a quiet, caressing sea. The past shed its perfume over him, to-day held his hand as it were a little child, and to-morrow shone like a white star: nothing was changed.

He drank opaline.

The man had known the obscure night of the soul, and lay even now in the valley of humiliation; and the tiger menace of the things to be was red in the skies. But for a little while he had forgotten.

Green changed to white, emerald to an opal: nothing was changed.

Ernest Dowson (1899)

The Pipe

Yesterday I found my pipe while pondering a long evening of work, of fine winter work. Thrown aside were my cigarettes, with all the childish joys of summer, into the past which the leaves shining blue in the sun, the muslins, illuminate, and taken up once again was the grave pipe of a serious man who wants to smoke for a long while without being disturbed, so as better to work: but I was not prepared for the surprise that this abandoned object had in store for me; for hardly had I drawn the first puff when I forgot the grand books I was planning to write, and, amazed, moved to a feeling of tenderness, I breathed in the air of the previous winter which was now coming back to me. I had not been in contact with my faithful sweetheart since returning to France, and now all of London, London as I had lived it a year ago entirely alone, appeared before my eyes: first the dear fogs that muffle one's brains and have an odor of their own there when they penetrate beneath the casements. My tobacco had the scent of a somber room with leather furniture sprinkled by coal dust, on which the thin black cat would curl and stretch; the big fires! and the maid with red arms pouring coals, and the noise of those coals falling from the sheet-iron bucket into the iron scuttle in the morning – when the postman gave the solemn double knock that kept me alive! Once again I saw through the windows those sickly trees of the deserted square – I saw the open sea, crossed so often that winter, shivering on the deck of the steamer wet with drizzle and blackened from the fumes – with my poor wandering beloved, decked out in traveller's clothes, a long dress, dull as the dust of the roads, a coat clinging damply to her cold shoulders, one of those straw hats with no feather and hardly any ribbons that wealthy ladies throw away upon arrival, mangled as they are by the sea, and that poor loved ones refurbish for many another season. Around her neck was wound the terrible handkerchief that one waves when saying goodbye forever.

Stéphane Mallarmé (1897), translated from the French
by Henry Weinfeld

The Disciple

When Narcissus died the pool of his pleasure changed from a cup of sweet waters into a cup of salt tears, and the Oreads came weeping through the woodland that they might sing to the pool and give it comfort.

And when they saw that the pool had changed from a cup of sweet waters into a cup of salt tears, they loosened the green tresses of their hair and cried to the pool and said, 'We do not wonder that you should mourn in this manner for Narcissus, so beautiful was he.'

'But was Narcissus beautiful?' said the pool.

'Who should know that better than you?' answered the Oreads. 'Us did he ever pass by, but you he sought for, and would lie on your banks and look down at you, and in the mirror of your waters he would mirror his own beauty.'

And the pool answered, 'But I loved Narcissus because, as he lay on my banks and looked down at me, in the mirror of his eyes I saw ever my own beauty mirrored.'

Oscar Wilde (1894)

The Master

Now when the darkness came over the earth Joseph of Arimathea, having lighted a torch of pinewood, passed down from the hill into the valley. For he had business in his own home.

And kneeling on the flint stones of the Valley of Desolation he saw a young man who was naked and weeping. His hair was the colour of honey, and his body was as a white flower, but he had wounded his body with thorns and on his hair had he set ashes as a crown.

And he who had great possessions said to the young man who was naked and weeping, 'I do not wonder that your sorrow is so great, for surely He was a just man.'

And the young man answered, 'It is not for Him that I am weeping, but for myself. I too have changed water into wine, and I have healed the leper and given sight to the blind. I have walked upon the waters, and from the dwellers in the tombs I have cast out devils. I have fed the hungry in the desert where there was no food, and I have raised the dead from their narrow houses, and at my bidding, and before a great multitude of people, a barren fig-tree withered away. All things that this man has done I have done also. And yet they have not crucified me.'

Oscar Wilde (1894)

from *By the Waters of Babylon*

Little Poems in Prose

I. The Exodus (August 3, 1492)

1. The Spanish noon is a blaze of azure fire, and the dusty pilgrims crawl like an endless serpent along treeless plains and bleached highroads, through rock-split ravines and castellated, cathedral-shadowed towns.

2. The hoary patriarch, wrinkled as an almond shell, bows painfully upon his staff. The beautiful young mother, ivory-pale, well-nigh swoons beneath her burden; in her large enfolding arms nestles her sleeping babe, round her knees flock her little ones with bruised and bleeding feet. 'Mother, shall we soon be there'?

3. The youth with Christ-like countenance speaks comfortably to father and brother, to maiden and wife. In his breast, his own heart is broken.

4. The halt, the blind, are amid the train. Sturdy pack-horses laboriously drag the tented wagons wherein lie the sick athirst with fever.

5. The panting mules are urged forward with spur and goad; stuffed are the heavy saddlebags with the wreckage of ruined homes.

6. Hark to the tinkling silver bells that adorn the tenderly-carried silken scrolls.

7. In the fierce noon-glare a lad bears a kindled lamp; behind its network of bronze the airs of heaven breathe not upon its faint purple star.

8. Noble and abject, learned and simple, illustrious and obscure, plod side by side, all brothers now, all merged in one routed army of misfortune.

9. Woe to the straggler who falls by the wayside! no friend shall close his eyes.

10. They leave behind, the grape, the olive, and the fig; the vines they planted, the corn they sowed, the garden-cities of Andalusia and Aragon, Estremadura and La Mancha, of Granada and Castile; the altar, the hearth, and the grave of their fathers.

11. The townsman spits at their garments, the shepherd quits his flock, the peasant his plow, to pelt with curses and stones; the villager sets on their trail his yelping cur.

12. Oh the weary march, oh the uptorn roots of home, oh the blankness of the receding goal!

13. Listen to their lamentation: *They that ate dainty food are desolate in the streets; they that were reared in scarlet embrace dunghills. They flee away and wander about. Men say among the*

nations, they shall no more sojourn there; our end is near, our days are full, our doom is come.

14. Whither shall they turn? for the West hath cast them out, and the East refuseth to receive.

15. O bird of the air, whisper to the despairing exiles, that to-day, to-day, from the many-masted, gayly-bannered port of Palos, sails the world-unveiling Genoese, to unlock the golden gates of sunset and bequeath a Continent to Freedom!

IV. The Test

1. Daylong I brooded upon the Passion of Israel.

2. I saw him bound to the wheel, nailed to the cross, cut off by the sword, burned at the stake, tossed into the seas.

3. And always the patient, resolute, martyr face arose in silent rebuke and defiance.

4. A Prophet with four eyes; wide gazed the orbs of the spirit above the sleeping eyelids of the senses.

5. A Poet, who plucked from his bosom the quivering heart and fashioned it into a lyre.

6. A placid-browed Sage, uplifted from earth in celestial meditation.

7. These I saw, with princes and people in their train; the monumental dead and the standard-bearers of the future.

8. And suddenly I heard a burst of mocking laughter, and turning, I beheld the shuffling gait, the ignominious features, the sordid mask of the son of the Ghetto.

V. Currents

1. Vast oceanic movements, the flux and reflux of immeasurable tides, oversweep our continent.

2. From the far Caucasian steppes, from the squalid Ghettos of Europe,

3. From Odessa and Bucharest, from Kief and Ekaterinoslav,

4. Hark to the cry of the exiles of Babylon, the voice of Rachel mourning for her children, of Israel lamenting for Zion.

5. And lo, like a turbid stream, the long-pent flood bursts the dykes of oppression and rushes hitherward.

6. Unto her ample breast, the generous mother of nations welcomes them.

7. The herdsman of Canaan and the seed of Jerusalem's royal shepherds renew their youth amid the pastoral plains of Texas and the golden valleys of the Sierras.

Emma Lazarus (1887)

After the Flood

No sooner had the notion of the Flood regained its composure,

Than a hare paused amid the gorse and trembling bellflowers and said its prayer to the rainbow through the spider's web.

Oh the precious stones that were hiding, – the flowers that were already peeking out.

Stalls were erected in the dirty main street, and boats were towed toward the sea, which rose in layers above as in old engravings.

Blood flowed in Bluebeard's house, – in the slaughterhouses, – in the amphitheaters, where God's seal turned the windows livid. Blood and milk flowed.

The beavers built. Tumblers of coffee steamed in the public houses.

In the vast, still-streaming house of windows, children in mourning looked at marvelous pictures.

A door slammed, and on the village square, the child waved his arms, understood by vanes and weathercocks everywhere, in the dazzling shower.

Madame xxx established a piano in the Alps. Mass and first communions were celebrated at the cathedral's hundred thousand altars.

The caravans left. And the Splendide Hotel was built amid the tangled heap of ice floes and the polar night.

Since then the Moon has heard jackals cheeping in thyme deserts, – and eclogues in wooden shoes grumbling in the orchard. Then, in the budding purple forest, Eucharis told me that spring had come.

– Well up, pond, – Foam, roll on the bridge and above the woods; – black cloths and organs, – lightning and thunder, – rise and roll; – Waters and sorrows, rise and revive the Floods.

For since they subsided, – oh the precious stones shoveled under, and the full-blown flowers! – so boring! and the Queen, the Witch who lights her coals in the clay pot, will never want to tell us what she knows, and which we do not know.

Arthur Rimbaud (1886), translated from the French
by John Ashbery

Sideshow

Very robust rascals. Several of them have exploited your worlds. With no pressing needs, and in no hurry to bring into play their brilliant faculties and their experience of your consciences. What mature men! Their eyes glazed like the midsummer night, red and black, tricolored, steel pierced with gold stars; facial features deformed, leaden, ashen, on fire; playful hoarseness! The cruel procedures of discarded finery! – There are a few young men – what would they think of Cherubino? – endowed with frightening voices and some dangerous resources. They are sent off to be buggered in cities, swathed in disgusting *luxury*.

O most violent Paradise of the enraged grimace! No comparison with your Fakirs and other theatrical buffoonery. Wearing improvised costumes in nightmarish taste they act out ballads, tragedies of thieves and demigods of a spirituality hitherto unknown to history or religions. Chinese, Hottentots, Gypsies, nincompoops, hyenas, Molochs, old dementias, sinister demons, they mingle populist, maternal tricks with bestial poses and tenderness. They would perform new plays and 'nice girl' songs. Expert jugglers, they transform people and places, and resort to magnetic comedy. The eyes flame, the blood sings, the bones swell, tears and trickles of red descend. Their raillery or their terror lasts a minute, or entire months.

I alone know the plan of this savage sideshow.

Arthur Rimbaud (1886), translated from the French
by John Ashbery

Genie

He is affection and the present since he opened the house to foaming winter and the hum of summer, he who purified drink and food, he who is the charm of fleeting places and the super-human deliciousness of staying still. He is affection and the future, strength and love that we, standing amid rage and trou-bles, see passing in the storm-rent sky and on banners of ecstasy.

He is love, perfect and reinvented measurement, wonderful and unforeseen reason, and eternity: machine beloved for its fatal qualities. We have all experienced the terror of his yield-ing and of our own: O enjoyment of our health, surge of our faculties, egoistic affection and passion for him, he who loves us for his infinite life.

And we remember him and he travels . . . And if the Adoration goes away, resounds, its promise resounds: 'Away with those superstitions, those old bodies, those couples and those ages. It's this age that has sunk!'

He won't go away, nor descend from a heaven again, he won't accomplish the redemption of women's anger and the gaiety of men and of all that sin: for it is now accomplished, with him being, and being loved.

O his breaths, his heads, his racing; the terrible swiftness of the perfection of forms and of action.

O fecundity of the spirit and immensity of the universe!

His body! The dreamed-of release, the shattering of grace crossed with new violence!

The sight, the sight of him! all the ancient kneeling and suffering *lifted* in his wake.

His day! the abolition of all resonant and surging suffering in more intense music.

His footstep! migrations more vast than ancient invasions.

O him and us! pride more benevolent than wasted charities.

O world! and the clear song of new misfortunes!

He has known us all and loved us all. Let us, on this winter night, from cape to cape, from the tumultuous pole to the castle, from the crowd to the beach, from glance to glance, our strengths and feelings numb, learn to hail him and see him, and send him back, and under the tides and at the summit of snowy deserts, follow his seeing, his breathing, his body, his day.

Arthur Rimbaud (1886), translated from the French
by John Ashbery

The End of the World

A Dream

I fancied I was somewhere in Russia, in the wilds, in a simple country house.

The room big and low pitched with three windows; the walls whitewashed; no furniture. Before the house a barren plain; gradually sloping downwards, it stretches into the distance; a grey monotonous sky hangs over it, like the canopy of a bed.

I am not alone; there are some ten persons in the room with me. All quite plain people, simply dressed. They walk up and down in silence, as it were stealthily. They avoid one another, and yet are continually looking anxiously at one another.

Not one knows why he has come into this house and what people there are with him. On all the faces uneasiness and despondency . . . all in turn approach the windows and look about intently as though expecting something from without.

Then again they fall to wandering up and down. Among us is a small-sized boy; from time to time he whimpers in the same thin voice, 'Father, I'm frightened!' My heart turns sick at his whimper, and I too begin to be afraid . . . of what? I don't know myself. Only I feel, there is coming nearer and nearer a great, great calamity.

The boy keeps on and on with his wail. Oh, to escape from here! How stifling! How weary! how heavy . . . But escape is impossible.

That sky is like a shroud. And no wind . . . Is the air dead or what?

All at once the boy runs up to the window and shrieks in the same piteous voice, 'Look! look! the earth has fallen away!'

'How? fallen away?' Yes; just now there was a plain before the house, and now it stands on a fearful height! The horizon has sunk, has gone down, and from the very house drops an almost overhanging, as it were scooped-out, black precipice.

We all crowded to the window . . . Horror froze our hearts. 'Here it is . . . here it is!' whispers one next me.

And behold, along the whole far boundary of the earth, something began to stir, some sort of small, roundish hillocks began heaving and falling.

'It is the sea!' the thought flashed on us all at the same instant. 'It will swallow us all up directly . . . Only how can it grow and rise upwards? To this precipice?'

And yet, it grows, grows enormously . . . Already there are not separate hillocks heaving in the distance . . . One continuous, monstrous wave embraces the whole circle of the horizon.

It is swooping, swooping, down upon us! In an icy hurricane it flies, swirling in the darkness of hell. Everything shuddered – and there, in this flying mass – was the crash of thunder, the iron wail of thousands of throats . . .

Ah! what a roaring and moaning! It was the earth howling for terror . . .

The end of it! the end of all!

The child whimpered once more . . . I tried to clutch at my companions, but already we were all crushed, buried, drowned, swept away by that pitch-black, icy, thundering wave! Darkness . . . darkness everlasting!

Scarcely breathing, I awoke.

March 1878

Ivan Turgenev (1883), translated from the Russian
by Constance Garnett

On the Sea

I was going from Hamburg to London in a small steamer. We were two passengers; I and a little female monkey, whom a Hamburg merchant was sending as a present to his English partner.

She was fastened by a light chain to one of the seats on deck, and was moving restlessly and whining in a little plaintive pipe like a bird's. Every time I passed by her she stretched out her little, black, cold hand, and peeped up at me out of her little mournful, almost human eyes. I took her hand, and she ceased whining and moving restlessly about.

There was a dead calm. The sea stretched on all sides like a motionless sheet of leaden colour. It seemed narrowed and small; a thick fog overhung it, hiding the very mast-tops in cloud, and dazing and wearying the eyes with its soft obscurity. The sun hung, a dull red blur in this obscurity; but before evening it glowed with strange, mysterious, lurid light.

Long, straight folds, like the folds in some heavy silken stuff, passed one after another over the sea from the ship's prow, and broadening as they passed, and wrinkling and widening, were smoothed out again with a shake, and vanished. The foam flew up, churned by the tediously thudding wheels; white as milk, with a faint hiss it broke up into serpentine eddies, and then melted together again and vanished too, swallowed up by the mist.

Persistent and plaintive as the monkey's whine rang the small bell at the stern.

From time to time a porpoise swam up, and with a sudden roll disappeared below the scarcely ruffled surface.

And the captain, a silent man with a gloomy, sunburnt face, smoked a short pipe and angrily spat into the dull, stagnant sea.

To all my inquiries he responded by a disconnected grumble. I was obliged to turn to my sole companion, the monkey.

I sat down beside her; she ceased whining, and again held out her hand to me.

The clinging fog oppressed us both with its drowsy dampness; and buried in the same unconscious dreaminess, we sat side by side like brother and sister.

I smile now . . . but then I had another feeling. We are all children of one mother, and I was glad that the poor little beast was soothed and nestled so confidingly up to me, as to a brother.

November 1879

Ivan Turgenev (1883), translated from the Russian
by Constance Garnett

The Stranger

'Whom lovest thou the best, enigmatical man, say, thy father, thy mother, thy sister, or thy brother?'

'I have neither father, nor mother, nor sister, nor brother.'

'Thy friends?'

'You use there a word whose sense has to this day remained unknown to me.'

'Thy fatherland?'

'I know not in what latitude it is situated.'

'Beauty?'

'I would fain love it, godlike and immortal.'

'Gold?'

'I hate it as you hate God.'

'Eh? What lovest thou, then, extraordinary stranger?'

'I love the clouds . . . the clouds that pass . . . over there . . . the marvellous clouds!'

Charles Baudelaire (1869), translated from the French
by Stuart Merrill

Windows

He who looks in through an open window never sees so many things as he who looks at a shut window. There is nothing more profound, more mysterious, more fertile, more gloomy, or more dazzling, than a window lighted by a candle. What we can see in the sunlight is always less interesting than what goes on behind the panes of a window. In that dark or luminous hollow, life lives, life dreams, life suffers.

Across the waves of roofs, I can see a woman of middle age, wrinkled, poor, who is always leaning over something, and who never goes out. Out of her face, out of her dress, out of her attitude, out of nothing almost, I have made up the woman's story, and sometimes I say it over to myself with tears.

If it had been a poor old man, I could have made up his just as easily.

And I go to bed, proud of having lived and suffered in others.

Perhaps you will say to me: 'Are you sure that it is the real story?' What does it matter, what does any reality outside of myself matter, if it has helped me to live, to feel that I am, and what I am?

Charles Baudelaire (1869), translated from the French
by Arthur Symons

The Bad Glazier

There are natures purely contemplative, completely unsuited for action, who nevertheless, under mysterious unknown impulses, act sometimes with a rapidity of which they would suppose themselves incapable.

Those for instance who, afraid their concierge may have bad news for them, pace an hour timorously before daring to go in; those who hold letters for two weeks before opening them, or wait six months to take some step that has been immediately necessary for a year already – but sometimes abruptly feel precipitated into action by an irresistible force, like an arrow leaving the bow. Moralists and doctors, who claim to know everything, fail to explain from whence so sudden a mad energy comes to these lazy, voluptuous souls and why, incapable of the simplest and most necessary things, they find at certain moments a spurt of first class courage to execute the most absurd and even most dangerous actions.

A friend of mine, as harmless a dreamer as ever was, one day set a forest on fire, in order to see, he said, if a fire would catch as easily as generally claimed. Ten times the experiment failed; but the eleventh it was all too successful.

Another lit a cigar next to a powder keg, *to see, to see if, to tempt fate*, to force himself to prove his own energy, to gamble, to feel the pleasures of anxiety, for nothing, caprice, to kill time.

This sort of energy springs from ennui and reverie; and those in whom it so unexpectedly appears are in general, as I have said, the most indolent and dreamy of mortals.

Another, timid to the extent of lowering his eyes before anybody's gaze, to the point of having to pull together his poor will to enter a cafe or go past the ticket office of a theater (where the managers seem to him invested with the majesty of Minos, of Aeacus and of Rhadamanthus) will all of a sudden fall on the neck of some geezer and embrace him enthusiastically, to the astonishment of passers-by.

Why? Because . . . because of an irresistibly sympathetic physiognomy? Maybe, but we may well suppose that he himself has no idea.

More than once I have been victim to these crises, these outbursts, that give some authority to the notion that malicious Demons slip into us and make us unwittingly accomplish their most absurd wishes.

One morning I got up on the wrong side, dejected, worn out from idleness, driven it seemed to me to perform some grand, some brilliant action. And, alas! I opened the window.

(Please note that the urge to practical jokes, in certain persons, the result neither of work nor planning, but of mere chance inspiration, belongs largely, even if only through the eagerness of desire, to that temper – hysterical according to doctors; by rather better minds than a doctor's, satanic – which drives us irresistibly towards a host of dangerous or indecent acts.)

The first person I noticed in the street was a glazier whose cry, piercing, discordant, came up to me through the oppressive and dirty Parisian atmosphere. Impossible for me to say why this poor fellow roused in me a hatred as sudden as despotic.

'– Hey there!' and I yelled for him to come up, meanwhile reflecting, not without amusement, that, my room being on the sixth floor and the stairs very narrow, the man would find it difficult to effect his ascent, to maneuver at certain spots the corners of his fragile merchandise.

Finally he appeared: I examined curiously all his glass and said to him: 'What? you have no colored glass? pink, red, blue glass, magical glass, the glass of paradise? Shameful! you dare promenade this poor district and you don't even have glass to suggest a better life!' And I pushed him smartly towards the staircase where he stumbled growling.

I went to the balcony, picked up a little pot of flowers, and when the man came out of the door below, I let my war machine fall straight down, onto the edge of his hooks. The shock sending him over backwards, he smashed under his back the whole petty fortune he carried, from which burst the sound of a crystal palace shattered by a bolt of lightning.

And, drunk with my folly, I shouted at him, madly, 'The beauty of life! the beauty of life!'

These nervous pleasantries are not without danger, and some-
times quite costly. But what's an eternity of damnation to one
who has found in such an instant infinite satisfaction?

Charles Baudelaire (1869), translated from the French
by Keith Waldrop

The Madman

One carolous coin; or, if you would like, a golden lamb.
    – MS in the King's Library

The moon was grooming her hair with an ebony comb, sprinkling the hills, the meadows, and the woods with fireflies like pieces of silver.

Scarbo, gnome sated with treasures, was up on my roof, and, to the crow of the weathercock, was winnowing his loot, separating the ducats and florins, which jingled in cadence, from the counterfeit coins, which showered over the street.

How the madman laughed, mockingly, as each night he wandered about the deserted city, his one eye on the moon and the other – burned out!

'Wealth of the moon,' he muttered. 'Scraping together these devil's tokens, I shall buy a pillory where I may warm myself in the sun.'

But, as always, there was the moon, the moon going down – and concealed in my cellar, Scarbo was turning out more ducats and florins with each echoing strike of his press.

Meantime, its two horns waving ahead, a snail, which must have been confused by the night, was pushing its way across my glistening windowpane.

Aloysius Bertrand (1842), translated from the French
by Thomas Ligotti

The Mason

The Master Mason: 'Come look at these bastions, these buttresses; they seem to have been built for all eternity.'
  – Schiller, *William Tell*

The Mason Abraham Knupfer is singing, trowel in hand, scaffolded up so high that, as he examines the gothic inscription on the great cathedral bell, even the soles of his feet stand high above the rooftops of the thirty-arched church, in this town of thirty churches.

He sees gargoyles spewing water from the slates down into the entangled abyss of galleries, windows, pendants, pinnacles, roofs, turrets and timberwork which the falcon's hovering wing punctuates with its one still point.

He sees the star-shaped outlines of the fortification-walls, the citadel sticking out like some fat hen inside a piecrust, the palace courtyards with their sun-dried fountains, and the monastery cloisters, where the sun revolves around the pillars.

The imperial guard is quartered at the edge of town. In the distance, a soldier is drumming. Abraham Knupfer can see his tri-cornered hat, his epaulets of red wool, his cockade crimped with a rosette, and his pigtail tied with a bow.

The next thing he sees are some soldiers who, in a far-off park surrounded by dense foliage, on wide, broad lawns, are firing with some blunderbusses at a wooden bird nailed to the top of a maypole.

And in the evening, when the echoing nave of the cathedral falls asleep, its arms folded in a cross, he sees from his lofty ladder a village set afire by troops, flaming like a comet in the deep-blue sky.

Aloysius Bertrand (1842), translated from the French
by Michael Benedikt

Haarlem

While Amsterdam's golden cockerel doth sing and spin,
Haarlem's golden chicken dwells within.
* – The Centuries of Nostradamus*

Haarlem, that fine free-hand sketch, birthplace of the Flemish school, Haarlem as painted by Breughel the Elder, Peter Neefs, David Teniers and Paul Rembrandt.

With its canal full of shimmering blue water, and its church with flaming, golden windows, and the stone porches with bed-linen drying in the sun, with its roofs, green with straw.

And the storks sailing around the town clock, stretching out their necks to catch raindrops in their beaks.

And the slow-moving burgomeister stroking his double chin, and the lovelorn florist growing thinner and thinner, her eye battened upon a tulip.

And the gypsy leaning over his mandolin, and the old man playing upon the Rommelpot, and the child filling up his wineskin-bladder.

And the drinkers smoking in some dark dive, and the hotel-keeper's servant hanging up a dead pheasant in the window.

Aloysius Bertrand (1842), translated from the French
by Michael Benedikt

Acknowledgements

The editor gratefully acknowledges the following for permission to reprint copyright materival:

PAIGE ACKERSON-KIELY: 'Cry Break' from *My Love is a Dead Arctic Explorer* (Ahsahta Press, 2012). MEENA ALEXANDER: 'Burnt Hair' from *House of a Thousand Doors* (Three Continents Press, 1988), reprinted by permission of the author. AGHA SHAHID ALI: 'Return to Harmony 3' from *The Veiled Suite: The Collected Poems* (W. W. Norton, 2009), reprinted by permission of the publisher. SIMON ARMITAGE: 'The Experience' from *Seeing Stars* (Faber & Faber, 2010), reprinted by permission of Faber & Faber Ltd. HANS ARP: 'Around the Star's Throne', trans. by Bethany Schneider, from *Models of the Universe*, ed. by Stuart Friebert and David Young (Oberlin College Press, 1995), reprinted by permission of the publisher. JOHN ASHBERY: 'For John Clare' from *Collected Poems 1956–1987* (Carcanet, 2010) and 'Homeless Heart' from *Quick Question* (Carcanet, 2013), reprinted by permission of the publisher. TIM ATKINS: *Folklore*, part 20 (Salt, 2008), reprinted by permission of the author. MARGARET ATWOOD: 'In Love with Raymond Chandler' (© O. W. Toad Ltd. 1983, 1992, 1994) from *Good Bones and Simple Murders* (Nan A. Talese, 1994), reprinted by permission of Nan A. Talese, an imprint of the Knopf Doubleday Publishing Group, a division of Penguin Random House LLC. W. H. AUDEN: 'Argument: I' from *The Orators*, in *The English Auden: Poems, Essays and Dramatic Writings, 1927–1939*, ed. by Edward Mendelson (Faber & Faber, 1977), reprinted by permission of Faber & Faber Ltd. CHARLES BAUDELAIRE: 'The Bad Glazier', trans. by Keith Waldrop, from *Paris Spleen* (Wesleyan University

Press, 2009), used by permission of the publisher (© Keith Waldrop 2009). EMILY BERRY: 'Some Fears' from *Dear Boy* (Faber & Faber, 2013), reprinted by permission of Faber & Faber Ltd. MEI-MEI BERSSENBRUGGE: 'Fairies', part 2, from *Hello, the Roses* (New Directions, 2013), reprinted by permission of the publisher. ALOYSIUS BERTRAND: 'Haarlem', trans. by Michael Benedikt, from *Short: An International Anthology*, ed. by Alan Ziegler (Persea Books, 2014), reprinted by permission of The Estate of Michael Benedikt. HERA LINDSAY BIRD: 'Children are the Orgasm of the World' from *Hera Lindsay Bird* (Penguin Books, 2017), reprinted by permission of the publisher. ELIZABETH BISHOP: 'Strayed Crab' from *Poems: The Centenary Edition* (Chatto & Windus, 2011), reprinted by permission of the publisher. ROBERT BLY: 'A Caterpillar' from *Collected Poems* (W. W. Norton, 2018), reprinted by permission of the publisher. CHRISTIAN BÖK: Extract from 'Chapter E', from *Eunoia* (Canongate and Coach House, 2008), reprinted by permission of the publishers. YVES BONNEFOY: 'The Dogs', trans. by Richard Stamelman, published in *Modern Poetry in Translation* (Summer 1992), reprinted by permission of the translator. SEAN BONNEY: Extract from 'Letter Against the Firmament', in *Letters Against the Firmament* (Enitharmon, 2015), reprinted by permission of the publisher. JORGE LUIS BORGES: 'Borges and I', trans. by James E. Irby, from *Labyrinths* (Penguin Modern Classics, 2000), reprinted by permission of The Random House Group. Copyright © 1995, Maria Kodama, used by permission of the Wylie Agency (UK) Limited. JENNY BORNHOLDT: 'Man with a Mower' from *Waiting Shelter* (Victoria University Press, 1991), reprinted by permission of the publisher. ANNE BOYER: 'A Woman Shopping' from *Garments Against Women* (Ahsahta Press, 2015), reprinted by permission of the publisher. CHARLES BOYLE: 'Hosea: A Commentary' from *The Age of Cardboard and String* (CB Editions, 2015), reprinted by permission of the publisher. BERTOLT BRECHT: 'The God of War', originally published in German in 1949 as 'Der kriegsgott', trans. by Thomas Mark Kuhn. Copyright © 1964, 1976 by Bertolt-Brecht-Erben / Suhrkamp Verlag. Translation copyright © 2015 by Tom Kuhn and David Constantine, from *Collected Poems* of Bertolt Brecht (W. W. Norton, 2015), used by permission of Liveright Publishing Corporation. ANDRÉ BRETON and PAUL ÉLUARD: 'Force of Habit' from *L'Immaculée Conception* (Oxford

University Press, 1970), reprinted by permission of Enitharmon Editions. PAM BROWN: 'How Everything Has Turned Around' from *This world / This place* (University of Queensland Press, 1994), reprinted by permission of the author. JOANNE BURNS: 'reading', from *blowing bubbles in the 7th lane* (Fab Press, 1988), reprinted by permission of the author. VAHNI CAPILDEO: 'Going Nowhere, Getting Somewhere' from *Measures of Expatriation* (Carcanet, 2016), reprinted by permission of the publisher. ANNE CARSON: 'Merry Christmas from Hegel' from *Float* (Jonathan Cape, 2016), reprinted by permission of The Random House Group; 'Short Talk on Homo Sapiens' and 'Short Talk on the Total Collection' from *Plainwater* (Vintage Contemporaries, 2000), reprinted by permission of Vintage Books, an imprint of the Knopf Doubleday Publishing Group, a division of Penguin Random House LLC; 'Short Talk on the Truth to Be had from Dreams' and 'Short Talk on the Sensation of Aeroplane Takeoff' from *Short Talks: Brick Books Classics* 1 (Brick Books, 2015), reprinted by permission of the publisher. BRIAN CATLING: Extract from *The Stumbling Block Its Index*, in *A Court of Miracles: Collected Poems* (Etruscan, 2009), reprinted by permission of the publisher. LUIS CERNUDA: 'Street Cries', trans. by Stephen Kessler, from *Written in Water* (City Lights, 2004), reprinted by permission of the publisher. AIMÉ CÉSAIRE: 'Phrase', trans. by Clayton Eshleman and A. James Arnold, from *The Complete Poetry of Aimé Césaire: Bilingual Edition* (Wesleyan University Press, 2017), used by permission of the publisher (© Clayton Eshleman and A. James Arnold 2017). RENÉ CHAR: 'The Swift', trans. by Mary Ann Caws, from *Poems of René Char* (Princeton University Press, 1976), reprinted by permission of the publisher. MAXINE CHERNOFF: 'Vanity, Wisconsin' (© Maxine Chernoff) from *Leap Year Day: New and Selected Poems* (Another Chicago Press, 1991), reprinted by permission of the author. INGER CHRISTENSEN: 'TEXT symmetries', parts 1-3, from *it*, trans. by Susanna Nied (Carcanet, 2007), reprinted by permission of the publisher. CLARK COOLIDGE: 'Letters' from *The Book of During* (The Figures, 1991), reprinted by permission of the author and the publisher. PETER DIDSBURY: 'A Vernacular Tale' from *Scenes from a Long Sleep: New and Collected Poems* (Bloodaxe, 2003), reprinted by permission of Bloodaxe Books. LINH DINH: 'A Hardworking Peasant from the Idyllic Countryside' from *All Around What Empties Out*

(Subpress, 2003), reprinted by permission of the publisher. RITA DOVE: 'Quaker Oats' from *Collected Poems* (W. W. Norton, 2016), reprinted by permission of the publisher. LAURIE DUGGAN: 'Hearts' from *Compared to What* (Shearsman, 2005), reprinted by permission of the publisher and author. RUSSEL EDSON: 'Ape' from *The Tunnel: Selected Poems* (Oberlin College Press, 1994), reprinted by permission of the publisher. T. S. ELIOT: 'Hysteria' from *Collected Poems 1909–1962* (Faber & Faber, 1963), reprinted by permission of Faber and Faber Ltd. ELKE ERB: 'Portrait of A. E. (An Artful Fairy Tale)', trans. by Rosmarie Waldrop, from *Mountains in Berlin* (Burning Deck, 1995), reprinted by permission of the publisher. CARRIE ETTER: 'Imagined Sons 9: Greek Salad' from *Imagined Sons* (Seren, 2014), reprinted by permission of the publisher. IAN HAMILTON FINLAY: 'Cinema-Going' from *Selections* (University of California Press, 2012), reprinted by permission of the publisher. ROY FISHER: Extract from *City*, in *The Dow Low Drop: New and Selected Poems* (Bloodaxe, 1997), reprinted by permission of Bloodaxe Books. CAROLYN FORCHÉ: 'The Colonel' from *The Country Between Us* (Harper and Row, 1981), reprinted by permission of the publisher. JOHN FULLER: 'Flower, Quartet, Mask' from *The Dice Cup* (Chatto & Windus, 2014), reprinted by permission of The Random House Group. ANZAI FUYE: 'Sunflowers are Already Black Gunpowder', trans. by Dennis Keene, from *The Modern Japanese Prose Poem* (Princeton University Press, 2014), reprinted by permission of the publisher. CLIFTON GACHAGUA: 'Reclaiming a Beloved City' from *Madman at Kilifi* (University of Nebraska Press, 2014), reprinted by permission of the publisher. DAVID GASCOYNE: 'Lozanne' from *Collected Poems, 1988* (Oxford University Press, 1988), reprinted by permission of the publisher. ALLEN GINSBERG: 'A Supermarket in California' (© Allen Ginsberg 1956, 1961) from *Howl* (City Lights, 1955), reprinted by permission of HarperCollins Publishers and by permission of The Wylie Agency (UK) Limited. PETER GIZZI: 'Antico Adagio' from *Archeophonics* (Wesleyan University Press, 2016), used by permission of the publisher (© Peter Gizzi 2016). BILL GRIFFITHS: 'The Hornsman' from *The Lion Man and Others* (Veer Books, 2008), reprinted by permission of The Estate of Bill Griffiths. BARBARA GUEST: 'The Cough' from *Collected Poems*, ed. by Hadley Haden Guest (Wesleyan University Press, 1999), used by permission of the publisher

(© The Estate of Barbara Guest 2008). JEN HADFIELD: 'The Wren' from *Nigh-No-Place* (Bloodaxe, 2008), reprinted by permission of Bloodaxe Books. GOLAN HAJI: 'The End of Days', trans. by the author and Stephen Watts, from *A Tree Whose Name I Don't Know* (A Midsummer Night's Press, 2017), reprinted by permission of the author and translator. JOY HARJO: 'Deer Dancer' from *In Mad Love and War* (Wesleyan University Press, 1990), used by permission of the publisher (© Joy Harjo 1990). LEE HARWOOD: 'The Land of Counterpane' from *Collected Poems* (Shearsman, 1985) reprinted by permission of the publisher and author. ROBERT HASS: 'Human Wishes' from *The Apple Trees at Olema: New and Selected Poems* (HarperCollins / Ecco, 2010), reprinted by permission of the author. SEAMUS HEANEY: 'Cloistered' from *Opened Ground: Poems 1966–1996* (Faber & Faber, 2002) and 'Fiddleheads' from *District and Circle* (Faber & Faber, 2006), reprinted by permission of Faber and Faber Ltd. LYN HEJINIAN: 'One begins as a student but becomes a friend of clouds' from *My Life*, in *My Life and My Life in the Nineties* (Wesleyan University Press, 1987), reprinted by permission of the publisher. ZBIGNIEW HERBERT: 'Hermes, Dog and Star' (© The Estate of Zbigniew Herbert 2007), trans. by Alyssa Valles, from *The Collected Poems 1956–1998* (Atlantic Books, 2008), reprinted by permission of Atlantic Books Ltd. and The Wylie Agency. GEOFFREY HILL: *Mercian Hymns*, parts I–V, XXV, XXVII and XVIII, from *Broken Hierarchies* (Oxford University Press, 2013), reprinted by permission of the publisher. JEFF HILSON: '*Troglodytes troglodytes* (wren)', '*Apus apus* (swift)' and '*Coccothraustes coccothraustes* (hawfinch)' from *Bird bird* (Landfill, 2008), reprinted by permission of the author. MIROSLAV HOLUB: 'Meeting Ezra Pound', trans. by Dana Hábova and Stuart Friebert, from *Saggital Section: Poems, New and Selected* (Oberlin College Press, 1980), reprinted by permission of the publisher. CATHY PARK HONG: 'Of Lucky Highrise Apartment 88' and 'Of the Millennial Promenade Along the River' from *Engine Empire* (W. W. Norton, 2013), reprinted by permission of the publisher. SARAH HOWE: 'There were barnacles . . .' from *Loop of Jade* (Chatto & Windus, 2015), reprinted by permission of The Random House Group. KIM HYESOON: 'Seoul's Dinner', trans. by Don Mee Choi, from *I'm OK, I'm Pig!* (Bloodaxe, 2014), reprinted by permission of Bloodaxe Books. MAX JACOB: 'Hell is Graduated', trans. by Elizabeth Bishop, from

Elizabeth Bishop, *Poems: The Centenary Edition* (Chatto & Windus, 2011), reprinted by permission of the publisher. ESTHER JANSMA: 'Thought (1)', trans. by Scott Rollins, published in *Modern Poetry in Translation* (Winter 1997), reprinted by permission of the author and translator. LISA JARNOT: 'Ode' from *Ring of Fire* (Zoland Books, 2001), reprinted by permission of the author. ELIZABETH JENNINGS: 'Catherine of Siena' from *Collected Poems*, ed. by Emma Mason (Carcanet, 2012), reprinted by permission of David Higham Associates. JUAN RAMÓN JIMÉNEZ: 'The Moon (April 23)', trans. by H. R. Hays, from *Selected Writings of Juan Ramón Jiménez* (Farrar, Straus & Giroux, 1957). Copyright © 1957 by Juan Ramón Jiménez. Copyright renewed 1985 by Farrar, Straus & Giroux, Inc. ANTHONY JOSEPH: 'Folkways' from *Bird Head Son* (Salt, 2009), reprinted by permission of the author. BHANU KAPIL: 'Notes Towards a Race Riot Scene' from *Ban en Banlieue* (Nightboat Books, 2015), reprinted by permission of the publisher. LAURA KASISCHKE: 'O elegant giant' (© Laura Kasischke 2011) from *Space, in Chains* (Copper Canyon Press, 2011), reprinted with the permission of The Permissions Company, Inc., on behalf of Copper Canyon Press, www.coppercanyonpress.org. LUKE KENNARD: 'Blue Dog' from *The Harbour Beyond the Movie* (Salt, 2007), reprinted by permission of the author. DANIIL KHARMS: 'Blue Notebook, No. 10', trans. by Robert Chandler, from *The Penguin Book of Russian Poetry* (Penguin Books, 2015), reprinted by permission of the translator. VELIMIR KHLEBNIKOV: 'Menagerie', trans. by James Womack, from *The Penguin Book of Russian Poetry* (Penguin, 2015), reprinted by permission of the translator. DAVID KINLOCH: 'Dustie-Fute' from *Dustie-Fute* (Vennel Press, 1992), reprinted by permission of the author. WULF KIRSTEN: 'abglanz/reflected gleam', trans. by Andrew Duncan, from *Depart, Kaspar: Modern German Poems* (Equipage, 1992), reprinted by permission of the publisher. MASAYO KOIKE: 'The Most Sensual Room', trans. by Hiroaki Sato, from *Japanese Women Poets: An Anthology*, (Routledge, 2015), reprinted by permission of the Taylor & Francis Group. YUSEF KOMUNYAKAA: 'The Hanoi Market' from *Pleasure Dome: New and Collected Poems* (Wesleyan University Press, 1988), used by permission of the publisher (© Yusef Komunyakaa 2001). ABDELLATIF LAÂBI: 'The Word-Gulag', trans. by André Naffis-Sahely, from *Beyond the Barbed Wire* (Carcanet, 2016), reprinted by permission of the publisher. JOHN LEHMANN: 'Vigils', part 1, from *Collected Poems 1930–1963* (Eyre & Spottiswoode, 1963), reprinted by permission of David Hingham Associates. ÁGNES LEHÓCZKY: 'Photographs, Undeveloped' from *Budapest to Babel* (Eggbox Press, 2008), reprinted by permission of the publisher. BEN LERNER: 'The first gaming system . . .' from *Angle of Yaw*, in *No Art: Poems* (Granta Books, 2016), reprinted by permission of the publisher. PATRICIA LOCKWOOD: 'Rape Joke' from *Motherland Fatherland Homelandsexuals* (Penguin Books, 2017), reprinted by permission of the publisher. DULCE MARÍA LOYNAZ: 'Love Letter to King Tutankamun', trans. by James O'Connor, from *Absolute Solitude* (Brooklyn, NY: Archipelago Books, 2016), reprinted by permission of the publisher. CHARLES MADGE: 'Bourgeois News' from *Of Love, Time and Place: Selected Poems* (Anvil Press, 1994), reprinted by permission of Carcanet. STÉPHANE MALLARMÉ: 'The Pipe', trans. by Henry Weinfeld, from *Collected Poems of Stéphane Mallarmé* (University of California Press, 1995), reprinted by permission of the publisher. PETER MANSON: 'My Funeral' from *Poems of Frank Rupture* (Sancho Panza Press, 2014), reprinted by permission of the publisher and author. D. S. MARRIOTT: 'Black Sunlight' from *The Bloods* (Shearsman, 2011), reprinted by permission of the publisher. BERNADETTE MAYER: 'Gay Full Story' from *A Bernadette Mayer Reader* (New Directions, 1992), reprinted by permission of New Directions Publishing Corp (© Bernadette Mayer 1964). CHRIS MCCABE: 'Birthweights' from *The Restructure* (Salt, 2012), reprinted by permission of the author. IAN MCMILLAN: 'The Ice House' from *To Fold the Evening Star: New and Selected Poems* (Carcanet, 2016), reprinted by permission of the publisher. ROD MENGHAM: 'Knife', published in *PN Review*, 222 (March–April 2015), reprinted by permission of the author. HENRI MICHAUX: 'My Pastimes', trans. by Richard Ellmann, from *Selected Writings* (New Directions, 1968), reprinted by permission of New Directions Publishing Corp (© New Directions Publishing Corp 1964). CHRISTOPHER MIDDLETON: 'Or Else' from *Collected Poems* (Carcanet, 2008), reprinted by permission of the publisher. KEI MILLER: 'Place Name: Flog Man' from *The Cartographer Tries to Map a Way to Zion* (Carcanet, 2014), reprinted by permission of the publisher. CZESŁAW MIŁOSZ: 'Christopher Robin', trans. by the author and Robert Hass, from *New and Collected Poems 1931–2001* (Allen

Lane, 2001; HarperCollins/Ecco 2001), reprinted by permission of The Random House Group and HarperCollins Publishers (© Czesław Miłosz Royalties Inc. 1988, 1991, 1995, 2001). CHELSEY MINNIS: 'The Skull Ring' from *Zirconia* (Fence Books, 2001), reprinted by permission of the publisher. GABRIELA MISTRAL: 'In Praise of Glass', trans. by Stephen Tapscott, *Selected Prose and Prose Poems* (University of Texas Press, 2002), reprinted by permission of the publisher. N. SCOTT MOMADAY: 'The Colors of Night', from *Again the Far Morning: New and Selected Poems* (University of New Mexico Press, 2011), reprinted by permission of the publisher. JANE MONSON: 'Via Negativa' from *The Line's Not for Turning* (Cinnamon Press, 2010), reprinted by permission of the publisher. EUGENIO MONTALE: 'Where the Tennis Court Was . . .', trans. by Charles Wright, from Eugenio Montale, *Poems* (Penguin Modern Classics, 2002), reprinted by permission of the publisher and Mondadori Editore. THYLIAS MOSS: 'An Anointing' from *Rainbow Remnants in Rock Bottom Ghetto Sky* (Persea Books, 1991), reprinted by permission of the publisher. HARRYETTE MULLEN: 'Denigration' from *Sleeping with the Dictionary* (University of California Press, 1995), reprinted by permission of the publisher. TOGARA MUZANENHAMO: 'Captain of the Lighthouse' from *Spirit Brides* (Carcanet, 2006), reprinted by permission of the publisher. EILEEN MYLES: 'The Poet' from *I Must Be Living Twice: New and Selected Poems 1975–2014* (Ecco, 2016), reprinted by permission of HarperCollins Publishers. ÁGNES NEMES NAGY: 'A Walk Through the Museum', trans. by George Szirtes, from *The Night of Akhenaton* (Bloodaxe, 2004), reprinted by permission of Bloodaxe Books. VIVEK NARAYANAN: 'Short Prayer to Sound' from *Life & Times of Mr Subramaniam* (HarperCollins India, 2012), reprinted by permission of the author. AMJAD NASSER: 'The Phases of the Moon in London' from *A Map of Signs and Scents: New and Selected Poems, 1979–2014*, trans. by Fady Joudah and Khaled Mattawa (Northwestern University Press, 2016), reprinted by permission of the publisher. PABLO NERUDA: 'The Flag', trans. by Nathaniel Tarn, from *Selected Poems* (Jonathan Cape, 1970), reprinted by permission of The Random House Group. BINK NOLL: 'Many Musicians Practice Their Mysteries While I Am Cooking' from *Selected Poems*, ed. by David R. Slavitt (Little Island Press, 2017), reprinted by permission of the pub-

Acknowledgements

lisher. NAOMI SHIHAB NYE: 'Hammer and Nail' from *Mint Snowball* (Anhinga Press, 2001), reprinted by permission of the publisher. FRANK O'HARA: 'Meditations in an Emergency' from *Collected Poems*, ed. by Donald Allen (University of California Press, 1995), reprinted by permission of the publisher. KRISTÍN ÓMARSDÓTTIR: 'Neglected Knives', trans. by Vala Thorodds, from *Waitress in Fall: Selected Poems* (Carcanet, 2018), reprinted by permission of the author and publisher. OTTÓ ORBÁN: 'Chile', trans. by Edwin Morgan, from *Collected Translations* (Carcanet, 1996), reprinted by permission of the publisher. RON PADGETT: 'Prose Poem' from *New and Selected Poems* (Godine, 1995), reprinted by permission of Coffee House Press. DAN PAGIS: 'The Souvenir', trans. by Stephen Mitchell, from *The Selected Poetry of Dan Pagis* (University of California Press, 1996), reprinted by permission of the publisher. ALVIN PANG: 'Other Things', from *When the Barbarians Arrive* (Arc, 2013), reprinted by permission of the publisher. DON PATERSON: 'Little Corona' from *God's Gift to Women* (Faber & Faber, 1997), reprinted by permission of the publisher. OCTAVIO PAZ: 'The Clerk's Vision', trans. by Eliot Weinberger, from *The Collected Poems* (Carcanet, 1988), reprinted by permission of the publisher. ELENA PENGA: 'Nightmare Pink', trans. by Karen Van Dyck, from *Austerity Measures: The New Greek Poetry* (Penguin Books, 2016), reprinted by permission of the author. SAINT-JOHN PERSE: 'Song', trans. by T. S. Eliot, from *Poems of T. S. Eliot*, Vol. II: *Practical Cats & Further Verses*, ed. by Christopher Ricks and Jim McCue (Faber & Faber, 2015), reprinted by permission of the publisher. FRANCIS PONGE: 'The Pleasures of the Door', trans. by C. K. Williams, from *Selected Poems*, ed. by Margaret Guiton (Faber & Faber, 1998), reprinted by permission of the publisher; 'Rain', trans. by Beverley Bie Brahic, from *Unfinished Ode to Mud* (CB Editions, 2008), reprinted by permission of the publisher; 'Crate', trans. by Joshua Corey and Jean-Luc Garneau, from *Partisan of Things* (Kenning Editions, 2016). SHANG QIN: 'The First Week of Mourning', trans. by Steve Bradbury, from *Feelings Above Sea Level* (Zephyr Press, 2006), reprinted by permission of The Permissions Company, on behalf of Zephyr Press. SINA QUEYRAS: 'If' from *Lemon Hound* (Coach House Books, 2006), reprinted by permission of the publisher. NATHALIE QUINTANE: Extract from *Joan of Arc*, trans. by Cynthia Hogue and

Acknowledgements

Sylvain Gallais, from *Joan Darc* (La Presse, 2018), reprinted by permission of the publisher and translators. CLAUDIA RANKINE: 'When you are alone and too tired . . .', 'The new therapist specializes in trauma counseling . . .' and 'A friend writes of the numbing effects . . .' from *Citizen: An American Lyric* (Penguin Books, 2015), reprinted by permission of The Random House Group. MANI RAO: Extract from *echolocation* (Math Paper Press, 2014), reprinted by permission of the publisher and author. TOM RAWORTH: 'Logbook', pages 106, 291, 298 and 253, from *Collected Poems* (Carcanet, 2003), reprinted by permission of the publisher. PETER READING: Extract from *C*, in *Collected Poems 1: Poems 1970–1984* (Bloodaxe, 1995), reprinted by permission of Bloodaxe Books. SRIKANTH REDDY: 'Corruption' from *Facts for Visitors* (University of California Press, 2004), reprinted by permission of the publisher. PIERRE REVERDY: 'Clock' ('Pendule'), trans. by Lydia Davis, from *Pierre Reverdy*, ed. by Mary Ann Caws (NYRB Poets, 2013), reprinted by permission of NYRB Books and Flammarion; 'Street Circus' ('Saltimbanques'), trans. by Ron Padgett, from *Pierre Reverdy*, ed. by Mary Ann Caws (NYRB Poets, 2013), reprinted by permission of NYRB Books. Copyright © Editions Flammarion, Paris, 2010. ADRIENNE RICH: 'Shooting Script', part 14, from *Collected Poems: 1950–2012* (W. W. Norton, 2016), reprinted by permission of the publisher. ARTHUR RIMBAUD: 'After the Flood', 'Sideshow' and 'Genie', trans. by John Ashbery, from *Illuminations* (Carcanet, 2011), reprinted by permission of the publisher. MAURICE RIORDAN: 'The Idylls', part 1, from *The Holy Land* (Faber & Faber, 2007), reprinted by permission of Faber and Faber Ltd. LISA ROBERTSON: 'Monday' from *The Weather* (Reality Street / New Star Books, 2002), reprinted by permission of the publisher. SOPHIE ROBINSON: 'Edith', reprinted by permission of the author. CAROL RUMENS: 'Inflation' from *From Berlin to Heaven* (Bloodaxe, 1989), reprinted by permission of Bloodaxe Books. JAMES SCHUYLER: 'Milk' from *Collected Poems*, 1993 (Farrar, Straus & Giroux, 1995). Copyright © 1993 by the Estate of James Schuyler. GEORGE SEFERIS: 'Nijinski', trans. by Edmund Keeley and Phillip Sherrard, from *Complete Poems* (Anvil Press, 1995), reprinted by permission of Carcanet. WARSAN SHIRE: 'Conversations About Home (at the Deportation Centre)' from *Teaching My Mother How to Give Birth* Mouthmark Series, No.10 (flipped eye, 2011), reprinted by permission of the publisher. CHARLES SIMIC: Extract from *The World Doesn't End: Prose Poems* (Houghton Mifflin, 1987), reprinted by permission of Houghton Mifflin Harcourt Publishing Company (© Charles Simic 1987). KEN SMITH: 'The Wild Rose', parts I and VII, from *Collected Poems* (Bloodaxe, 1973), reprinted by permission of Bloodaxe Books. ROD SMITH: 'Ted's Head' from *Deed* (University of Iowa Press, 2007), reprinted by permission of the author. ANDRZEJ SOSNOWSKI: 'In the Off-Season', trans. by Rod Mengham, from *Speedometry* (Contraband, 2014), reprinted by permission of the publisher and author. WOLE SOYINKA: 'Chimes of Silence' from *A Shuttle in the Crypt* (Methuen, 1972), reprinted by permission of the publisher. JACK SPICER: 'Dear James, It is absolutely clear and absolutely sunny . . .' from 'Letters to James Alexander', in *My Vocabulary Did This to Me: The Collected Poetry of Jack Spicer*, ed. by Peter Gizzi and Kevin Killian (Wesleyan University Press, 2010), used by permission of the publisher (© The Estate of Jack Spicer 2008). MARK STRAND: 'Chekhov' and 'The Mysterious Arrival of an Unusual Letter' from *Collected Poems* (Knopf, 2014), reprinted by permission of Alfred A. Knopf, an imprint of the Knopf Doubleday Publishing Group, a division of Penguin Random House LLC, and by permission of The Wylie Agency (UK) Limited (© Mark Strand 2012). ÉRIC SUCHÈRE: '24', trans. by Sandra Doller, from *Mystérieuse* (Anomalous Press, 2007), reprinted by permission of the publisher. KESTON SUTHERLAND: Extract from *Odes to TL61P*, 5 (I.i) (Enitharmon, 2013), reprinted by permission of the publisher. WISŁAWA SZYMBORSKA: 'Vocabulary', trans. by Stanisław Barańczak and Clare Cavanagh, from *View with a Grain of Sand* (Faber & Faber, 1996), reprinted by permission of Faber and Faber Ltd. RABINDRANATH TAGORE: 'A Day', trans. by Aurobindo Bose, from *Lipika* (Peter Owen, 1977), reprinted by permission of the publisher. SHUNTAR TANIKAWA: 'Scissors' from *New Selected Poems*, trans. by William I. Elliott and Kazuo Kawamura (Carcanet, 2015), reprinted by permission of the publisher. JAMES TATE: 'Goodtime Jesus' from *Selected Poems* (Wesleyan University Press, 1991), used by permission of the publisher (© James Tate 1991). ROSEMARY TONKS: 'An Old-Fashioned Traveller on the Trade Routes' from *Bedouin of the London Evening: Collected Poems* (Bloodaxe, 2014), reprinted by permission of Bloodaxe Books. GEORG TRAKL: 'Winter

Night', trans. by James Wright, from James Wright, *Collected Poems* (Wesleyan University Press, 2007), reprinted by permission of the publisher. TOMAS TRANSTRÖMER: 'The Bookcase', trans. by Robert Fulton, from *New Collected Poems* (Bloodaxe, 2011), reprinted by permission of Bloodaxe Books. GAEL TURNBULL: 'A Case' from *There Are Words: Collected Poems* (Shearsman Books, 2006), reprinted by permission of the publisher and The Estate of Gael Turnbull. UDAYAN VAJPEYI: 'The Well' and 'Sari' from *Kuchh Vakya* (Vani Prakashan, 1995), trans. by Alok Bhalla, reprinted by permission of the publisher and translator. CÉSAR VALLEJO: 'The Right Meaning', trans. by Robert Bly, from *Models of the Universe* (Oberlin College Press, 1995), reprinted by permission of the publisher. CATHY WAGNER: 'Chicken' from *Nervous Device* (City Lights, 2012), reprinted by permission of the publisher. ROSMARIE WALDROP: *Lawn of Excluded Middle*, parts 1–6, from *Curves to the Apple* (New Directions, 2006), reprinted by permission of New Directions Publishing Corp (© Rosmarie Waldrop 1993). MATTHEW WELTON: 'Virtual Airport', parts 1, 2, 4, 6, 9, 11, 13, 14, 17, 18, 21 and 24, from *'We needed coffee but . . .'* (Carcanet, 2009), reprinted by permission of the publisher. JOE WENDEROTH: 'September 2, 1996', 'September 5, 1996', 'September 21, 1996', 'February 8, 1997', 'June 3, 1997' and 'June 28, 1997' from *Letters to Wendy's* (Verse Press, 2000), reprinted by permission of Wave Books. WILLIAM CARLOS WILLIAMS: *Kora in Hell: Improvisations*, part II, from *Imaginations* (New Directions, 1971), reprinted by permission of New Directions Publishing Corp (© Florence H. Williams 1970). C. D. WRIGHT: 'What No One Could Have Told Them' from *Like Something Flying Backwards* (Bloodaxe, 2007), reprinted by permission of Bloodaxe Books. JAMES WRIGHT: 'Honey' from *Collected Poems* (Wesleyan University Press, 2007), reprinted by permission of the publisher. ZHOU YAPING: 'dropped on the ground • the small coin', trans. by Jeff Twitchell-Waas, reprinted by permission of the translator.

Every effort has been made to trace and contact the copyright-holders prior to publication. If notified, the publisher undertakes to rectify any errors or omissions at the earliest opportunity.

Editor's Acknowledgements

I am indebted to everyone who has pointed me in the direction of prose poems over the last three years, including the generous suggestions of many people on Twitter, both known to me and anonymous. Among those people who also offered thoughts and texts either in conversation or by correspondence, I must particularly thank: Rachael Allen, Emily Berry, Jen Calleja, Vahni Capildeo, Simon Collings, Patricia Debney, Nathan Hamilton, Beau Hopkins, Daniel Kane, Amy Key, Dominic Leonard, Andrew McDonnell, Leo Mellor, Rod Mengham, Jane Monson, Vivek Narayanan, Sandeep Parmar, Sam Riviere, Michael Robbins, Andy Spragg, Toh Hsien Min, and David Wheatley. Peter Gizzi was a good friend to this project from the start, as was Carrie Etter, who kindly shared her own teaching anthology of prose poems as I was beginning to assemble a first draft.

The idea for this book took shape during research leave granted by the University of East Anglia, and many UEA colleagues have contributed to how my thinking about it has developed, including Stephen Benson, Tom Boll, Giles Foden, Ross Hair, Thomas Karshan, David Nowell Smith, Rachel Potter, Cecilia Rossi, and Sophie Robinson. I am also grateful to both the Centre for Modern Poetry at the University of Kent and the School of Arts, English and Languages at Queen's University, Belfast, for inviting me to speak at their research seminars, and for the stimulating discussions with staff and students that followed. Warm thanks for hot meals to my hosts David Herd, Ben Hickman, and Robbie Richardson (Kent), and Gail McConnell and Alex Murray (Belfast).

Editor's Acknowledgements

The invitation from Gatehouse Press to guest-edit the Spring 2016 issue of *Lighthouse* magazine on the subject of 'poetry into prose' gave me a chance to begin thinking about ideas developed in my introduction, as did writing a chapter for *British Prose Poetry: The Poems Without Lines* (Palgrave Macmillan, 2018), ed. by Jane Monson.

I am indebted also to my editors at Penguin, without whom this book would not exist in its current form, and to Keiron Pim and Ralf Webb, who lent invaluable support in the final stages. All errors are, of course, my own.

Finally, my love as always, for everything, to my wife, Beccy, and to my children – Edie, Violet, and Norah – who made good use of the scrap paper that editing an anthology inevitably generates. I hope that one day they will find something here to enjoy.

Jeremy Noel-Tod

Index of Poets

Index of Titles